▶ Concept Applications

Siegfried Engelmann • Susan Hanner • Phyllis Haddox

**SRA
McGraw-Hill**

Columbus, Ohio

A Division of The **McGraw·Hill** *Companies*

PHOTO CREDITS
Cover Photo: KS Studios

SRA/McGraw-Hill

A Division of The **McGraw·Hill** *Companies*

Send all inquiries to:
SRA/McGraw-Hill
250 Old Wilson Bridge Road
Suite 310
Worthington, Ohio 43085

Printed in the United States of America.

ISBN 0-02-674819-3

1 2 3 4 5 6 7 8 9 POH 04 03 02 01 00 99 98

A Here's what we know:

> **Mary loves all kinds of sports.**

If Mary loves all kinds of sports, here are some things we could expect.

- **Mary loves tennis.**
- **Mary loves to go to the ball park.**
- **Mary spent last Saturday buying ski equipment.**

Name two more things we could expect if Mary loves all kinds of sports.

If Mary loves all kinds of sports, here are some things we would not expect.

- **Mary threw away her ski equipment.**
- **Mary hates to go to the ball park.**
- **Mary said that she'd rather read than play tennis.**

Name two more things we would not expect if Mary loves all kinds of sports.

The things we would not expect are **inconsistent** with what we know about Mary.

Two items below seem inconsistent with what we know about Mary. Write the word **inconsistent** for each of them. Leave the other items blank. Spell the word **inconsistent** correctly.

1. Mary felt sad because she couldn't go to the

   track meet. _____

2. Mary was late for dinner because she was at the swimming pool.

   _____

3. Mary wants to sew a new skirt instead of playing baseball.

   _____

4. Mary spent $30 for a season basketball

   ticket. _____

5. Mary saw every game of the World Series.

   _____

6. Mary turns off the television when a football game comes on.

   _____

 B These lines are **horizontal.**

These lines are **not** horizontal.

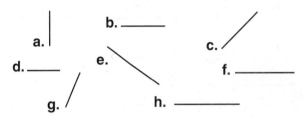

Which of these lines are horizontal?

a. | b. ———   c. /

d. ——   e. \   f. ———

g. /   h. ———

These lines are not horizontal. They are **vertical.**

Slanted lines are not horizontal and not vertical.

Identify each of these lines as **horizontal, vertical,** or **slanted.**

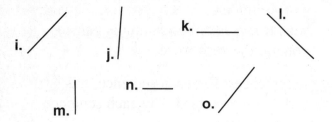

Follow the directions.

1. Draw a horizontal line.
2. Below that line, draw a second horizontal line of the same length.
3. Write the word **perhaps** above the left end of the upper line.

 You're going to use facts as evidence to explain why different things may happen. Here are the facts:

| Fact A. **Susan liked to play sports.** |
| Fact B. **Susan was a lawyer.** |
| Fact C. **Susan was not tall.** |

Read the facts over until you can say them without looking.

1. Here's what happened: **Susan never played center in basketball.** Say the fact that best explains why that happened.
2. Here's what happened: **She bought five pairs of tennis shoes.** Say the fact that best explains why that happened.

3. Here's what happened: **She knew the judge in Lincoln City.** Say the fact that best explains why that happened.
4. Here's what happened: **She kept her baseball equipment in the garage.** Say the fact that best explains why that happened.

For each item, write the **letter of the fact** that best explains what happened.

5. She never played center in basketball. _____

6. She bought five pairs of tennis shoes. _____

7. She knew the judge in Lincoln City. _____

8. She kept her baseball equipment in the garage. _____
9. She stood on a stool to reach the shelves.

_____

 Let's draw a conclusion about the shoes. Here's the evidence:

The shoes are in the closet.
And the closet is in the house.

Here's the conclusion we can draw about the shoes:

The shoes are in the house.

• Draw a conclusion about the dogs. Here's the evidence:

The dogs are in the pen.
And the pen is in the yard.

What's the conclusion about the dogs?

- Draw a conclusion about Miami. Here's the evidence:

  Miami is in the state of Florida.
  The state of Florida is in the United States.

What's the conclusion about Miami?

- Draw a conclusion about all carrots. Here's the evidence:

  All carrots are vegetables.
  All vegetables are plants.

What's the conclusion about all carrots?

Read the evidence and write the conclusion for each item.

1. Here's the evidence:

  The bird is in the nest.
  And the nest is in the tree.

What's the conclusion about the bird?

_____

_____

2. Here's the evidence:

  All carrots are vegetables.
  All vegetables are plants.

What's the conclusion about all carrots?

_____

_____

E The verb in each sentence below is underlined. The writer of the sentences has trouble with verbs. What the writer doesn't know is that if only one thing is named in the sentence, you use the verb **was.** If more than one thing is named, you use the verb **were.**

Read the sentences. For each sentence, tell which verb the writer used. Say each sentence with the correct verb.

1. **The girls <u>was sitting</u>.**
   What verb did the writer use?
   Say the sentence with the correct verb.
2. **The girls <u>were swimming</u>.**
   What verb did the writer use?
   Say the sentence with the correct verb.
3. **The girl <u>were running</u>.**
   What verb did the writer use?
   Say the sentence with the correct verb.
4. **The girl <u>was eating</u>.**
   What verb did the writer use?
   Say the sentence with the correct verb.

Write the verb **was** or the verb **were** in each blank.

5. The girls _____ sitting.

6. The girls _____ swimming.

7. The girl _____ running.

8. The girl _____ eating.

9. The boys _____ eating.

10. The dogs _____ sitting.

11. They _____ running.

12. He _____ sleeping.

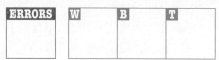
ERRORS	W	B	T

 A Let's draw a conclusion about the dishes. Here's the evidence:

The dishes are in the cupboard.
The cupboard is in the kitchen.

Here's the conclusion we can draw about the dishes:

The dishes are in the kitchen.

● Draw a conclusion about Gino. Here's the evidence:

Gino is a person.
Every person has a scapula.

What's the conclusion about Gino?

● Draw a conclusion about all cups. Here's the evidence:

All cups are containers.
All containers can hold things.

What's the conclusion about all cups?

● Draw a conclusion about a Siamese cat. Here's the evidence:

Every feline eats meat.
A Siamese cat is a feline.

What's the conclusion about a Siamese cat?

Read the evidence and write the conclusion for each item.

1. Here's the evidence:

> **All mammals have hair.**
> **Whales are mammals.**

What's the conclusion about whales?

_____

2. Here's the evidence:

> **Every feline eats meat.**
> **A Siamese cat is a feline.**

What's the conclusion about a Siamese cat?

_____

 B The verb in each sentence below is underlined. The writer of the sentences has trouble with verbs. What the writer doesn't know is that if only one thing is named in the sentence, you use the verb **was.** If more than one thing is named, you use the verb **were.**
Read the sentences. For each sentence, tell which verb the writer used. Say each sentence with the correct verb.

1. The boys <u>was eating</u>.
What verb did the writer use?
Say the sentence with the correct verb.

2. The girls <u>were swimming</u>.
What verb did the writer use?
Say the sentence with the correct verb.

3. All the boys <u>was eating</u>.
What verb did the writer use?
Say the sentence with the correct verb.

Write the verb **was** or the verb **were** in each blank.

4. The boys _____ eating.

5. The boy _____ eating.

6. All the boys _____ eating.

7. Two of the girls _____ tired.

8. One of the girls _____ sleeping.

9. Most of the girls _____ happy.

10. Two of those girls _____ sick.

 You're going to use facts as evidence to explain why different things may happen. Here are the facts:

Fact A.	**It was noon.**
Fact B.	**It was midnight.**
Fact C.	**It was pouring rain.**

Read the facts over until you can say them without looking.

1. Here's what happened: **The street lamps were lit.** Say the fact that best explains why that happened.
2. Here's what happened: **The picnic was canceled.** Say the fact that best explains why that happened.
3. Here's what happened: **Sue got splashed when the car drove past.** Say the fact that best explains why that happened.
4. Here's what happened: **It surprised him when the phone rang.** Say the fact that best explains why that happened.
5. Here's what happened: **Everyone went out to eat.** Say the fact that best explains why that happened.

For each item, write the **letter of the fact** that best explains what happened.

Fact D.	**Jill never ate meat.**
Fact E.	**Jill worked in the city.**
Fact F.	**Jill had four children to support.**

6. She had two jobs. _____

7. She saw tall buildings every day. _____

8. She ate lots of vegetables. _____

9. She never went to the butcher shop. _____

 Here's what we know:

George is the best student in his class.

If George is the best student in his class, we expect certain things to happen, and we don't expect other things to happen. What do we call sentences that tell something we don't expect to happen?
Name three things that are inconsistent with the idea that George is the best student in his class.

Some items below seem inconsistent with what we know about George. Write the word **inconsistent** for each of them. Leave the other items blank. Spell the word **inconsistent** correctly.

1. He spends a lot of time studying.

_____

2. George got three F's last term.

_____

3. George is usually late for school.

_____

4. George turns in all his assignments.

_____

5. He refuses to answer when the teacher calls

on him. _____

6. He got 100 percent on his final exam.

_____

7. He tutors three students in science.

_____

8. He spends a lot of time daydreaming in

class. _____

9. George often forgets to do his homework.

_____

10. He turned in a report that was so messy the
teacher couldn't read it.

_____

E Identify each of these lines as **horizontal, vertical,** or **slanted.**

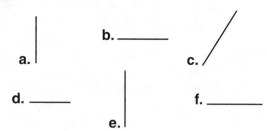

Follow the directions.

1. Draw a square.
2. Draw a slanted line from the upper left corner of the square to the lower right corner of the square.
3. On the slanted line, write the first four letters of the alphabet in order.

Let's draw a conclusion about all lizards. Here's the evidence:

All lizards are reptiles.
All reptiles are animals.

Here's the conclusion we can draw about all lizards:

All lizards are animals.

● Draw a conclusion about the vena cava. Here's the evidence:

Every vein carries blood to the heart.
The vena cava is a vein.

What's the conclusion about the vena cava?

Read the evidence and write the conclusion for each item.

1. Here's the evidence:

Every vein carries blood to the heart.
The vena cava is a vein.

What's the conclusion about the vena cava?

_____

_____

2. Here's the evidence:

The socks are in the drawer.
The drawer is in the dresser.

What's the conclusion about the socks?

_____

_____

3. Here's the evidence:

Idaho is a state.
Every state has a capital.

What's the conclusion about Idaho?

_____

_____

4. Here's the evidence:

All bananas are fruit.
All fruit contains seeds.

What's the conclusion about all bananas?

_____

_____

LESSON 3

B Here's what we know:

Frankie earns $5000 a year.

If Frankie earns $5000 a year, we expect certain things to happen, and we don't expect other things to happen. What do we call sentences that tell something we don't expect to happen? Name three things that are inconsistent with the idea that Frankie earns $5000 a year.

Some items below seem inconsistent with what we know about Frankie. Write the word **inconsistent** for each of them. Leave the other items blank. Spell the word **inconsistent** correctly.

1. Frankie goes to Hawaii every Easter

   vacation. _____

2. Frankie drives a car that's twelve years old.

   _____

3. She brings her lunch to work in a paper bag.

   _____

4. She hired a housekeeper to do all her

   housework. _____

5. Frankie cuts her own hair.

   _____

6. She saved no money last year.

   _____

7. She wears stockings with holes in them.

   _____

8. She has steak for dinner five nights a week.

   _____

9. Frankie gave her mother a diamond ring.

   _____

C You have two minutes to copy the paragraph below. Be sure to copy capital letters and punctuation marks. Spell all the words correctly. Don't start until the teacher tells you to start.

> **Some lines are horizontal and some lines are vertical. Slanted lines are neither horizontal nor vertical. They can slant up to the right or up to the left.**

_____

_____

_____

_____

_____

★ **D** You're going to use facts as evidence to explain why different things may happen. For each item, write the **letter of the fact** that best explains what happened. Here are the facts:

> Fact A. **The horses broke out of the corral.**
>
> Fact B. **It was the worst blizzard in history.**
>
> Fact C. **The electricity went out in the farmhouse.**

1. There were strong winds. _____
2. The refrigerator stopped running. _____
3. The fence was in pieces. _____
4. Snow hid the hoofprints. _____
5. We burned a lot of candles. _____

E Write the verb **was** or the verb **were** in each blank.

1. All the men _____ working.
2. One of the men _____ working.
3. Not one of the men _____ working.
4. All the students _____ studying.
5. We _____ studying.
6. Some of them _____ studying.
7. Not one of them _____ studying.
8. They _____ awake.
9. We _____ awake.

F Follow the directions.

1. Draw a circle.
2. Put a dot in the center of the circle.
3. Draw a horizontal line from one side of the circle to the other. The line must pass through the dot.

G Write **horizontal, vertical,** or **slanted** next to each line. Spell the words correctly.

1. —— _____
2. / _____
3. \ _____
4. | _____
5. | _____

A   Here is a diagram:

Here are instructions for the diagram:

1. Draw a horizontal line.
2. Draw a square above the left end of the line.
3. Draw an oval above the right end of the line.

The instructions tell to draw the line, to draw the square, and to draw the oval. But the instructions are not complete.

Make up the instructions for telling about the triangle. Tell **what** to draw and **where** to draw it.

Make up the instructions for telling about the circle. Tell **what** to draw and **where** to draw it.

4. Write instructions for the triangle.

_____

_____

5. Write instructions for the circle.

_____

_____

B   What kind of sentence tells something we don't expect to happen?
   To combine two sentences that are inconsistent, we can use the word **but** or the word **however.** Here's what we know:

Sally is only twelve years old.

Here's a sentence that seems inconsistent with the sentence in the box:

She is a college student.

Here are the two sentences combined with the word **but:**

> **Sally is only twelve years old, but she is a college student.**

Here are the two sentences combined with the word **however:**

> **Sally is only twelve years old; however, she is a college student.**

Here's what we know:

Owen is really friendly.

Read the sentences below and find the one that seems inconsistent with the sentence in the box.

•   **He gets many calls from his friends.**
•   **He got in a fight at his birthday party.**
•   **He always says hello to strangers.**

Use the word **but** to combine the sentence in the box with the inconsistent sentence.
Use the word **however** to combine the sentence in the box with the inconsistent sentence.

Here's what we know:

Sam is a famous movie star.

Read the sentences below and find the one that seems inconsistent with the sentence in the box.

•   **He hates to act.**
•   **He gets lots of fan mail.**

Use the word **but** to combine the sentence in the box with the inconsistent sentence.
Use the word **however** to combine the sentence in the box with the inconsistent sentence.

Look at diagram 1.

Diagram 1

You can't see any dots in the diagram. But pretend that there are some dots in the diagram. Here is a fact about those dots:

Some dots are inside the circle.

Let's say that we were trying to find a dot. Would it be inside the circle? Maybe. But maybe it would be outside the circle. All we know is that **some** dots are inside the circle. Here's a diagram that shows some dots inside the circle.

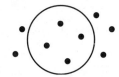

• Look at diagram 2.

Diagram 2

You can't see the dots in the diagram. But here's a fact about the dots:

Some dots are in the square.

Draw dots in diagram 2 to show that some dots are in the square.
We're looking for a dot. Here's the conclusion about where that dot is:

Maybe the dot is in the square.

• Look at diagram 3.

Diagram 3

You can't see the little boxes, but here's a fact about them:

Some of the boxes are inside the circle.

Draw little boxes in diagram 3 to show that some of the boxes are in the circle.
We're looking for a box. What's the conclusion about where that box is?

• Look at diagram 4.

Diagram 4

You can't see the dots in the diagram, but here's a fact about the dots:

All the dots are in the circle.

Draw dots in diagram 4 to show that all the dots are in the circle.
We're looking for a dot. What's the conclusion about where that dot is?

D You have two minutes to copy the paragraph below. Be sure to copy capital letters and punctuation marks. Spell all the words correctly. Don't start until the teacher tells you to start.

> **If you know something is true, you expect certain things to happen, but you don't expect other things. The things you don't expect are inconsistent with what you know.**

_____

_____

_____

_____

_____

_____

_____

★ **E** Read the evidence and write the conclusion for each item.

1. Here's the evidence:

   The gift is in the box.
   The box is under the Christmas tree.

   What's the conclusion about the gift?

   _____

   _____

2. Here's the evidence:

   All cars are vehicles.
   Vehicles can transport people.

   What's the conclusion about all cars?

   _____

   _____

3. Here's the evidence:

   All butterflies are living things.
   All living things breathe.

   What's the conclusion about all butterflies?

   _____

   _____

4. Here's the evidence:

   Every burning thing needs oxygen.
   Fires are burning things.

   What's the conclusion about fires?

   _____

   _____

F You're going to use facts as evidence to explain why different things may happen. For each item write the **letter of the fact** that best explains what happened. Here are the facts:

Fact A. **It was Christmas Eve.**

Fact B. **It had been snowing for two days.**

Fact C. **Students were driving home from college that night.**

1. There was ice on the roads. _____

2. There was a pine tree in the living room. _____

3. The younger kids kept looking up the chimney. _____

4. The phone lines were down. _____

5. The car was loaded with books and clothes. _____

G Write the verb **was** or the verb **were** in each blank.

1. The woman _____ eating.

2. All the men _____ taking a break.

3. One of the men _____ resting.

4. That deer _____ old.

5. Most of them _____ old.

6. Some sheep _____ running around.

7. We _____ having fun.

8. Some of them _____ eating hamburgers.

H Write **horizontal, vertical,** or **slanted** next to each line. Spell the words correctly.

1. \   _____

2. —   _____

3. | _____

4. —   _____

I Follow the directions.

1. Draw a circle.
2. Draw a square around the circle. The square must not touch the circle.
3. Write the letter **Q** so that it is inside the square, but outside the circle.

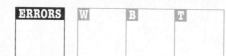

ERRORS | W | B | T

A What kind of sentence tells something we don't expect to happen?

To combine two sentences that are inconsistent, we can use the word **but** or the word **however.** Here's what we know:

> **My cat doesn't like water.**

Here's a sentence that seems inconsistent with the sentence in the box:

> **It likes to play in the river.**

Here are the two sentences combined with the word **but:**

> **My cat doesn't like water, but it likes to play in the river.**

Here are the two sentences combined with the word **however:**

> **My cat doesn't like water; however, it likes to play in the river.**

Here's what we know:

> **Jerry ate five hot dogs for lunch.**

Read the sentences below and find the one that seems inconsistent with the sentence in the box.

- **He has a stomach ache.**
- **He doesn't want hot dogs for dinner.**
- **He is still hungry.**

Use the word **but** to combine the sentence in the box with the inconsistent sentence.
Use the word **however** to combine the sentence in the box with the inconsistent sentence.

Here's what we know:

> **Lila hates to travel.**

Read the sentences below and find the one that seems inconsistent with the sentence in the box.

- **She's going to Mexico for Easter.**
- **She doesn't have any suitcases.**
- **She always spends her vacations at home.**

Use the word **but** to combine the sentence in the box with the inconsistent sentence.
Use the word **however** to combine the sentence in the box with the inconsistent sentence.

B You're going to figure out whether information is relevant to a fact. Here's the rule:

> Information that helps explain a fact is relevant to the fact.
>
> Information that does not help explain a fact is not relevant to the fact.

What do we call information that helps explain a fact?
What do we call information that doesn't help explain a fact?

Here's a fact:

> **The dog bit the mail carrier.**

Here's information about what happened before the dog bit the mail carrier:

1. **The mail carrier had kicked the dog three times.**
   Does that information help explain why the dog bit the mail carrier?
   So, what do you know about that information?

2. **The dog was born with brown spots.**
   Does that information help explain why the dog bit the mail carrier?
   So, what do you know about that information?

3. **The mail carrier had her forty-second birthday a month before.**
   Does that information help explain why?
   So, what do you know about that information?

4. **The dog had bitten five other people.**
   Does that information help explain why?
   So, what do you know about that information?

 Look at diagram 1.

Diagram 1

You can't see the dots in the diagram, but here's a fact about them:

Some dots are in the triangle.

Draw dots in diagram 1 to show that some dots are in the triangle.

● Look at diagram 2.

Diagram 2

You can't see the dots in the diagram, but here's a fact about them:

All the dots are in the circle.

Draw dots in diagram 2 to show that all the dots are in the circle.

● Look at diagram 3.

Diagram 3

You can't see the little boxes, but here's a fact about them:

Some boxes are in the triangle.

Draw little boxes in diagram 3 to show that some boxes are in the triangle.
We're looking for a box. What's the conclusion about where that box is?

● Look at diagram 4.

Diagram 4

You can't see the dots, but **all the dots are in the circle.**
Here's a deduction that is based on the diagram:

All the dots are in the circle.
The circle is in the square.
So, all the dots are in the square.

To check the conclusion, draw dots in diagram 4 so that all the dots are in the circle.
Is the conclusion correct? Are all the dots in the square?

LESSON 5

- Look at diagram 5.

You can't see the boxes, but **all the boxes are in the circle.**
Complete the deduction based on the diagram.

All the boxes are in the circle.
The circle is in the triangle.

So, _____

_____

To check your conclusion, draw boxes in diagram 5 so that all the boxes are in the circle. Is the conclusion correct? Are all the boxes in the triangle?

 Here is a diagram:

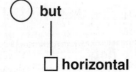

Here are instructions for the diagram:

1. Draw a vertical line.
2. Write the word **but** above the top of the vertical line.
3. Draw a circle to the left of the word **but.**

The instructions tell to draw the line, to write the word **but,** and to draw the circle. But the instructions are not complete.

Make up the instructions for telling about the square. Tell **what** to draw and **where** to draw it.

Make up the instructions for telling about the word **horizontal.** Tell **what** to write and **where** to write it.

4. Write the instructions for the square.

_____

_____

5. Write the instructions for the word **horizontal.**

_____

_____

E Here are two sentences that seem inconsistent with each other:

He was hungry. He didn't eat.

Here are the sentences combined with **but:**

He was hungry, but he didn't eat.

Here's the rule for combining two sentences with the word **but:**

Change the period of the first sentence to a comma.
Follow the comma with the word **but.**

Tell how you would make a combined sentence from the two sentences below. First say the combined sentence. Then tell about the punctuation.

She was happy. She cried a lot.

Combine each pair of sentences below with the word **but.** Be sure to punctuate the sentences correctly.

1. She was happy. She cried a lot.

_____

_____

2. He had an Irish name. He lived in Chile.

_____

_____

3. He was out of shape. He could run faster than anybody on the track team.

_____

_____

_____

4. Dale had green hair. Nobody paid any attention to him.

_____

_____

5. Joan did not sew well. She made all her clothes.

_____

_____

_____

F You have two minutes to copy the paragraph below. Be sure to copy capital letters and punctuation marks. Spell all the words correctly. Don't start until the teacher tells you to start.

> **If an event does not help to explain a fact, that event is not relevant. Sometimes you need more information to know if the event is not relevant.**

_____

_____

_____

_____

_____

★ **G** Information that helps explain a fact is called **relevant.** Information that does not help explain a fact is **not relevant.**

Write **relevant** or **not relevant** for each piece of information. Spell the words correctly.

> Fact: **The dog bit the mail carrier.**

Information about what happened before the dog bit the mail carrier:

1. The mail carrier had kicked the dog three times. _____

2. The dog was born with brown spots.

_____

3. The mail carrier had her forty-second birthday a month before._____

4. The dog had bitten five other people.

_____

LESSON 5

H Read the evidence and write the conclusion for each item.

1. Here's the evidence:

All beavers are rodents.
All rodents are mammals.

What's the conclusion about all beavers?

_____

_____

2. Here's the evidence:

The coffee is in the cup.
The cup is on the table.

What's the conclusion about the coffee?

_____

_____

3. Here's the evidence:

All valleys were cut by moving water.
The Grand Canyon is a valley.

What's the conclusion about the Grand Canyon?

_____

_____

4. Here's the evidence:

Every canine eats meat.
A wolf is a canine.

What's the conclusion about a wolf?

_____

_____

I Many writers have trouble with the words **each** and **every.** These words name only one thing.

This is correct: Each man **was** tired.
This is incorrect: Every man **were** tired.

Write the verb **was** or the verb **were** in each blank.

1. Each of the women _____ happy.

2. Every dinosaur _____ cold-blooded.

3. Not every man _____ working.

4. Each of the men _____ tired.

5. All men _____ working.

6. Not all men _____ working.

7. Each of the four sisters _____ smart.

8. Every sister _____ smart.

9. All the sisters _____ rich.

10. One of the sisters _____ an engineer.

You're going to figure out whether information is relevant to a fact.

What do we call information that helps explain a fact?

What do we call information that doesn't help explain a fact?

Here's a fact:

> **The cook burned the potatoes.**

Here's information about what happened before the cook burned the potatoes:

1. **He hadn't put any butter in the pan.**
   What kind of information is that?
   How do you know?
2. **He had set the burner on high.**
   What kind of information is that?
   How do you know?
3. **He had been wearing a big white hat.**
   What kind of information is that?
   How do you know?
4. **He had never cooked potatoes before.**
   What kind of information is that?
   How do you know?

 Look at diagram 1.

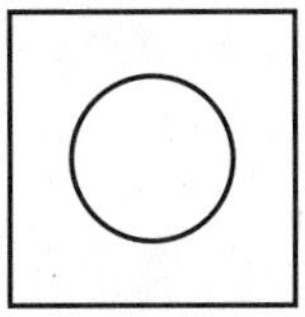

Diagram 1

You can't see the dots, but **all the dots are in the circle.**

Here's a deduction that is based on the diagram:

> **All the dots are in the circle.**
> **The circle is in the square.**
> **So, all the dots are in the square.**

To check the conclusion, draw dots in diagram 1 so that all the dots are in the circle.

Is the conclusion correct? Are all the dots in the square?

- Look at diagram 2.

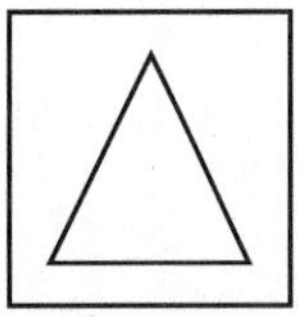

Diagram 2

You can't see the dots, but all the dots are in the triangle.

Complete the deduction based on the diagram:

All the dots are in the triangle.
The triangle is in the square.

So, _____

_____

Draw the dots in diagram 2.

- Look at diagram 3.

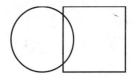

Diagram 3

You can't see the dots, but **all the dots are in the circle.**

Here's the deduction that is based on the diagram:

> **All the dots are in the circle.**
> **Part of the circle is in the square.**
> **So, maybe all the dots are in the square.**

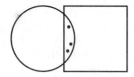

Look at diagram A and diagram B. Diagram A shows where the dots could be if all the dots were in the square. Diagram B shows where the dots could be if only some of the dots were in the square.

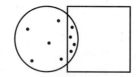

Diagram A   **Diagram B**

We want to draw a conclusion about all the dots. We don't know which diagram is correct, so we draw this conclusion:

Maybe all the dots are in the square.

• Look at diagram 4.

Diagram 4

You can't see the dots, but **all the dots are in the circle.**
Draw a conclusion about all the dots:

All the dots are in the circle.
Part of the circle is in the triangle.

So, _____

_____

Complete diagram C and diagram D.
For diagram C, show where the dots could be if all the dots were in the triangle. For diagram D, show where the dots could be if only some of the dots were in the triangle.

Diagram C   **Diagram D**

• Look at diagram 5.

Diagram 5

You can't see the dots, but **all the dots are in the square.**
Draw a conclusion about all the dots:

All the dots are in the square.
Part of the square is in the circle.

So, _____

_____

 Here are two sentences that seem inconsistent:

Herman and Sal are friends. They are always fighting.

What two words can you use to combine those sentences?
Combine those sentences with the word **however.**
Combine those sentences with the word **but.**

Here are the sentences combined with **but:**

Herman and Sal are friends, but they are always fighting.

Here's the rule for combining sentences with the word **but:**

Change the period of the first sentence to a comma.
Follow the comma with the word **but.**

Tell how you would make a combined sentence from the two sentences below. First say the combined sentence. Then tell about the punctuation.

I love to cook. I haven't cooked in a year.

Combine each pair of sentences below with the word **but.** Be sure to punctuate the sentences correctly.

1. I love to cook. I haven't cooked in a year.

_____

_____

2. Kelly is a careful driver. He had four accidents this year.

_____

_____

_____

3. Maria hates to talk on the phone. She called Elena yesterday.

_____

_____

_____

4. The teacher gave a good explanation. I still didn't understand.

_____

_____

_____

D You have two minutes to copy the paragraph below. Be sure to copy capital letters and punctuation marks. Spell all the words correctly. Don't start until the teacher tells you to start.

Before you combine two sentences, figure out if one sentence is inconsistent with the other. If the two are inconsistent, you can use "but" or "however" to combine the sentences.

_____

_____

_____

_____

_____

★ **E** Here is a diagram:

relevant

○ □

evidence

Here are instructions for the diagram:

1. Draw a line that slants down to the right.

2. Draw a triangle below the bottom of the slanted line.

3. Write the word **evidence** to the right of the triangle.

4. Write instructions for the square.

_____

_____

5. Write instructions for the word **relevant.**

_____

_____

6. Write instructions for the circle.

_____

_____

F Write **relevant** or **not relevant** for each piece of information. Spell the words correctly.

Fact: **Fred did not eat dinner that**

night.

Information about what happened **before** the fact:

1. He ate three hamburgers after school.

_____

2. He ran to school that morning.

_____

3. He felt very sick to his stomach.

_____

4. He wore a red shirt.

_____

5. His brother always ate well.

_____

G Read the evidence and write the conclusion for each item.

1. Here's the evidence:

Dayton is in Ohio.
Ohio is in the United States.

What's the conclusion about Dayton?

_____

_____

2. Here's the evidence:

> **A DC-10 is a jet.**
> **All jets need fuel.**

What's the conclusion about a DC-10?

_____

3. Here's the evidence:

> **All butterflies come from caterpillars.**
> **A monarch is a butterfly.**

What's the conclusion about a monarch?

_____

_____

4. Here's the evidence:

> **Every river flows to the sea.**
> **The Skagit is a river.**

What's the conclusion about the Skagit?

_____

_____

H Some writers have trouble using the verbs **is** and **are**. These words work the same way as **was** and **were**. Use the verb **is** when only one thing is named. Use the verb **are** when more than one thing is named.

Don't be fooled. This sentence is not correct: **Each of the planes are big.** This is correct: **Each of the planes is big.** Remember, the word **each** names only one thing.

Write the verb **is** or the verb **are** in each blank.

1. Five women _____ laughing.

2. All the animals _____ racing.

3. Each of the boys _____ hiding under the bushes.

4. They _____ jumping in the cage.

5. It _____ jumping in the cage.

6. He _____ at home.

7. My brothers _____ at home.

8. Every girl _____ at the game.

9. Two police officers _____ riding to work.

10. Each of the rooms _____ full of people.

11. One of the elephants _____ making noise.

12. Rats _____ making noise.

13. One of the rats _____ making noise.

14. Every one of the picnic tables _____ covered with ants.

15. Every elephant _____ warm-blooded.

16. All elephants _____ warm-blooded.

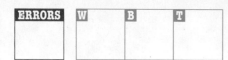
A When you combine sentences with the word **but,** what do you do with the period of the first sentence? What follows the comma?

Tell how you would make a combined sentence from the two sentences below. First say the combined sentence. Then tell about the punctuation.

Her brother was older. She was taller.

Combine each pair of sentences below with the word **but.** Be sure to punctuate the sentences correctly.

1. Dogs make her sneeze. She has two collies.

   _____

   _____

2. Fred is very sick. He won't go to the doctor.

   _____

   _____

3. Gina has a good job. She wants to quit.

   _____

   _____

4. Frank likes to have roommates. He lives alone.

   _____

   _____

5. Freda has a terrible cough. She won't stop smoking.

   _____

   _____

B Look at diagram 1.

Diagram 1

You can't see the dots in the diagram, but **all the dots are in the circle.** Complete the deduction:

All the dots are in the circle.
The circle is in the triangle.

So, _____

_____

To check your conclusion, draw dots in diagram 1 so that all the dots are in the circle.

• Look at diagram 2.

Diagram 2

You can't see the dots, but all the dots are in the circle. Draw a conclusion about all the dots:

All the dots are in the circle.
Part of the circle is in the triangle.

So, _____

_____

• Look at diagram 3.

Diagram 3

You can see the dots and the circle in the diagram, but you can't see the square. Here's a fact about the square:

The circle is in the square.

Complete the deduction:

All the dots are in the circle.
The circle is in the square.

So, _____

_____

To check your conclusion, draw a square in diagram 3 so that the circle is in the square.

• Look at diagram 4.

Diagram 4

You can see the dots and the circle in the diagram, but you can't see the triangle. Complete the deduction:

All the dots are in the circle.
The circle is in the triangle.

So, _____

_____

To check your conclusion, draw a triangle in diagram 4 so that the circle is in the triangle.

• Look at diagram 5.

Diagram 5

You can see the dots and the circle, but you can't see the triangle.

Here's the deduction:

All the dots are in the circle.
Part of the circle is in the triangle.
So, maybe all the dots are in the triangle.

Look at diagram A and diagram B.
Diagram A shows where the triangle could be if all the dots were in the triangle.
Diagram B shows where the triangle could be if only some of the dots were in the triangle.

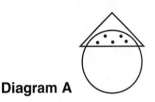

Diagram A   **Diagram B**

• Look at diagram 6.

Diagram 6

You can see the dots and the square, but you can't see the oval. Draw a conclusion about all the dots:

All the dots are in the square.
Part of the square is in the oval.

So, _____

_____

Complete diagram C and diagram D.
For diagram C, show where the oval could be if all the dots were in the oval.
For diagram D, show where the dots could be if only some of the dots were in the oval.

Diagram C   **Diagram D**

You're going to figure out whether information is relevant to a fact.

What do we call information that helps explain a fact?

What do we call information that doesn't help explain a fact?

Here's a fact:

> **The woman honked her horn.**

Here's information about what happened before the woman honked her horn:

1. **Another car almost ran into her.**
   What kind of information is that?
   How do you know?
2. **She was mad at the driver in front of her.**
   What kind of information is that?
   How do you know?
3. **She was wearing a silk hat.**
   What kind of information is that?
   How do you know?
4. **She passed her driver's test five days before.**
   What kind of information is that?
   How do you know?

 You have two minutes to copy the paragraph below. Be sure to copy capital letters and punctuation marks. Spell all the words correctly. Don't start until the teacher tells you to start.

> **Some writers have trouble using the verbs "is" and "are." Use the verb "is" when one thing is named. Use the verb "are" when more than one thing is named.**

★ **E** Answer the questions.

1. What do we call information that does not help explain a fact? _____

   _____

2. What do we call information that helps explain a fact? _____

Write **relevant** or **not relevant** for each piece of information.

| Fact: **There were mice in the kitchen.** |

Information about what happened before there were mice in the kitchen:

3. The walls had been painted white.

   _____

4. Someone had left the back door open.

   _____

5. No one had covered the food.

   _____

6. No one had set the traps.

   _____

7. The heat was turned off in the kitchen.

   _____

F Some writers have trouble using the verbs **is** and **are.** These words work the same way as **was** and **were.** Use the verb **is** when only one thing is named. Use the verb **are** when more than one thing is named.

Don't be fooled. This sentence is not correct: **Every one of the plants are blooming.** This is correct: **Every one of the plants is blooming.** Remember, the word **every** names only one thing.

Write the verb **is** or the verb **are** in each blank.

1. Not all of the children _____ playing in the yard.

2. All of the children _____ playing in the yard.

3. Not every child _____ playing in the yard.

4. Three of my uncles _____ living in Canada.

5. It _____ building a nest.

6. Her brothers _____ playing baseball.

7. Every sister _____ watching the game.

Write the verb **was** or the verb **were** in each blank.

8. All the girls _____ solving puzzles.

9. Every girl _____ solving puzzles.

10. One of the girls _____ solving puzzles.

11. Each of the boys _____ solving puzzles.

12. They _____ flying above the clouds.

13. Each of the planes _____ flying above the clouds.

14. I _____ going to the game.

G Here is a diagram:

slanted
vertical

△

conclusion

○

Here are instructions for the diagram:

1. Draw a square.
2. Write the word **conclusion** below the square.
3. Write the word **vertical** above the square.
4. Write instructions for the triangle.

_____

_____

5. Write instructions for the word **slanted.**

_____

_____

6. Write instructions for the circle.

_____

_____

H Read the evidence and write the conclusion for each item.

1. Here's the evidence:

**Every country has a capital.
Brazil is a country.**

What's the conclusion about Brazil?

_____

_____

2. Here's the evidence:

**All living things need water.
An antelope is a living thing.**

What's the conclusion about an antelope?

_____

_____

3. Here's the evidence:

**Every ocean is made up of salt water.
The Atlantic is an ocean.**

What's the conclusion about the Atlantic?

_____

_____

4. Here's the evidence:

**All birds are warm-blooded.
Penguins are birds.**

What's the conclusion about penguins?

_____

_____

A When you combine two sentences with the word **but,** what do you do with the period of the first sentence?
What follows the comma?

The two sentences below seem inconsistent. Tell how you would combine them with **but.** First say the combined sentence. Then tell about the punctuation.

Her brother was older. She was taller.

We can combine the same sentences with the word **however.** Here's the rule for doing that:

Change the period of the first sentence to a semicolon (;).

Follow the semicolon with the word **however.**

Follow **however** with a comma.

What do you do with the period of the first sentence?
What follows the semicolon?
What follows the word **however?**

Here are two sentences that seem inconsistent.

Her brother was older. She was taller.

Here are the sentences combined with **however.**

Her brother was older; however, she was taller.

Tell how you would combine the following sentences with the word **however.** First say the combined sentence. Then tell about the punctuation.

He was out of shape. He could run faster than anyone else I know.

Combine each pair of sentences below with the word **however.** Be sure to punctuate the sentences correctly.

1. He was out of shape. He could run faster than anyone else I know.

   _____

   _____

   _____

2. Tina did not cook well. She often had guests for dinner.

   _____

   _____

   _____

3. She had a Chinese name. She lived in Mexico.

   _____

   _____

   _____

Here is a diagram:

②conclusion

①

③evidence

1. (what)
2. (what and where)
3. (what and where)

For the word **(what)**, tell **what** the circled number shows. For the words **(what and where)**, tell **what** the circled number shows and **where** that part is.

For item 1, the word in parentheses is **what,** so you have to tell **what** to make for circle 1. Say the instructions for circle 1.

For item 2, the words in parentheses are **what and where,** so you have to tell **what** to make and **where** to make it for circle 2. Say the instructions for circle 2.

What are the words in parentheses for item 3?

Tell **what** to make and **where** to make it for circle 3.

Write the instructions for the diagram above.

1. (what) _____

_____

2. (what and where) _____

_____

_____

3. (what and where) _____

_____

_____

 Information that is not relevant is called **irrelevant.** What is the word for information that is not relevant? So, information that does not help explain a fact is **irrelevant** to the fact.

Here's a fact:

> **The woman walked with a limp.**

Here's information about what happened before the woman walked with a limp:

1. **She had pulled a muscle in her leg playing football.**
   Is that information relevant or irrelevant?
2. **She had been wearing red socks.**
   Is that information relevant or irrelevant?
3. **She had pulled a muscle in her arm playing basketball.**
   Is that information relevant or irrelevant?

D Here's the evidence:

> **The dog is in the pen.**
> **Part of the pen is in the yard.**

Can we be sure that the dog is in the yard? So, we start the conclusion with the word **maybe.**

> **Maybe the dog is in the yard.**

• Here's the evidence for a new conclusion:

> **The ant is in the sugar.**
> **Part of the sugar is in the cup.**

Can we be sure that the ant is in the cup? So, what word do we use to start the conclusion? Here's the conclusion about the ant:

> **Maybe the ant is in the cup.**

- Draw a conclusion about Joe. Here's the evidence:

Joe is in the car.
Part of the car is in the garage.

What's the conclusion about Joe?
We aren't sure that Joe is in the garage.
Which piece of evidence explains why we can't be sure?

- Draw a conclusion about the White House. Here's the evidence:

The White House is in Washington.
Part of Washington is on a hill.

What's the conclusion about the White House?
We aren't sure that the White House is on a hill.
Which piece of evidence explains why we can't be sure?

E You have two minutes to copy the paragraph below.

> **Some events are relevant to a fact; other events are irrelevant to that fact. If an event helps explain a fact, that event is relevant to the fact.**

_____

_____

_____

_____

_____

★ **F** Many writers have trouble with the words **everybody, anybody,** and **nobody.** These words name only one thing.

Write the verb **is** or the verb **are** in each blank.

1. Everybody _____ at the party.

2. Nobody _____ tired.

3. Anybody who fights them _____ beaten.

4. Nobody _____ waiting in line.

5. Anybody _____ glad to get a raise.

6. Everybody _____ playing tennis.

7. Anybody who cooks in these restaurants _____ a better cook than I am.

8. Nobody from these companies _____ working today.

9. Everybody in my classes _____ glad to be out of school.

G Read the evidence and write the conclusion. Here's the evidence:

Joe is in the car.
Part of the car is in the garage.

What's the conclusion about Joe?

_____

_____

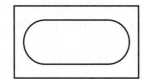

H Look at diagram 1.

Diagram 1

You can't see the dots, but **all the dots are in the oval.**

1. Complete the deduction.

All the dots are in the oval.
The oval is in the rectangle.

So, _____

_____

2. Draw dots in diagram 1.

• Look at diagram 2.

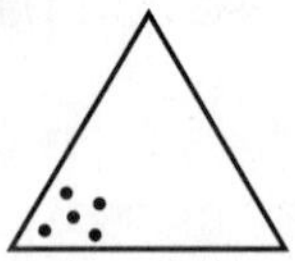

Diagram 2

You can see the dots and the triangle, but you can't see the circle.

3. Complete the deduction.

All the dots are in the triangle.
Part of the triangle is in the circle.

So, _____

_____

I Answer the questions.

1. What do we call information that does not help explain a fact?

_____

2. What do we call information that helps

explain a fact? _____

Write **relevant** or **irrelevant** for each piece of information.

| Fact: **The woman walked with a limp.** |

Information about what happened before the fact:

1. She had pulled a muscle in her leg playing football.

_____

2. She had been wearing red socks.

_____

3. She had pulled a muscle in her arm playing baseball.

_____

4. Her boots were squeezing her feet.

_____

A Here is a diagram:

relevant ——————— irrelevant
③   ①   ②

1. (what)
2. (what and where)
3. (what and where)

For the word **(what),** tell **what** the circled number shows. For the words **(what and where),** tell **what** the circled number shows and **where** that part is.

For item 1, the word in parentheses is **what,** so you have to tell **what** to make for circle 1. Say the instructions for circle 1.

What are the words in parentheses for item 2?

Tell **what** to make and **where** to make it for circle 2.

What are the words in parentheses for item 3?

Tell **what** to make and **where** to make it for circle 3.

 B When you combine two sentences with the word **but,** what do you do with the period of the first sentence?
What follows the comma?

The two sentences below seem inconsistent. Tell how you would combine them with **but.** First say the combined sentence. Then tell about the punctuation.

> **He wants to go out with Jolene. He won't ask her for a date.**

We can combine the same sentences with the word **however.** Here's the rule for doing that:

Change the period of the first sentence to a semicolon (;).
Follow the semicolon with the word **however.**
Follow **however** with a comma.

What do we do with the period of the first sentence?
What follows the semicolon?
What follows the word **however?**

Here are two sentences that seem inconsistent:

> **He wants to go out with Jolene. He won't ask her for a date.**

Here are the sentences combined with **however:**

> **He wants to go out with Jolene; however, he won't ask her for a date.**

Tell how you would combine the following two sentences with the word **however.** First say the combined sentence. Then tell about the punctuation.

> **Irene is fourteen years old. She is a college student.**

Combine each pair of sentences below with the word **however.** Be sure to punctuate the sentences correctly.

1. Irene is 14 years old. She is a college student.

   _____

   _____

2. David is a movie star. He hates to act.

   _____

   _____

3. Hal loves to play tennis. He doesn't have a tennis racket.

   _____

   _____

   _____

C Draw a conclusion about Rover. Here's the evidence:

   Some dogs are terriers.
   Rover is a dog.

What's the conclusion about Rover?
We aren't sure that Rover is a terrier.
Which piece of evidence explains why we can't be sure?

Draw a conclusion about the horse. Here's the evidence:

   The horse is in the barn.
   Part of the barn is on our land.

What's the conclusion about the horse?
We aren't sure that the horse is on our land.
Which piece of evidence explains why we can't be sure?

D You have two minutes to copy the paragraph below.

> **Here's the rule for combining two sentences with the word "but." Change the period of the first sentence to a comma. Follow the comma with the word "but."**

   _____

   _____

   _____

   _____

   _____

   _____

★ **E** Write the instructions for this diagram.

   relevant ———————— irrelevant
   ③   ①   ②

1. (what) _____

2. (what and where) _____

   _____

3. (what and where) _____

   _____

   _____

F Combine each pair of sentences below with the word **but.** Be sure to punctuate the sentences correctly.

1. Sometimes she seems really stupid. She usually gets the right answer.

_____

_____

_____

2. The moon is far away. It has been visited by humans.

_____

_____

_____

3. Olga hates to spend her money. She bought a new coat.

_____

_____

_____

4. Cora got mad. She kept smiling.

_____

_____

G Read the evidence and write the conclusion for each item.

1. Here's the evidence:

The dog is in the pen.
Part of the pen is in the yard.

What's the conclusion about the dog?

_____

_____

2. Here's the evidence:

The White House is in Washington.
Part of Washington is on a hill.

What's the conclusion about the White House?

_____

_____

H Write the verb **is** or the verb **are** in each blank.

1. Some of the dogs _____ howling.

2. Not all of my dreams _____ pleasant.

3. Each of the candles _____ a different color.

4. Everybody _____ going to swim.

5. Arlene _____ winning the race.

6. It _____ after midnight.

Write the verb **was** or the verb **were** in each blank.

7. Anybody _____ welcome to the party.

8. Ten toads _____ hiding in her sleeping bag.

9. Every day this winter _____ gloomy.

10. We _____ bored by his story.

11. Nobody _____ willing to go out in the cold.

12. All those cars _____ jamming the highway.

Answer the questions.

1. What do we call information that does not help explain a fact?

_____

2. What do we call information that helps explain a fact?

_____

Write **relevant** or **irrelevant** for each piece of information.

> Fact: **The driver jammed on her brakes.**

Information about what happened before the fact:

1. She owned a sports car.

_____

2. A dog ran in front of her car.

_____

3. She didn't want to hit the dog.

_____

4. She had been to the grocery store.

_____

5. Her car had bright brake lights.

_____

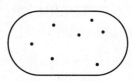 Look at diagram 1.

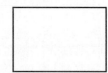

Diagram 1

You can see the dots and the oval, but you can't see the rectangle.

1. Complete the deduction.

> **All the dots are in the oval.**
> **The oval is in the rectangle.**

So, _____

_____

2. Draw the square in diagram 1.

- Look at diagram 2.

Diagram 2

You can't see the dots in the diagram, but **some dots are in the rectangle.**

3. We're looking for a dot. What's the conclusion about where that dot is?

_____

_____

A When you combine two sentences with the word **but,** what do you do with the period of the first sentence?
What word follows the comma?

When you combine two sentences with the word **however,** what do you do with the period of the first sentence?
What follows the semicolon?
What follows the word **however?**

B You have two minutes to copy the paragraph below.

> It is important to understand that certain events are relevant to a fact and other events are irrelevant. This understanding can help you in discussions with other people.

_____

_____

_____

_____

_____

_____

_____

★ **C** Here's what we know:

> **Jana doesn't swim very well.**

One of these sentences seems inconsistent with the sentence in the box:

- **She doesn't go to the pool very often.**
- **She won a swimming race.**

1. Use the word **but** to combine the sentence in the box with the inconsistent sentence.

_____

_____

_____

2. Use the word **however** to combine the sentence in the box with the inconsistent sentence.

_____

_____

_____

D Write the verb **was** or the verb **were** in each blank.

1. I _____ eating dinner when the tornado struck.

2. Each of the students _____ going to the show.

3. Some of the astronauts _____ in the parade.

4. Four of my chickens _____ killed by a fox.

5. Each of these movies _____ filmed in Hollywood.

6. Nobody _____ listening to Mr. Glump.

Write the verb **is** or the verb **are** in each blank.

7. Every one of those drivers _____ an air polluter.

8. One of the boys _____ the best flute player.

9. Anybody who lives in those hills _____ crazy.

10. They _____ going to jail for robbing that bank.

11. Maria _____ singing in the shower.

12. Everybody _____ laughing at you.

E Answer the questions.

1. What do we call information that does not help explain a fact? _____

2. What do we call information that helps explain a fact? _____

Write **relevant** or **irrelevant** for each piece of information.

Fact: Mr. Jones walked home from work today.

Information about what happened before the fact:

3. He liked his job.

_____

4. He thought he needed more exercise.

_____

5. He lived in an old house.

_____

6. His car broke down yesterday.

_____

7. He saw a good movie last week.

_____

F Write the instructions for this diagram.

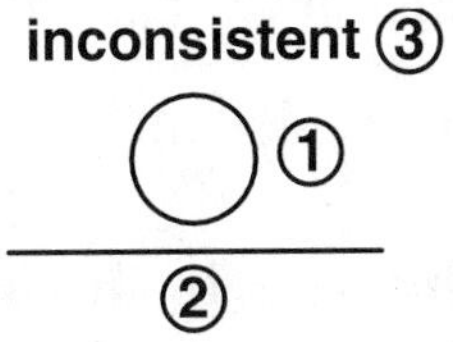

inconsistent ③

◯ ①
___
②

1. (what) _____

_____

2. (what and where) _____

_____

_____

3. (what and where) _____

_____

_____

G Look at diagram 1.

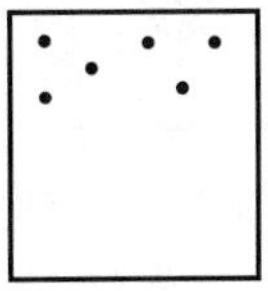

Diagram 1

You can see the dots and the square, but you can't see the oval.

1. Complete the deduction.

**All the dots are in the square.
Part of the square is in the oval.**

So, _____

_____

• Look at diagram 2.

Diagram 2

You can't see the dots in the diagram, but **all the dots are in the triangle.**

2. Complete the deduction.

**All the dots are in the triangle.
Part of the triangle is in the circle.**

So, _____

_____

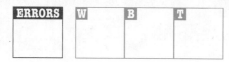
A If a question asks about your marital status, it is asking whether you are married, single, widowed, or divorced. If a question asks about your qualifications for a job, it is asking you to tell why you would be good at the job.

Use the facts to fill out the form.

Facts: Your name is Lois Meyer. You were a waitress before you got married. You are divorced and have three children. You know how to type. Your address is 104 Willow Lane, Kent, Washington. You are applying for a secretarial job at a newspaper. You would like to be a reporter.

B Read the evidence and write the conclusion for each item.

1. Here's the evidence:

The horse is in the barn.
Part of the barn is on our land.

What's the conclusion about the horse?

_____

_____

2. Here's the evidence:

Some trees bear fruit.
A mimosa is a tree.

What's the conclusion about a mimosa?

_____

_____

★
 a. Print your name on line 2.
 b. On line 1, print your present home address.
 c. State your marital status on line 4.
 d. On line 5, state any qualifications you have for this job.
 e. List your former work experience on line 3.
 f. On line 6, list the facts you didn't use in filling out this form.

1. _____

2. _____

3. _____

4. _____

5. _____

6. _____

Here's what we know:

Mr. Franko is building a house.

One of these sentences seems inconsistent with the sentence in the box:

- **He doesn't own many tools.**
- **He bought a lot of lumber.**

1. Use the word **but** to combine the sentence in the box with the inconsistent sentence.

_____

_____

_____

_____

2. Use the word **however** to combine the sentence in the box with the inconsistent sentence.

_____

_____

_____

_____

 Look at diagram 1.

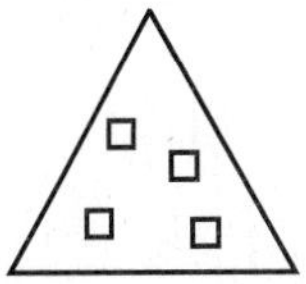

Diagram 1

You can see the boxes and the triangle, but you can't see the circle.

1. Complete the deduction.

**All the boxes are in the triangle.
The triangle is in the circle.**

So, _____

_____

- Look at diagram 2.

Diagram 2

You can't see the dots in the diagram, but **some of the dots are in the rectangle.**

2. We're looking for a dot. What's the conclusion about where that dot is?

_____

_____

E Write the verb **is** or the verb **are** in each blank.

1. Not one of my friends _____ a movie star.

2. Nobody in those houses _____ willing to enter that deserted mansion.

3. We _____ spending too much.

4. Every member of my family _____ sick.

5. One of the senators _____ up for reelection this year.

Write the verb **was** or the verb **were** in each blank.

6. Everybody who drove those cars _____ in an accident.

7. One of the restaurants _____ twice as expensive as the others.

8. I _____ ordering dinner when the roof collapsed.

9. The clothes my aunt bought _____ all too big for me.

10. Everybody _____ dancing and singing.

A If a question asks about your monthly income, it is asking how much money you make each month.
If a question asks about your monthly expenses, it is asking how much you have to pay out each month for things such as rent and food and car maintenance.

What does a question about your marital status ask?
What does a question about your job qualifications ask?

Use the facts to fill out the form.

Facts: Your name is Chris Curtis. You and your husband are applying for a loan to open a theater. You were a social worker before you decided to start your own business. Your husband teaches high school and makes $2500 a month. The two of you have $13,000 in a savings account. You make payments of $200 a month on a 1995 sedan. Your monthly house payment is $700, and your other monthly expenses come to $500.

★ 1. Why are you applying for this loan? _____

2. Indicate your marital status by checking one of these boxes.
   ☐ single   ☐ divorced   ☐ married   ☐ widowed

3. If you are married, what is the combined monthly income of you and your spouse?

   _____

4. If you have a car, indicate the following: year _____ model _____

5. What are your monthly expenses? _____

6. If you have any savings, indicate the amount. _____

7. State your present (or most recent) job. _____

8. If you are married, state your spouse's job. _____

LESSON 12

B Assume that this statement is true:

Jason always sleeps until 9 A.M.

Then this statement is a contradiction:

Jason went fishing today at 6 A.M.

Fill in the blanks to tell why the statement is a contradiction.

If _____

_____ ,

then _____

_____ .

● Assume that this statement is true:

Gina loved to eat all vegetables.

Then this statement is a contradiction:

Gina hated to eat broccoli.

Fill in the blanks to tell why the statement is a contradiction.

If _____

_____ ,

then _____

_____ .

C Write the instructions for this diagram.

③ **but**
② **however**
①

1. (what) _____

_____

2. (what and where) _____

_____

_____

3. (what and where) _____

_____

_____

Check your instructions and make sure they don't tell about making this diagram.

③ **but**
② **however**
①

D Write the verb **was** or the verb **were** in each blank.

1. Each of the chefs _____ planning a special dish for the king's wedding.

2. She _____ glad to be back home.

3. Not all the cows _____ ready to be milked.

4. Mr. Duval _____ smoking a pipe at the time of the accident.

5. They _____ looking for someone to help them.

Write the verb **is** or the verb **are** in each blank.

6. Everybody _____ interested in her opinions.

7. Anybody who flies in airplanes _____ crazy.

8. Every one of those plants _____ dying.

9. It _____ unlikely that I will ever see you again.

10. Your shoes _____ untied.

E Here's what we know:

> **Marie has a terrible cold.**

One of these sentences seems inconsistent with the sentence in the box:

- **Her nose is red.**
- **She came to school today.**

1. Use the word **but** to combine the sentence in the box with the inconsistent sentence.

_____

_____

_____

2. Use the word **however** to combine the sentence in the box with the inconsistent sentence.

_____

_____

_____

F Read the evidence and write the conclusion for each item.

1. Here's the evidence:

   Carrots are vegetables.
   All vegetables are food.

   What's the conclusion about carrots?

   _____

   _____

2. Here's the evidence:

   Carrots are vegetables.
   Some vegetables contain vitamin A.

   What's the conclusion about carrots?

   _____

   _____

3. Here's the evidence:

   The spiders are in the dirt.
   Some of the dirt is on the table.

   What's the conclusion about the spiders?

   _____

   _____

LESSON 13

★ **A** Here's what we know:

> **There is no electricity in Henry's house.**

One of these sentences seems inconsistent with the sentence in the box:

- **He cooks on a wood stove.**
- **He just bought a new washer and dryer.**

1. Use the word **but** to combine the sentence in the box with the inconsistent sentence.

   _____

   _____

   _____

2. Use the word **however** to combine the sentence in the box with the inconsistent sentence.

   _____

   _____

   _____

B Write the verb **is** or the verb **are** in each blank.

1. The girls _____ hungry.

2. Each of the girls _____ hungry.

3. Each of the dogs _____ running.

4. The dogs _____ running.

5. All of the chairs _____ in the basement.

6. Every one of the oak trees _____ dying.

C Assume that this statement is true:

Emma could not type.

1. Make up a contradiction.

   _____

   _____

2. Tell why your statement is a contradiction.

   If _____ ,

   then _____

   _____ .

- Assume that this statement is true:

  Fred always gets to work at 8 A.M.

1. Make up a contradiction.

   _____

   _____

2. Tell why your statement is a contradiction.

   If _____

   _____ ,

   then _____

   _____ .

• Assume that this statement is true:

Ziggy loved all kinds of trees.

1. Make up a contradiction.

_____

_____

2. Tell why your statement is a contradiction.

If _____

_____ ,

then _____

_____

_____ .

D Read the evidence and write the conclusion for each item.

1. Here's the evidence:

The boy was in the sand.
Some of the sand was in the shade.

What's the conclusion about the boy?

_____

_____

2. Here's the evidence:

All cows are mammals.
An Angus is a cow.

What's the conclusion about an Angus?

_____

_____

3. Here's the evidence:

Some cows are bred for beef.
An Angus is a cow.

What's the conclusion about an Angus?

_____

_____

LESSON 13

E Tuition is the fee that people must pay to attend a school. When people receive financial aid for their schooling, they get the money they need to pay their tuition or living expenses. Without financial aid, some people wouldn't be able to stay in college.

Use the facts to fill out the form.

Facts: Your name is Joe W. Brown, and you are tired of working in a bank. You have decided to go back to school to get a degree in economics. You attended West Lake Junior College from 1976 to 1978 and studied business. You have saved money for your living expenses, but you need a loan to pay your school tuition. Your social security number is 243-34-5521. Your address is 1501 South First Street, Santa Cruz, California. Your telephone number is 344-9037. You live alone. You like your apartment and want to keep it.

1. _____
   Last Name   First Name   Middle Initial

2. Social Security Number _____

3. Fill out the following: If more space is needed, use a separate sheet of paper.

Colleges you have attended	Years attended	Major subject studied
a.		
b.		

4. Do you plan to apply for student housing? Yes ☐ No ☐

5. Will you be applying for financial aid? Yes ☐ No ☐

6. _____
   Street Address   City   State

7. Phone Number _____

A Here's what we know:

| Owen is trying to lose weight. |

One of these sentences seems inconsistent with the sentence in the box:

- **He eats four large meals a day.**
- **He exercises two hours a day.**

1. Use the word **but** to combine the sentence in the box with the inconsistent sentence.

_____

_____

_____

2. Use the word **however** to combine the sentence in the box with the inconsistent sentence.

_____

_____

_____

B Answer the questions.

1. What do we call an event that does not help explain a fact? _____

2. What do we call an event that helps explain a fact? _____

Write **relevant** or **irrelevant** for each event.

Fact: **Peter's mother told him he should stop eating candy bars.**

Events that happened before the fact:

3. Peter came home from the dentist with six cavities. _____

4. Peter's mother read a book about the dangers of sugar. _____

5. Peter was a good baseball player.

_____

6. Peter was getting a little bit chubby.

_____

7. Peter sometimes spent his lunch money on the movies. _____

LESSON 14

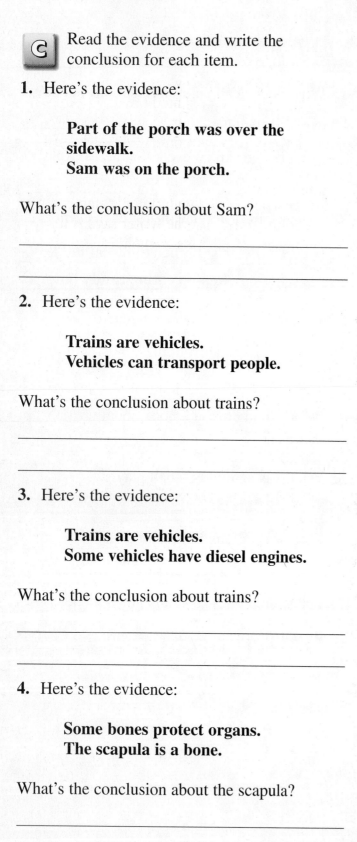

C   Read the evidence and write the conclusion for each item.

1. Here's the evidence:

Part of the porch was over the sidewalk.
Sam was on the porch.

What's the conclusion about Sam?

_____

_____

2. Here's the evidence:

Trains are vehicles.
Vehicles can transport people.

What's the conclusion about trains?

_____

_____

3. Here's the evidence:

Trains are vehicles.
Some vehicles have diesel engines.

What's the conclusion about trains?

_____

_____

4. Here's the evidence:

Some bones protect organs.
The scapula is a bone.

What's the conclusion about the scapula?

_____

_____

 D   Here's what we know:

> **Terry has been a writer for ten years.**

Write whether each sentence below seems **consistent** or **inconsistent** with the sentence in the box.

1. She doesn't like to write.

_____

2. She usually works at home.

_____

3. She has had five books published.

_____

4. She has used a lot of paper.

_____

E   Write the verb **was** or the verb **were** in each blank.

1. Each of the players _____ resting.

2. The players _____ resting.

3. Some of the children _____ sick.

4. Each of the cups _____ broken.

5. None of the girls _____ asleep.

6. Everybody in my classes _____ getting free tickets.

The name of our organization is the Fair-Minded Organization. Like the name says, we're fair-minded. We work hard. We take on difficult community projects. We keep women out of our organization because the work is too hard for them.

F | Here's a passage:

> The name of our organization is the Fair-Minded Organization. Like the name says, <u>we're fair-minded</u>. We work hard. We take on difficult community projects. We keep women out of our organization because the work is too hard for them.

1. We assume that the underlined statement is true. Something else the writer says is a contradiction. Which statement is a contradiction?

   _____

   _____

   _____

2. Explain the contradiction using an if-then statement.

   If _____

   _____ ,

   then _____

   _____ .

• Here's another passage:

> <u>I went to the ballet when I was in France</u>. There was painted scenery of the beautiful French countryside. I've never been away from my home in Kansas, but I would like to travel.

1. We assume that the underlined statement is true. Something else the writer says is a contradiction. Which statement is a contradiction?

   _____

   _____

2. Explain the contradiction using an if-then statement.

   If _____

   _____ ,

   then _____

   _____

   _____ .

Copyright © SRA/McGraw-Hill

LESSON 14 53

ERRORS | W | B | T

★ **A** Here's a passage:

> The Baseball Hall of Fame is in Cooperstown, New York. The exhibits there show the equipment that was used in famous games or by great players. Each year many people visit California, where they see the exhibits in the Baseball Hall of Fame.

1. We assume that the underlined statement is true. Something else the writer says is a contradiction. Which statement is a contradiction?

_____

_____

_____

_____

2. Explain the contradiction using an if-then statement.

If _____

_____ ,

then _____

_____ .

• Here's another passage:

> Mrs. Ramirez had spent all day preparing Thanksgiving dinner for her family. Now she was setting the dinner table. She was really excited about having everyone together again—her four daughters and their husbands, her eight grandchildren, herself, and Mr. Ramirez. It would be a wonderful way to celebrate New Year's Day. She could hardly wait.

1. We assume that the underlined statement is true. Something else the writer says is a contradiction. Which statement is a contradiction?

_____

_____

_____

2. Explain the contradiction using an if-then statement.

If _____

_____

_____ ,

then _____

_____ .

B Read the evidence and write the conclusion for each item.

1. Here's the evidence:

All mammals have hair.
Whales are mammals.

What's the conclusion about whales?

_____

_____

2. Here's the evidence:

Part of the army was in Germany.
Sidney was in the army.

What's the conclusion about Sidney?

_____

_____

3. Here's the evidence:

All trucks have wheels.
Todd has a truck.

What's the conclusion about Todd's truck?

_____

_____

4. Here's the evidence:

Some trucks are green.
Todd has a truck.

What's the conclusion about Todd's truck?

_____

_____

C Answer the questions.

1. What do we call an event that helps explain a fact? _____

2. What do we call an event that does not help explain a fact? _____

Write **relevant** or **irrelevant** for each event.

Fact: **Sally is mad at Tom.**

Events that happened before the fact:

3. Sally kissed her mother this morning.

_____

4. Tom spilled ink on Sally's final exam.

_____

5. She watched Tom play basketball.

_____

6. He told her she was fat.

_____

LESSON 15

 D Here's what we know:

Jeffrey is a nurse.

Write whether each sentence below seems **consistent** or **inconsistent** with the sentence in the box.

1. He doesn't like to work with people.

   _____

2. He works with doctors.

   _____

3. The sight of blood makes him sick.

   _____

4. He knows a lot about illnesses.

   _____

E Write the verb **is** or the verb **are** in each blank. Remember which verb always goes with the word **each.**

1. Each of the pencils _____ broken.

2. The girls _____ hungry.

3. Each of the dogs _____ running.

4. Each player _____ resting.

5. The men _____ tired.

6. Each of the older lions _____ sleeping.

 F Here's what we know:

Alvin doesn't read very well.

One of these sentences seems inconsistent with the sentence in the box:

- **He works at a library.**
- **He never reads.**

1. Use the word **but** to combine the sentence in the box with the inconsistent sentence.

   _____

   _____

   _____

2. Use the word **however** to combine the sentence in the box with the inconsistent sentence.

   _____

   _____

   _____

G This lesson presented a fact that you will be tested on. The fact is:

A boar is a wild pig with large tusks.

Study the fact. Repeat it to yourself. Writing the fact may help you to remember it.

★ **A** Read the evidence and write the conclusion for each item.

1. Here's the evidence:

> **The children were in the flowers.**
> **Some of the flowers were in the schoolyard.**

What's the conclusion about the children?

_____

_____

2. Here's the evidence:

> **Some trees bear fruit.**
> **A mimosa is a tree.**

What's the conclusion about a mimosa?

_____

_____

3. Here's the evidence:

> **All trees are living things.**
> **A mimosa is a tree.**

What's the conclusion about a mimosa?

_____

_____

4. Here's the evidence:

> **Some countries have a king.**
> **Brazil is a country.**

What's the conclusion about Brazil?

_____

_____

B Here's a passage:

> Frank was getting ready for his fishing trip. At 5:30 in the afternoon, he waterproofed his boots. Then he made six sandwiches, filled a jug with hot cocoa, and put everything in a basket. When Frank drove off a few minutes later, the sunrise was turning the sky pink.

1. We assume that the underlined statement is true. Something else the writer says is a contradiction. Circle the contradiction.

2. Make up an if-then statement that explains the contradiction.

_____

_____

_____

_____

_____

_____

LESSON 16

- Here's another passage:

> All people need a certain amount of sugar in their diets. The natural sugar found in fruits and vegetables is a good source of energy. But other types of sugar are not good for you. It would be best if everyone stopped eating sugar. However, the average American consumes about 50 kilograms of sugar a year.

1. We assume that the underlined statement is true. Something else the writer says is a contradiction. Circle the contradiction.
2. Make up an if-then statement that explains the contradiction.

_____

_____

_____

_____

_____

C Write the verb **was** or the verb **were** in each blank.

1. The pencils _____ broken.

2. Each of the tires _____ flat.

3. The men _____ working hard.

4. Each of the boys _____ singing.

5. Those pins _____ sharp.

 D Here's what we know:

> **Sharon went out to gather firewood.**

One of these sentences seems inconsistent with the sentence in the box:

- **She heats her house with wood.**
- **She doesn't have a fireplace.**

1. Use the word **but** to combine the sentence in the box with the inconsistent sentence.

_____

_____

_____

2. Use the word **however** to combine the sentence in the box with the inconsistent sentence.

_____

_____

_____

E This lesson presented a fact that you will be tested on. The fact is:

> **A nook is a small place.**

Study the fact. Repeat it to yourself. Writing the fact may help you to remember it.

★ **A**

When you name somebody as a reference, that person is supposed to give evidence about what kind of worker you are and how reliable you are. The person you give as a reference should say good things about you.

Use the facts to fill out the form.

Facts: Your name is Susan Wilson. You live at $203\frac{1}{2}$ West 5th, in Toledo, Ohio. You are filling out a credit application form to buy a washer. You pay $500 a month for rent and $500 for bills. You are a car mechanic and make $2000 a month. You have been working at Joe's Garage for three years. Your boss is George Simpson. He thinks you are a very good mechanic.

1. What is your monthly income? _____

2. What are your monthly expenses? _____

3. Subtract line 2 from line 1. _____
4. State your present job and how long you have worked there.

_____

5. Print your name, last name first. _____

6. Name one person as a reference. _____
7. Write the first fact you didn't use in filling out this form.

_____

LESSON 17

B Here's what we know:

> **He was tired.**

Here's a sentence that seems consistent with the sentence in the box:

> **He went to bed.**

1. Combine the sentences with **so.**

   _____

   _____

2. Combine the sentences with **and.**

   _____

   _____

3. Combine the sentences with **therefore.**

   _____

   _____

Make sure you punctuated the sentences correctly.

C Look at diagram 1.

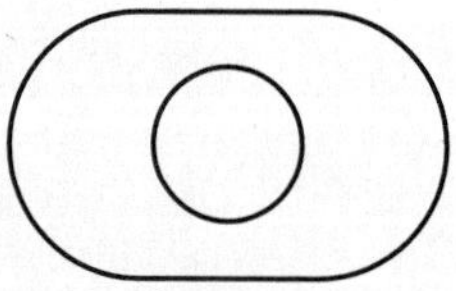

Diagram 1

You can't see the boxes, but **all the boxes are in the circle.**

1. Complete the deduction.

   > **All the boxes are in the circle.**
   > **The circle is in the oval.**

   So, _____

   _____

2. Draw boxes in diagram 1.

● Look at diagram 2.

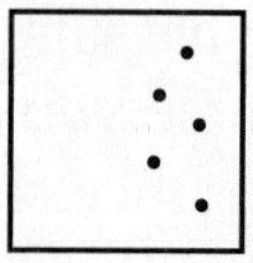

Diagram 2

You can see the dots and the square, but you can't see the circle.

3. Complete the deduction.

   > **All the dots are in the square.**
   > **Part of the square is in the circle.**

   So, _____

   _____

D Write the verb **was** or the verb **were** in each blank.

1. Each of the pencils _____ sharpened.

2. Each of the dogs _____ tired.

3. All the chairs _____ covered with chewing gum.

4. Each piece of paper _____ yellow.

5. The rugs _____ brown and white.

Here's a passage:

> All reptiles are cold-blooded. This means that their body temperature goes down when it is cold outside and up when the weather is warm. Mammals, which include humans, are warm-blooded. They have nearly the same body temperature all the time. A few kinds of reptiles in Africa are warm-blooded, but they are now almost extinct.

1. We assume that the underlined statement is true. Something else the writer says is a contradiction. Circle the contradiction.
2. Make up an if-then statement that explains the contradiction.

_____

_____

_____

• Here's another passage:

> The most common plant in Oregon is the blackberry bush. It produces dark purple berries in late August and early September. People pick the berries for free and eat blackberry jam and fresh blackberry pie all through the spring. Some people think the only bad thing about the blackberry bush is that it grows everywhere—even in their backyards.

1. We assume that the underlined statement is true. Something else the writer says is a contradiction. Circle the contradiction.
2. Make up an if-then statement that explains the contradiction.

_____

_____

_____

_____

_____

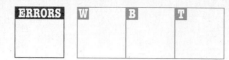

ERRORS W B T

★ **A** Here's a passage:

> "Seymour, I wish you'd stop hitting your sister. <u>Hitting people is stupid and ugly.</u> If you can't find some other way to express your unhappiness with Sarah, I'm going to slug you."

1. We assume that the underlined statement is true. Something else the writer says is a contradiction. Circle the contradiction.
2. Make up an if-then statement that explains the contradiction.

_____

_____

_____

• Here's another passage:

> <u>Linda wrote several short stories that she decided to send to seven different magazines</u>. Six magazines each sent back a letter that said, "I'm sorry, but we cannot use your stories." But Linda received a check for $25 from the eighth magazine. She celebrated by going out to dinner and spending the $25.

1. We assume that the underlined statement is true. Something else the writer says is a contradiction. Circle the contradiction.

2. Make up an if-then statement that explains the contradiction.

_____

_____

_____

_____

_____

B Here's what we know:

> **Nina is hungry.**

Here's a sentence that seems consistent with the sentence in the box:

She is eating a lot.

1. Combine the sentences with **so.**

_____

_____

2. Combine the sentences with **and.**

_____

_____

3. Combine the sentences with **therefore.**

_____

_____

Make sure you punctuated the sentences correctly.

Use the facts to fill out the form.

Facts: Your name is Arnold Tillum and you are 28 years old. You've shared an apartment with Larry Romez for five years. You are applying for car insurance for your 1994 station wagon. You live at 2515 W. 23rd Street in Houston, Texas. Your home phone number is 689-1538. Your driver's license number is M454360, and your license plate number is HEZ 152. Your old insurance company was Bump Auto in Chicago. Bump Auto canceled your insurance when you moved. Your doctor's name is Pedro Petron.

1. Name _____ Age _____

2. Type of insurance you want _____

3. Address _____

4. If applying for health insurance, who is your doctor? _____
5. If applying for car insurance, tell about your car:

   Year _____ Model _____

6. Have you had insurance before? _____

7. If so, with whom? _____

8. If so, why are you changing companies? _____

   _____

9. Give the name and address of a personal reference.

   _____

LESSON 18

D For each item, write a new sentence that means the same thing by changing the underlined words.

1. By pausing, she lost her chance.

_____

_____

2. Although he paused, he did not give up his chance.

_____

_____

_____

3. The dog had four chances to catch the fly.

_____

_____

4. Don't pause before eating.

_____

_____

E Write the instructions for this diagram.

③ **hesitating**
① △
② **opportunity**
④ ☐

1. (what) _____

_____

2. (what and where) _____

_____

_____

3. (what and where) _____

_____

4. (what and where) _____

_____

F This lesson presented a fact that you will be tested on. The fact is:

The Greek word paragraphos means by the side of writing.

Study the fact. Repeat it to yourself. Writing the fact may help you to remember it.

★ **A**   Here's a passage:

> Many people are becoming vegetarians. Basketball star Bill Digby says, "Eating meat is bad for me. Being a vegetarian has made me a great athlete." Among Digby's favorite foods are dandelion roots, cantaloupes, and antelope. He is also fond of cucumber cookies and eggplant pie.

1. We assume that the underlined statement is true. Something else the writer says is a contradiction. Circle the contradiction.
2. Make up an if-then statement that explains the contradiction.

_____

_____

_____

_____

● Here's another passage:

> SAM: This math problem is too hard for me. I need some help.
> PAM: Well, what do you know! My big brother needs help from little me! I'll bet mom would think this is pretty funny. Hey, mom—
> SAM: Hush up, Pam. I don't need you. I can do this myself.

1. We assume that the underlined statement is true. Something else the writer says is a contradiction. Circle the contradiction.
2. Make up an if-then statement that explains the contradiction.

_____

_____

_____

_____

B For each item, write a new sentence that means the same thing by changing the underlined words.

1. By <u>pausing</u>, the old woman lost her <u>chance</u>.

_____

_____

2. How many <u>chances</u> do you think you'll get?

_____

_____

3. The minute Claude <u>paused</u>, his sister jumped at the <u>chance</u>.

_____

_____

_____

4. Stop <u>pausing</u> before diving into the pool.

_____

_____

C Write the verb **is** or the verb **are** in each blank.

1. Nobody I know _____ going to that party.

2. Each of the flowers _____ a different color and shape.

3. Some of my friends _____ going to the game.

4. All my clothes _____ gone.

5. Ms. Kaplan _____ the best trumpet player in Idaho.

Write the verb **was** or the verb **were** in each blank.

6. I _____ being followed by some thug in a pickup truck.

7. Not one of the athletes _____ playing fair.

8. Everybody _____ dressed up like a Roman soldier.

9. He _____ the ugliest person I had ever seen.

10. The animals in the circus _____ escaping.

D Here's what we know:

Julia doesn't know how to type.

One of the sentences below seems consistent with the sentence in the box. One of the sentences seems inconsistent with the sentence in the box.

- **She has a typewriter.**
- **She's going to take a typing class.**

1. Use the word **so** to combine the sentence in the box with the consistent sentence.

   _____

   _____

   _____

2. Use **therefore** to combine the sentence in the box with the consistent sentence.

   _____

   _____

   _____

3. Use **but** to combine the sentence in the box with the inconsistent sentence.

   _____

   _____

   _____

4. Use **however** to combine the sentence in the box with the inconsistent sentence.

   _____

   _____

   _____

Make sure you punctuated the sentences correctly.

E Answer the questions.

1. What do we call an event that helps explain a fact? _____

2. What do we call an event that does not help explain a fact? _____

Write **relevant** or **irrelevant** for each event.

   Fact: "The murder obviously occurred quite recently," declared Inspector Bonedigger.

3. The ice in the victim's drink had not melted.

   _____

4. The murder was committed with a candlestick. _____

5. The body was still warm.

   _____

6. Although a large window was broken, the room was much warmer than the outside air.

   _____

7. The victim was a rich French baron.

   _____

F Tomorrow you will be tested on facts you have learned. The test will include facts presented in Lessons 15–19. The facts are:

1. **A boar is a wild pig with large tusks.** 2. **A nook is a small place.** 3. **The Greek word <u>paragraphos</u> means <u>by the side of writing.</u>**

ERRORS	W	B	T

★ **A** Here's a passage:

> I really care about my health. Every morning I take two vitamin C tablets and one multivitamin tablet. A lot of people don't like to take pills. I'll admit it's difficult to choke down five vitamin pills every morning, but I think it's worth it.

1. We assume that the underlined statement is true. Something else the writer says is a contradiction. Circle the contradiction.
2. Make up an if-then statement that explains the contradiction.

_____

_____

_____

_____

_____

_____

• Here's another passage:

> On the planet Bloop, things are different colors from what they are on Earth. Bushes are blue. And everything that is red on Earth is white on Bloop.
> Venro lived on Bloop. It was a beautiful fall day, so he decided to go for a drive. He was going along, looking at the leaves of the trees, which had changed colors. As he was driving, he didn't notice that the traffic light had changed from green to red. A car struck his car as he went through the intersection.

1. We assume that the underlined statement is true. Something else the writer says is a contradiction. Circle the contradiction.
2. Make up an if-then statement that explains the contradiction.

_____

_____

_____

_____

B Write the verb **was** or the verb **were** in each blank.

1. Each of the spaceships _____ scooping up many people.

2. Everybody who read those books _____ bored.

3. Jody Epstein _____ the biggest show-off in the seventh grade.

4. It _____ the hottest day of the year.

5. Twelve radios _____ stolen from that store.

Write the verb **is** or the verb **are** in each blank.

6. Every one of these students _____ learning how to read.

7. We _____ going to fight for our freedom.

8. Nobody _____ going to tell me what to do.

9. All my friends _____ willing to help.

10. She _____ on her way to Spain.

C Answer the questions.

1. What do we call an event that does not help explain a fact?

_____

2. What do we call an event that helps explain a fact?

_____

Write **relevant** or **irrelevant** for each event.

Fact: In 1969, American astronauts set foot on the moon.

3. The phases of the moon are related to ocean tides.

_____

4. The United States government spends billions of dollars on research and equipment for space travel.

_____

5. The word **lunatic** once meant someone who had been driven crazy by the moon.

_____

6. There has been enormous progress in science and technology in the last twenty years.

_____

7. Since the earliest times, people have wondered what it would be like to visit someplace far from Earth.

_____

Here's what we know:

> **Frank loves going to school.**

One of the sentences below seems consistent with the sentence in the box. One of the sentences seems inconsistent with the sentence in the box.

- **He never cuts any classes.**
- **He failed three tests last week.**

1. Use the word **but** to combine the sentence in the box with the inconsistent sentence.

   _____

   _____

   _____

2. Use the word **so** to combine the sentence in the box with the consistent sentence.

   _____

   _____

   _____

3. Use the word **however** to combine the sentence in the box with the inconsistent sentence.

   _____

   _____

   _____

4. Use the word **and** to combine the sentence in the box with the consistent sentence.

   _____

   _____

   _____

Make sure you punctuated the sentences correctly.

A Here's a passage:

> "I'm eight and Kevin's only six," whined Rachel. "That means I'm bigger and I need more food to keep me going. That's why I should get the last piece of pie."
>
> "But, mom," countered Kevin, "she's already had two pieces today and I haven't had any!"
>
> "Rachel," said their mother calmly, "if you don't want to share the last piece with your older brother, then I don't think either of you should have any."

1. We assume that the underlined statement is true. Something else the writer says is a contradiction. Circle the contradiction.
2. Make up an if-then statement that explains the contradiction.

_____

_____

_____

_____

B In the passage below, the verbs **is** and **are** and the verbs **was** and **were** are used incorrectly five times. Cross out each incorrect word. Write the correct word above it.

> Four fire engines streaked toward the burning building. Three of them was long and had ladders. All of them were red. Gallons of water was spraying from a crack in a pipe. Soon one of the firefighters were climbing into a sewer and turning off the water. Anybody who does those kinds of things are pretty brave. Not one of the fire engines were able to pump water on the fire now, because there was no water.

 C For each item, write a sentence that means the same thing by changing the underlined word or words.

1. I got lost because his directions were underlined unclear.

_____

_____

2. The teacher's questions were underlined unclear and repetitive.

_____

_____

3. Repetitive books are not much fun to read.

_____

_____

4. His <u>unclear</u> and <u>repetitive</u> speech made the time drag.

_____

_____

5. By <u>pausing</u>, the hungry alligator lost its <u>chance</u>.

_____

_____

6. If Elena <u>pauses</u> too long, will you consider me?

_____

_____

7. Julio will have a <u>chance</u> to buy that car today.

_____

_____

_____

8. Ernie had a <u>chance</u> and acted without <u>pausing</u>.

_____

_____

_____

D Here's what we know:

> **Minnie is three years old.**

One of the sentences below seems consistent with the sentence in the box. One of the sentences seems inconsistent with the sentence in the box.

- **She takes a nap every day.**
- **She knows how to read.**

1. Use the word **therefore** to combine the sentence in the box with the consistent sentence.

_____

_____

2. Use the word **but** to combine the sentence in the box with the inconsistent sentence.

_____

_____

3. Use the word **however** to combine the sentence in the box with the inconsistent sentence.

_____

_____

4. Use the word **and** to combine the sentence in the box with the consistent sentence.

_____

_____

Make sure you punctuated the sentences correctly.

This lesson presented some facts that you will be tested on. These facts are:

---

1. **Eohippus was the earliest-known close relative of the modern horse.**
2. **We know that eohippus was related to the horse because its skeleton resembles the skeleton of a modern horse.**

Study these facts. Repeat them to yourself. Writing the facts may help you to remember them.

★ **A** Here's what we know:

Carol hates to cook.

One of the sentences below seems consistent with the sentence in the box. One of the sentences seems inconsistent with the sentence in the box.

- **She buys lots of TV dinners.**
- **She buys lots of cookbooks.**

1. Use the word **so** to combine the sentence in the box with the consistent sentence.

_____

_____

2. Use the word **but** to combine the sentence in the box with the inconsistent sentence.

_____

_____

3. Use the word **therefore** to combine the sentence in the box with the consistent sentence.

_____

_____

4. Use the word **however** to combine the sentence in the box with the inconsistent sentence.

_____

_____

Make sure you punctuated the sentences correctly.

B Here's a passage:

> <u>I have four cats and a dog at my house</u> because I really like animals. Some of my friends don't get along with them, though. I even have a couple of friends who can't visit me anymore because they are allergic to cats. The worst news came in a letter today. I invited my mom down for Thanksgiving, and she wrote back saying, "I would really like to come down for the holiday, but I just couldn't bear to stay in that house with ten animals crawling all over. Why don't you come here for the holiday instead?" Sometimes it seems that those animals are just too much trouble.

1. We assume that the underlined statement is true. Something else the writer says is a contradiction. Circle the contradiction.
2. Make up an if-then statement that explains the contradiction.

_____

_____

_____

C In the passage below, the verbs **is** and **are** and the verbs **was** and **were** are used incorrectly six times. Cross out each incorrect word. Write the correct word above it.

The impression that you get from western movies are really not very accurate. Most cowboys was lonely and overworked. A person living in the Old West was sometimes forced to go without food or shelter for days at a time. As for the glamorous gunfighter, he are more a myth than a historical fact. Many gunfighters was sneaky and cowardly men who survived by shooting others in the back without warning. In the early settlements, acts such as cheating and stealing was as common as trying to make an honest living. Perhaps western movies is best thought of as Early American fairy tales.

D For each item, write a sentence that means the same thing by changing the underlined word or words.

1. His directions were <u>unclear</u> and <u>repetitive</u>.

_____

_____

2. Her <u>repetitive</u> sentences made her argument <u>unclear</u>.

_____

_____

3. <u>Unclear</u> questions are hard to answer.

_____

_____

4. We were bored by her <u>repetitive</u> comments.

_____

_____

5. By <u>pausing</u>, the shopkeeper lost her <u>chance</u>.

_____

_____

6. Bill <u>paused</u> and then made a redundant comment.

_____

_____

7. His remarks about Tony's <u>chance</u> were ambiguous.

_____

_____

8. Vera lost her <u>chance</u> for that job because she <u>paused</u> too long.

_____

_____

E This lesson presented some facts that you will be tested on. These facts are:

1. **Eohippus defended itself by outrunning its enemies.**
2. **The feet of eohippus changed over the centuries to make it a better runner.**

Study these facts. Repeat them to yourself. Writing the facts may help you to remember them.

ERRORS | W | B | T

A For each item, write a sentence that means the same thing by changing the underlined word or words.

1. His directions were <u>unclear</u> and <u>repetitive</u>.

_____

_____

2. Many textbooks are <u>unclear</u> and <u>repetitive</u>.

_____

_____

3. The class was confused by the teacher's <u>unclear</u> explanation.

_____

_____

4. In giving her speech, she <u>paused</u> often and spoke very softly.

_____

_____

_____

B Read the evidence and write the conclusion for each item.

1. Here's the evidence:

   All planets orbit the sun.
   Venus is a planet.

   What's the conclusion about Venus?

   _____

2. Here's the evidence:

   Some planets have moons.
   Venus is a planet.

   What's the conclusion about Venus?

   _____

3. Here's the evidence:

   Toronto is in Ontario.
   Ontario is in Canada.

   What's the conclusion about Toronto?

   _____

4. Here's the evidence:

   The C5X is a car.
   Some cars run on diesel fuel.

   What's the conclusion about the C5X?

   _____

   _____

Read the facts and the items. If an item is relevant to fact A, write **relevant to fact A.** If an item is relevant to fact B, write **relevant to fact B.** If an item is irrelevant to both facts, write **irrelevant.**

Fact A. **Sally is mad at Tom.**

Fact B. **Sally is going to Europe this fall.**

1. Sally is studying conversational French.

2. Tom spilled salad dressing on Sally's dress.

3. Sally and Tom play violin duets.

4. Sally's desk is covered with travel brochures.

In the passage below, the verbs **is** and **are** and the verbs **was** and **were** are used incorrectly six times. Cross out each incorrect word. Write the correct word above it.

> Chickens swallow small bits of sand and gravel when they eat. The tiny rocks is used to help the chicken digest food. Some dinosaurs was rock eaters too, but the rocks they ate was much larger. A stone that were inside a dinosaur's stomach for a few years began to change in appearance. The juices in the dinosaur's stomach was able to change a rough stone into one that was smooth and shiny. Stones like this are called gastroliths, or gizzard stones. Naturally, most fossil collectors is very happy when they find a gizzard stone.

ERRORS | W | B | T

A Read the facts and the items. If an item is relevant to fact A, write **relevant to fact A.** If an item is relevant to fact B, write **relevant to fact B.** If an item is irrelevant to both facts, write **irrelevant.**

Fact A. **Mack drives a logging truck.**

Fact B. **In twenty years of driving, Mack has never had an accident.**

1. Mack got a special safety award and a $100 bonus in last month's check.

_____

2. Other truckers feel safe riding with Mack.

_____

3. Mack spends a lot of time in the woods.

_____

4. Mack repaints his car every three years.

_____

B For each item, write a sentence that means the same thing by changing the underlined word or words.

1. His directions were <u>unclear</u> and <u>repetitive</u>.

_____

_____

2. Her <u>unclear</u> and <u>repetitive</u> remarks wasted a lot of time.

_____

_____

3. Television commercials are very <u>repetitive</u>.

_____

_____

4. Her description of the marvelous <u>chance</u> they had was <u>unclear</u>.

_____

_____

_____

C In the passage below, the verbs **is** and **are** and the verbs **was** and **were** are used incorrectly six times. Cross out each incorrect word. Write the correct word above it.

Not all animals is as intelligent as elephants. At the London Zoo, elephants was separated from viewers by two fences. When people threw peanuts to the elephants, they sometimes didn't throw the nuts hard enough. Many nuts was on the ground between the two fences. Neither the people nor the elephants was able to reach them. One of the elephants were clever enough to give the throwers another chance. With a blast of air from its trunk, it blew the peanuts back to the crowd. Soon, every elephant in the zoo were blowing poorly thrown peanuts back to the startled visitors.

D This lesson presented some facts that you will be tested on. These facts are:

> 1. **Modern horses and other similar animals belong to a group called equus.**
> 2. **Some types of equus became large and others became slender, depending on what climate they lived in.**

Study these facts. Repeat them to yourself. Writing the facts may help you to remember them.

E Tomorrow you will be tested on facts you have learned. The test will include all of the facts presented in Lessons 20–24 and some of the facts from earlier lessons. These facts are:

1. A boar is a wild pig with large tusks.
2. A nook is a small place.
3. The Greek word **paragraphos** means **by the side of writing.**
4. Eohippus was the earliest-known close relative of the modern horse.
5. We know that eohippus was related to the horse because its skeleton resembles the skeleton of a modern horse.
6. Eohippus defended itself by outrunning its enemies.
7. The feet of eohippus changed over the centuries to make it a better runner.
8. Modern horses and other similar animals belong to a group called equus.
9. Some types of equus became large and others became slender, depending on what climate they lived in.

A Here's a deduction with no irrelevant words:

> **Every country in Africa is smaller than Canada.**
> **Libya is a country in Africa.**
> **Therefore, Libya is smaller than Canada.**

Here's a deduction with words that are irrelevant to the conclusion. The irrelevant words are in the second piece of evidence:

> **Every country in Africa is smaller than Canada.**
> **Libya is a country in Africa that has lots of oil.**
> **Therefore, Libya is smaller than Canada.**

Which words in the second piece of evidence are irrelevant?

• Here's another deduction with irrelevant words in the second piece of evidence:

> **She loved to eat all vegetables.**
> **Carrots are orange vegetables that grow in the ground.**
> **Therefore, she loved to eat carrots.**

Which words in the second piece of evidence are irrelevant?
Cross out those words.
Now say the entire deduction with the irrelevant words removed.

• Here's another deduction with irrelevant words in the second piece of evidence:

> **All dogs are mammals.**
> **An Afghan is a dog that has long hair.**
> **Therefore, an Afghan is a mammal.**

Which words in the second piece of evidence are irrelevant?
Cross out those words.
Now say the entire deduction with the irrelevant words removed.

B Look at this diagram:

The diagram contradicts instruction 1 or instruction 2.

1. Draw a vertical line.
2. Draw a square to the right of the line.

Say the instruction that the diagram contradicts.
What does the diagram show?
How would you change the diagram so that it is consistent with the instructions?

- Look at this diagram:

This diagram contradicts part of these instructions.

1. Draw a horizontal line.
2. Make a **T** in the middle of the line.

Circle the instruction that the diagram contradicts.
Draw a new diagram that follows the instructions.

- Look at this diagram:

This diagram contradicts part of these instructions.

1. Draw a square.
2. To the right of the square, draw a vertical line.
3. Draw a horizontal line above the vertical line.

Circle the instruction that the diagram contradicts.
Draw a new diagram that follows the instructions.

★ For each deduction, cross out the irrelevant words in the second piece of evidence.

1. **Every country in Africa is smaller than Canada.**
   Libya is a country in Africa that has lots of oil.
   Therefore, Libya is smaller than Canada.
2. **Valleys were cut by moving water.**
   The Grand Canyon is a valley in Arizona.
   Therefore, the Grand Canyon was cut by moving water.

D Here's what we know:

> **Jack has a burglar alarm.**

One of the sentences below seems consistent with the sentence in the box. One of the sentences seems inconsistent with the sentence in the box.

- **He isn't bothered by burglars.**
- **He was robbed last night.**

1. Use the word **but** to combine the sentence in the box with the inconsistent sentence.

   _____

   _____

2. Use the word **therefore** to combine the sentence in the box with the consistent sentence.

   _____

   _____

   _____

3. Use the word **and** to combine the sentence in the box with the consistent sentence.

_____

_____

_____

4. Use the word **however** to combine the sentence in the box with the inconsistent sentence.

_____

_____

_____

Make sure you punctuated the sentences correctly.

E For each item, write a sentence that means the same thing by changing the underlined word or words.

1. She had a marvelous <u>chance</u>, but her response was <u>unclear</u>.

_____

_____

_____

2. By <u>pausing</u>, she lost her <u>chance</u>.

_____

_____

3. Sophie had several <u>chances</u> to publish her book, even though it is very <u>repetitive</u>.

_____

_____

_____

_____

4. Ian <u>paused</u> before answering, and his position was still <u>unclear</u> when he finished.

_____

_____

_____

_____

F Read the facts and the items. If an item is relevant to fact A, write **relevant to fact A.** If an item is relevant to fact B, write **relevant to fact B.** If an item is irrelevant to both facts, write **irrelevant.**

Fact A. **Horace is a brilliant piano player.**

Fact B. **Horace is fifteen years old.**

1. Horace would rather go to Europe by boat than by plane.

_____

2. Horace has been to dozens of famous concert halls.

_____

3. Horace didn't vote in last year's election.

_____

4. Horace has his hands insured for a million dollars.

_____

A Here's a deduction with no irrelevant words:

> **Some planets have moons.**
> **Jupiter is a planet.**
> **Therefore, maybe Jupiter has moons.**

Here's a deduction with words that are irrelevant to the conclusion. The irrelevant words are in the second piece of evidence:

> **Some planets have moons.**
> **Jupiter is a large planet in our solar system.**
> **Therefore, maybe Jupiter has moons.**

Which words in the second piece of evidence are irrelevant?

- Here's another deduction with irrelevant words in the second piece of evidence:

> **All mammals have hair.**
> **A shrew is a small mammal that has a long, pointed nose.**
> **Therefore, a shrew has hair.**

Which words in the second piece of evidence are irrelevant?
Cross out those words.
Now say the entire deduction with the irrelevant words removed.

- Here's another deduction with irrelevant words in the second piece of evidence:

> **Some glaciers are getting smaller.**
> **The Mendenhall is a glacier in Alaska.**
> **Therefore, maybe the Mendenhall is getting smaller.**

Which words in the second piece of evidence are irrelevant?
Cross out those words.
Now say the entire deduction with the irrelevant words removed.

★ **B** In the passage below, the verbs **is** and **are** and the verbs **was** and **were** are used incorrectly six times. Cross out each incorrect word. Write the correct word above it.

> Rats are a nuisance all over the world. Rats and the fleas they carry is at this moment spreading twenty deadly diseases. Among these diseases is typhus and the plague. The plague were responsible for the death of one-fourth of the people in Europe during the Middle Ages. Last year, food that could have fed millions of people were eaten by rats. Each year, huge areas of South America, Asia, and Africa is overrun by hungry rats. Like humans, they are capable of eating almost anything and living almost anywhere. Like humans, their population grows and spreads each year. Like humans, the rat population are threatening to overrun and destroy portions of the environment.

LESSON 26

C For each deduction, cross out the irrelevant words in the second piece of evidence.

1. Some planets have moons.
   Jupiter is a large planet in our solar system.
   Therefore, maybe Jupiter has moons.

2. All animals breathe oxygen.
   An antelope is a long-horned animal.
   Therefore, an antelope breathes oxygen.

D Look at this diagram:

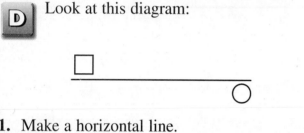

1. Make a horizontal line.
2. Make a circle above the right end of the line.
3. Make a square above the left end of the line.

Circle the instruction that the diagram contradicts.
Draw a new diagram that follows the instructions.

E For each item, write a sentence that means the same thing by changing the underlined word or words.

1. Thelma was not excited about her <u>chance</u> to be in the play because the script was so <u>repetitive</u>.

   _____

   _____

   _____

   _____

2. He <u>paused</u> and then said that his recollection of the accident was <u>unclear</u>.

   _____

   _____

   _____

3. His directions were <u>unclear</u> and <u>repetitive</u>.

   _____

   _____

4. The lawyer had her <u>chance</u> to ask questions about the parts of the contract that were <u>unclear</u>.

   _____

   _____

   _____

   _____

F Here's a passage:

Round Robert lives in a simply beautiful round house. <u>Everything in the house is round.</u> Round Robert is always tired because if he tries to sit on his round chairs, he rolls off. When he tries to sleep, he rolls off his round bed. Round Robert's pet starfish lives in a round aquarium. The starfish can sleep because it floats in the aquarium.

1. We assume that the underlined statement is true. Something else the writer says is a contradiction. Circle the contradiction.
2. Make up an if-then statement that explains the contradiction.

_____

_____

_____

_____

G Here's what we know:

> **Tilly loves to ski.**

One of the sentences below seems consistent with the sentence in the box. One of the sentences seems inconsistent with the sentence in the box.

- **She hasn't been skiing for three years.**
- **She just bought new ski equipment.**

1. Use the word **so** to combine the sentence in the box with the consistent sentence.

_____

_____

2. Use the word **however** to combine the sentence in the box with the inconsistent sentence.

_____

_____

3. Use the word **and** to combine the sentence in the box with the consistent sentence.

_____

_____

4. Use the word **but** to combine the sentence in the box with the inconsistent sentence.

_____

_____

Make sure you punctuated the sentences correctly.

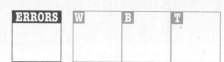

ERRORS | W | B | T

 A Here's a deduction with irrelevant words in the second piece of evidence.

> **Butterflies develop from caterpillars.**
> **Monarchs are orange and black butterflies.**
> **Therefore, monarchs develop from caterpillars.**

Which words in the second piece of evidence are irrelevant?

Cross out those words.

Now say the entire deduction with the irrelevant words removed.

• Here's some evidence that leads to a conclusion. There are irrelevant words in the second piece of evidence.

> **Some mammals can fly.**
> **A bandicoot is a mammal that carries its young in a pouch.**

Which words in the second piece of evidence are irrelevant?

Cross out those words.

Read the evidence with the irrelevant words removed and then say the conclusion.

★ **B** Here's a passage:

> Frieda saw Frank on a street corner and shouted to him to come over. When he did, she said to him, "Frank, I hear you're going to Europe this fall. I'd like to go with you. I can be your translator. <u>I speak French, German, Italian, and Greek</u>. I'm sure I'd be a big help."

> "Well," said Frank, "I don't really want to go alone anyway. Besides, anyone who can speak seven languages is probably really interesting to be with. I'll give you a copy of my schedule so that you can make plane reservations and everything. This trip is going to be tons of fun."

1. We assume that the underlined statement is true. Something else the writer says is a contradiction. Circle the contradiction.
2. Make up an if-then statement that explains the contradiction.

_____

_____

_____

_____

C Look at this diagram:

1. Draw a vertical line.
2. Draw a horizontal line below the vertical line.
3. Draw a line that slants down to the left from the top of the vertical line.

Circle the instruction that the diagram contradicts.
Draw a new diagram that follows the instructions.

D Cross out the irrelevant words in the evidence and write the conclusion for each item.

1. **Every person has a skull.**
   John is a tall person who lives next door.

   _____

   _____

2. **Burning things need oxygen.**
   Fires are burning things that can be dangerous.

   _____

   _____

3. **Some secretaries can type.**
   Sue is a secretary in our office.

   _____

   _____

E Here's what we know:

Fred hates to spend money.

For each item, combine one of the sentences below with the sentence in the box.

- **He bought three winter coats.**
- **He has a large savings account.**

1. Make a combined sentence with **but.**

   _____

   _____

   _____

2. Make a combined sentence with **however.**

   _____

   _____

   _____

3. Make a combined sentence with **and.**

   _____

   _____

   _____

4. Make a combined sentence with **so.**

   _____

   _____

   _____

Make sure you punctuated the sentences correctly.

F In the passage below, the verbs **is** and **are** and the verbs **was** and **were** are used incorrectly nine times. Cross out each incorrect word. Write the correct word above it.

Millions of Americans every year is fooled by clever advertisers. This does not mean that all commercials are sneaky or bad. Many of them is honest and informative. However, nearly everyone are tricked now and then by dishonest advertising. Toys or gadgets is sometimes shown doing something that they is not capable of doing, which is against the law. If you think you are being misled by an advertisement, there are an agency you can complain to. The Federal Trade Commission (FTC) is an agency that are trying to control misleading advertising. It are always interested in hearing your complaints. Here are the address of the FTC:

Federal Trade Commission

Pennsylvania Ave. at Sixth St. NW

Washington, DC 20580

G For each item, write a sentence that means the same thing by changing the underlined word or words.

1. They changed their Swiss money into Canadian money.

   _____

   _____

2. She needed a lot of money to change the garage into a store.

   _____

   _____

3. The Bruno family is changing their garage into a bedroom.

   _____

   _____

4. We changed our Mexican money into Japanese money.

   _____

   _____

A Here's a deduction with irrelevant words in the second piece of evidence.

> **Some mushrooms are poisonous.**
> **A morel is a brown mushroom that feels spongy.**
> **Therefore, maybe a morel is poisonous.**

Which words in the second piece of evidence are irrelevant?
Cross out those words.
Now say the entire deduction with the irrelevant words removed.

• Here's some evidence that leads to a conclusion. There are irrelevant words in the second piece of evidence.

> **All mountains are older than we are.**
> **The Rockies are mountains in North America.**

Which words in the second piece of evidence are irrelevant?
Cross out those words.
Read the evidence with the irrelevant words removed and then say the conclusion.

★ **B** For each item, write a sentence that means the same thing by changing the underlined word or words.

1. They changed their Swiss money into Canadian money.

   _____

   _____

   _____

2. Camilla had money problems when she was in Spain.

   _____

   _____

   _____

3. She went to the bank to change her money into savings bonds.

   _____

   _____

   _____

4. Jesse changed his money into diamonds.

   _____

   _____

C Read the facts and the items. If an item is relevant to fact A, write **relevant to fact A.** If an item is relevant to fact B, write **relevant to fact B.** If an item is irrelevant to both facts, write **irrelevant.**

Fact A. **Nancy is a firefighter.**

Fact B. **Nancy hates crowds.**

1. Nancy has a college degree in biology.

   _____

2. Nancy's husband worries about her when she is at work.

   _____

3. Nancy refuses to go to baseball games.

   _____

4. Nancy and Barney have been married for ten years.

   _____

D Cross out the irrelevant words in the evidence and write the conclusion for each item.

1. **Rivers flow to the sea.**
   The Mississippi is a wide river in the United States.

   _____

   _____

2. **Some reptiles are herbivorous.**
   The Gila monster is a reptile that lives in northern Mexico.

   _____

   _____

3. **She sells every kind of car.**
   The Bobcat is a small car that gets excellent mileage.

   _____

   _____

E Here's what we know:

Sheila enjoys walking in the rain.

For each item, combine one of the sentences below with the sentence in the box.

- **Her shoes are often wet.**
- **She stayed inside during the recent storm.**

1. Make a combined sentence with **therefore.**

   _____

   _____

   _____

2. Make a combined sentence with **so.**

   _____

   _____

   _____

3. Make a combined sentence with **however.**

   _____

   _____

   _____

4. Make a combined sentence with **but.**

   _____

   _____

   _____

F This lesson presented a fact that you will be tested on. This fact is:

When you haze people, you torment them.

Study this fact. Repeat it to yourself. Writing the fact may help you to remember it.

A Cross out the irrelevant words in the evidence and write the conclusion for each item.

1. Some chemical elements have been found on Mars.
Oxygen is a chemical element that all animals need.

_____

_____

2. Luis grows every kind of fruit tree.
The mango is a tropical evergreen fruit tree.

_____

_____

3. All veins carry blood to the heart.
The vena cava is a large vein that carries blood from the head and arms.

_____

_____

B For each item, write a sentence that means the same thing by changing the underlined word or words.

1. They <u>changed</u> their Swiss <u>money</u> into Canadian <u>money</u>.

_____

_____

2. Hector is <u>changing</u> his <u>money</u> into stocks.

_____

_____

3. The bags of <u>money</u> were locked in the safe.

_____

_____

4. She will <u>change</u> the dress into a skirt by cutting off the top.

_____

_____

_____

C Look at this diagram:

1. Draw a circle.
2. Make an **M** above the circle.
3. Make an **X** to the left of the circle.

Circle the instruction that the diagram contradicts.
Draw a new diagram that follows the instructions.

D Read the facts and the items. If an item is relevant to fact A, write **relevant to fact A.** If an item is relevant to fact B, write **relevant to fact B.** If an item is irrelevant to both facts, write **irrelevant.**

| Fact A. **Neil is a local TV newscaster.** |
| Fact B. **Neil was a college diving champion.** |

1. Everyone in town recognizes Neil's voice.

_____

2. Neil has a dozen trophies over his fireplace.

_____

3. Neil usually comes home with makeup on his collar.

_____

4. Neil is exceptionally intelligent.

_____

E This lesson presented some facts that you will be tested on. These facts are:

> 1. **A clue is a hint that helps you find your way out of a puzzle.**
> 2. **In Middle English the word for thread was <u>clewe</u>.**

Study these facts. Repeat them to yourself. Writing the facts may help you to remember them.

F Tomorrow you will be tested on facts you have learned. The test will include all of the facts presented in Lessons 25–29 and some of the facts from earlier lessons. These facts are:

1. A boar is a wild pig with large tusks.
2. A nook is a small place.
3. The Greek word **paragraphos** means **by the side of writing.**
4. Eohippus was the earliest-known close relative of the modern horse.
5. We know that eohippus was related to the horse because its skeleton resembles the skeleton of a modern horse.
6. Eohippus defended itself by outrunning its enemies.
7. The feet of eohippus changed over the centuries to make it a better runner.
8. Modern horses and other similar animals belong to a group called equus.
9. Some types of equus became large and others became slender, depending on what climate they lived in.
10. When you haze people, you torment them.
11. A clue is a hint that helps you find your way out of a puzzle.
12. In Middle English, the word for thread was **clewe.**

A ★ Here's what we know:

> **Brown rice is good for you.**

For each item, combine one of the sentences below with the sentence in the box.

- **Most people eat white rice.**
- **You should eat more of it.**

1. Make a combined sentence with **but.**

_____

_____

_____

2. Make a combined sentence with **however.**

_____

_____

_____

3. Make a combined sentence with **so.**

_____

_____

_____

B In the passage below, the verbs **is** and **are** and the verbs **was** and **were** are used incorrectly five times. Cross out each incorrect word. Write the correct word above it.

Even in our modern world, many people think that if they do something to a picture of someone, it will actually affect that person. This idea is extremely old, and one that were very important in the lives of the cave people who was alive fifteen thousand years ago. Before they was to leave on a hunt, these people drew pictures of bison or deer on the walls of caves. Then they would draw spears and arrows in the animals to show how they was going to kill them. The early hunters believed this would help them in the hunt. It were a way to give them the courage and confidence they needed to attack the large animals.

C Cross out the irrelevant words in the evidence and write the conclusion for each item.

1. **Living things need water.**
   An antelope is a fast-running living thing that is native to Africa and Asia.

   _____

   _____

2. **Some plants grow flowers.**
   The Venus's-flytrap is a plant that traps and digests flies.

   _____

   _____

3. **Some volcanoes are still active.**
   Izalco is a volcano in Central America.

   _____

   _____

D This lesson presented a fact that you will be tested on. This fact is:

> **When you tantalize someone, you tease that person by putting something just out of reach.**

Study this fact. Repeat it to yourself. Writing the fact may help you to remember it.

★ **A** Read the passage below.

> Many forest animals eat fish. Bears have a special method of hunting fish. Instead of standing in the water and reaching for the fish, they wait near waterfalls. Fish that are trying to swim upstream jump straight up out of the water to get over the falls. So, a bear can get its meal just by standing near a waterfall and catching the fish as they leap.

1. Here is a conclusion based on the passage:

> **It's easier for a bear to catch its dinner near a waterfall.**

The evidence that supports this conclusion is in one of the sentences. Which one?

_____

_____

_____

_____

_____

2. Here is another conclusion:

> **Fish sometimes swim against the current.**

The evidence that supports this conclusion is in one of the sentences. Which one?

_____

_____

_____

_____

B Some words, such as **sand,** are usually treated as if they name only one thing. These words go with **is** or **was.** We say, "The sand is hot," whether there is a lot of sand or just a little bit.

Here are some other words that are treated as if they name only one thing: **dirt, water, sugar, salt, gravel, hair, ice,** and **milk.** All these words go with **is** or **was.**

Write the verb **is** or **are** in each blank.

1. His hair _____ dirty.

2. The salt _____ on the table.

3. Five sacks _____ on the table.

4. Five sacks of salt _____ on the table.

5. The water in the sinks _____ overflowing.

6. The gravel _____ in our driveway.

7. Two mounds of gravel _____ in our driveway.

LESSON 31

C For each item, write a sentence that means the same thing by changing the underlined word or words.

1. They changed their Swiss money into Canadian money.

_____

_____

_____

2. A lot of money was needed to change the old house into a museum.

_____

_____

_____

3. The United States is changing to the metric system.

_____

_____

4. The money of some countries is colorful.

_____

_____

D Look at diagram 1.

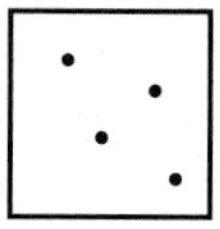

Diagram 1

You can see the dots and the square, but you can't see the rectangle.

1. Complete the deduction.

All the dots are in the square.
The square is in the rectangle.

So, _____

_____

2. Draw the rectangle in diagram 1.

• Look at diagram 2.

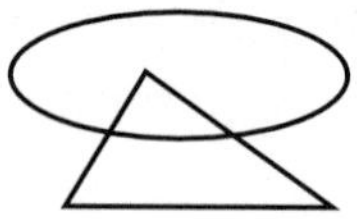

Diagram 2

You can't see the dots in the diagram, but **all the dots are in the triangle.**

3. Complete the deduction.

All the dots are in the triangle.
Part of the triangle is in the oval.

So, _____

_____

Here's what we know:

> **Jack has excellent job qualifications.**

For each item, combine one of the sentences below with the sentence in the box.

- **He has found a good job.**
- **He was turned down by three companies.**

1. Make a combined sentence with **but.**

_____

_____

_____

2. Make a combined sentence with **however.**

_____

_____

_____

3. Make a combined sentence with **so.**

_____

_____

_____

4. Make a combined sentence with **and.**

_____

_____

_____

ERRORS | W | B | T

★ **A** Read the evidence and write the conclusion for each item.

1. Here's the evidence:

   Whooping cranes are birds.
   Birds have feathers.

   What's the conclusion? _____
   _____

2. Here's the evidence:

   Some birds can swim.
   A whooping crane is a bird.

   What's the conclusion? _____
   _____

3. Here's the evidence:

   All birds are warm-blooded.
   A whooping crane is a bird.

   What's the conclusion? _____
   _____

B Write the verb **was** or **were** in each blank.

1. The dirt _____ dropped into the trucks.

2. Three loads of dirt _____ dropped into the trucks.

3. Sand _____ in my sleeping bag.

4. The corn _____ ripe last week.

5. The corn in those fields _____ ripe last week.

6. The hay _____ ready for storage.

7. Five baskets of grass _____ piled in her yard.

C For each item, write a sentence that means the same thing by changing the underlined word or words.

1. She will <u>change</u> the <u>repetitive</u> title into one that is more interesting.

   _____
   _____
   _____

2. He <u>paused</u> before turning in the stolen <u>money</u>.

   _____
   _____

3. They <u>changed</u> their Swiss <u>money</u> into Canadian <u>money</u>.

   _____
   _____
   _____

4. She has a <u>chance</u> to <u>change</u> the basement into a family room.

   _____
   _____
   _____

Read the passage below.

> Just by looking at dogs, wolves, and foxes, you can tell that they are closely related. However, if you just looked, you might not guess that dogs and bears are also closely related. By studying the fossils of bears and dogs, scientists called **paleontologists** have observed that the skeletons of these animals were quite similar twelve million years ago. In fact, early ancestors of today's bears and dogs have the name "bear-dogs." In other words, scientists cannot classify bear-dogs as either bear or dog.

1. Here is a conclusion based on the passage:

The fossil remains of bears and dogs show that these animals changed over time.

The evidence that supports this conclusion is in one of the sentences. Which one?

_____

_____

_____

_____

_____

2. Here is another conclusion:

Some relationships are not obvious at first glance.

The evidence that supports this conclusion is in one of the sentences. Which one?

_____

_____

_____

_____

_____

E Which reference book would you use to find each of the following pieces of information?

1. How much corn grows in Mexico every year

_____

2. The number of people who live in Houston

_____

3. When the airplane was invented

_____

4. How to pronounce the word **competitive**

_____

5. What de Gaulle is famous for

_____

6. What the **stock market** is

_____

F Some words, such as **dirt** and **ice,** are treated as if they name only one thing. List four more words like these.

1. _____

2. _____

3. _____

4. _____

G This lesson presented some facts that you will be tested on. These facts are:

1. **Donkeys and zebras descended from equus.**
2. **Two other names for a donkey are a burro and an ass.**

Study these facts. Repeat them to yourself. Writing the facts may help you to remember them.

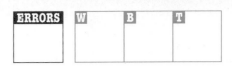

ERRORS W B T

★ **A** Some words, such as **dirt** and **ice**, are treated as if they name only one thing. List four more words like these.

1. _____

2. _____

3. _____

4. _____

B Which reference book would you use to find each of the following pieces of information?

1. Another word that means **over**

   _____

2. The largest industry in Venezuela

   _____

3. When the city of Venice was founded

   _____

4. Parts of speech for the word **thrill**

   _____

5. When the first submarine was used

   _____

6. Which state is bigger, Washington or Oregon

   _____

C Look at this diagram:

<u>T_____</u> **currency**

The diagram contradicts part of these instructions:

1. Write the word **currency.**
2. To the left of the word, draw a horizontal line.
3. Make a **T** below the left end of the line.

Circle the instruction that the diagram contradicts.
Draw a new diagram that follows the instructions.

D Write the verb **is** or **are** in each blank.

1. The grain in those silos _____ worth a lot of money.

2. Concrete _____ made from gravel, cement, and water.

3. The hail _____ ruining the crops.

4. Rice _____ the main food for many people in the world.

5. Two spoonfuls of sugar _____ added to this tea.

6. Sugar _____ in this tea.

7. The ice on those hills _____ melting.

LESSON 33

E For each item write a sentence that means the same thing by changing the underlined word or words.

1. The <u>rule</u> <u>limited</u> their parking.

_____

_____

2. Lawn sprinkling was <u>limited</u> because of the water shortage.

_____

_____

3. A <u>rule</u> <u>limited</u> her voting rights.

_____

_____

4. <u>Rules</u> <u>limit</u> the amount of interest a lender may charge on a loan.

_____

_____

_____

F Read the passage below.

During the 1940s, millions of Americans admired and imitated Hollywood film stars. Knowing this, some tobacco companies paid the film studios enormous amounts of money to show the stars' particular brands of cigarettes in movies. In the 1970s, more cigarettes per person were smoked in the United States than in any other country in the world.

1. Here is a conclusion based on the passage:

The tobacco companies were probably very successful in the 1940s.

The evidence that supports this conclusion is in one of the sentences. Which one?

_____

_____

_____

_____

_____

_____

_____

2. Here is another conclusion:

The average German smoked less than the average American.

The evidence that supports this conclusion is in one of the sentences. Which one?

_____

_____

_____

_____

_____

★ **A** Write the instructions for this diagram.

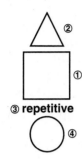

③ **repetitive**

1. (what) _____

_____

2. (what and where) _____

_____

_____

3. (what and where) _____

_____

_____

4. (what and where) _____

_____

_____

B Write the verb **was** or **were** in each blank.

1. The ice on the river _____ breaking up.

2. Five cups of flour _____ in the sack.

3. The rain _____ soaking through the tent roof.

4. The barley in those fields _____ dead by June.

5. Steel _____ used to make those beams.

6. Water _____ leaking from those pipes.

 C Read the passage below.

In an effort to improve working conditions for their employees, some companies have introduced "flex-time" work schedules. Instead of working from 9 A.M. to 5 P.M. every day, each employee puts in eight hours sometime between 6 A.M. and 10 P.M. The choice of when to start and when to finish the workday is up to the employee. Having control over their work time seems to make employees happier and better workers.

1. Here is a conclusion based on the passage:

People are more productive when they control their working hours.

The evidence that supports this conclusion is in one of the sentences. Which one?

_____

_____

_____

2. Here is another conclusion:

One problem with flex-time is that the office must be heated and lit for much longer periods of time.

The evidence that supports this conclusion is in one of the sentences. Which one?

_____

_____

_____

_____

D For each item, write a sentence that means the same thing by changing the underlined word or words.

1. The rule limited their parking.

_____

_____

2. To limit gasoline usage, the committee passed a rule.

_____

_____

_____

3. Some countries limit public meetings.

_____

_____

4. The rule limited campfires to a small area.

_____

_____

_____

E Which reference book would you use to find each of the following pieces of information?

1. How many ways **desert** can be pronounced

_____

2. What kind of weather London has in the winter

_____

3. When Henry Ford died

_____

4. How many miles it is from Iceland to New York

_____

5. When Shakespeare wrote *Hamlet*

_____

6. What a **kipper** is

_____

F Tomorrow you will be tested on facts you have learned. The test will include all of the facts presented in Lessons 30–34 and some of the facts from earlier lessons. These facts are:

1. A boar is a wild pig with large tusks.
2. A nook is a small place.
3. The Greek word **paragraphos** means **by the side of writing.**
4. Eohippus was the earliest-known close relative of the modern horse.
5. We know that eohippus was related to the modern horse because its skeleton resembles the skeleton of a modern horse.
6. Eohippus defended itself by outrunning its enemies.
7. The feet of eohippus changed over the centuries to make it a better runner.
8. Modern horses and other similar animals belong to a group called equus.
9. Some types of equus became large and others became slender, depending on what climate they lived in.
10. When you haze people, you torment them.
11. When you tantalize someone, you tease that person by putting something just out of reach.
12. A clue is a hint that helps you find your way out of a puzzle.
13. In Middle English the word for thread was **clewe.**
14. Donkeys and zebras descended from equus.
15. Two other names for a donkey are a burro and an ass.

ERRORS | W | B | T

A Use the rule in the box and the evidence to answer the questions.

> **The faster something moves, the harder it is to stop it.**

- **An airplane is going faster and faster.**

1. Will the plane be harder to stop?

_____

2. How do you know?

_____

_____

- **At noon a dog is running eight kilometers an hour. At 6 o'clock the dog is running fifteen kilometers an hour.**

3. What's the conclusion?

_____

_____

4. How do you know?

_____

_____

- **My car goes faster outside the city than it goes inside the city.**

5. What's the conclusion?

_____

_____

6. How do you know?

_____

_____

B Which reference book would you use to find each of the following pieces of information?

1. Who discovered the Engelmann spruce

_____

2. Whether **zinsnay** is a real word

_____

3. The population of Chicago, Illinois

_____

4. How many books Ernest Hemingway wrote

_____

5. What kinds of animals live in Australia

_____

6. Whether New York City is closer to Seattle or to London

_____

 A The verbs **has** and **have** work something like the verbs **is** and **are**. Here are the rules:

- If you name one thing, use the verb **has**.
- If you name more than one thing, use the verb **have**.
- If you use the word **you** or **I**, use the verb **have**.

Tell whether you would use the verb **has** or **have** with each item below.

I Ⓐ
You Ⓑ
That man Ⓒ
My sister Ⓓ
We Ⓔ
Those girls Ⓕ

Write the verb **has** or **have** in each blank.

1. You _____ lots of friends.

2. Jolene _____ gone home.

3. I _____ three dogs and two cats.

4. Everybody _____ left for work.

5. They _____ built their own homes.

6. These men _____ sports cars.

★ **B** Read the argument and write the conclusion.

> He must have a terrible temper. You should have heard him yelling on the phone this morning.

What does the writer of this argument want us to conclude?

_____

_____

C Use the rule in the box and the evidence to answer the questions.

The higher you go, the less oxygen there is in the air.

- **Mount Rainier is higher than Mount Adams.**

1. What's the conclusion?

_____

2. How do you know?

_____

_____

- **Bill's plane went up 3000 feet.**

3. What's the conclusion?

_____

_____

4. How do you know?

_____

_____

- **Mount Everest is 30,000 feet high. Mount Shasta is 15,000 feet high.**

5. What's the conclusion?

_____

_____

6. How do you know?

_____

_____

LESSON 36

D For each item, write a sentence that means the same thing by changing the underlined word or words.

1. The <u>rule</u> <u>limited</u> their parking.

_____

_____

2. The theater <u>rule</u> <u>limited</u> the movie to people over eighteen.

_____

_____

_____

3. To <u>limit</u> the use of the lunchroom to eating, the principal set strict <u>rules</u>.

_____

_____

_____

4. The <u>rule</u> <u>limited</u> campfires to a small area.

_____

_____

_____

E Read the passage below.

> Evidence can usually be found to support both sides of an argument. If you drink coffee, you should know that medical research in Boston has shown that heavy coffee drinking may double your risk of suffering a heart attack. On the other hand, equally reliable research done by the National Heart and Lung Institute shows that coffee drinking makes no difference to your health.

1. Here is a conclusion based on this passage:

According to medical research, you would be smart not to drink coffee.

The evidence that supports this conclusion is in one of the sentences. Which one?

_____

_____

_____

_____

_____

2. Here is another conclusion:

Finding out the truth about something can be very difficult.

The evidence that supports this conclusion is in one of the sentences. Which one?

_____

_____

_____

F Use the facts to fill out the form.

Facts: **Your name is Dina Kaplan. You have three siblings. Your brother Frank is 24 and works in a warehouse. Your sister Cassy is 18 and is in college. Your brother Paul is 3. You have completed two years of college at the University of Oregon in Eugene, Oregon, where you earned a 3.4 grade point average (GPA). You have saved $250 from a summer job, but you are no longer working. You are hoping to earn a degree in English. You enjoy wood carving and scuba diving.**

APPLICATION FOR SCHOLARSHIP TO CLARKSTONE COLLEGE

1. _____ 2. _____
   Print your name, last name first.   Indicate your sex (optional).

3. List all colleges or universities you have attended.

   a. _____   _____   _____
      Name of college or university   Years attended   GPA

   b. _____   _____   _____

   c. _____   _____   _____

4. Do you have any savings?   YES   NO   If yes, how much? _____
5. Are you currently employed?   YES   NO

6. How many siblings do you have? _____ How many attending college? _____

I hereby state that the information given above is complete and accurate to the best of my knowledge. I understand that willful falsification of the facts is illegal and punishable by law.

_____
                              Signature

ERRORS | W | B | T

★ **A** Here are the rules for using the verbs **has** and **have.**

- If you name one thing, use the verb **has.**
- If you name more than one thing, use the verb **have.**
- If you use the word **you** or **I,** use the verb **have.**

Write the verb **has** or **have** in each blank.

1. Nobody _____ tickets for the game.

2. I _____ to go to class now.

3. The team _____ won three games this year.

4. We _____ run out of ideas.

5. You _____ already eaten three hot dogs.

6. Retha _____ played trumpet for three years.

B For each item, write a sentence that means the same thing by changing the underlined word or words.

1. By pausing before she answered, she made the situation more unclear.

_____

_____

_____

2. The rule limited their parking.

_____

_____

3. The chance to buy a saxophone changed Olga into a music lover.

_____

_____

_____

4. The words in the song were repetitive.

_____

_____

Read the facts and the information. If the information is relevant to fact A, write **relevant to fact A.** If the information is relevant to fact B, write **relevant to fact B.** If the information is irrelevant to both facts, write **irrelevant.**

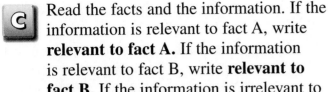

Fact A. **Alvin wants to be a jazz musician.**

Fact B. **Alvin is over six feet tall.**

1. Alvin devotes an hour out of each day to his trumpet playing.

_____

2. The coach wants Alvin to play basketball next winter.

_____

3. Alvin saves his paper route money for trumpet lessons.

_____

4. Alvin is afraid of the dark.

_____

D Use the rule in the box and the evidence to answer the questions.

> **A scruple is equal to 1.296 grams.**

1. **Jill has something that weighs one scruple.**
   How many grams does it weigh?

   _____

2. **Suzanne has something that weighs less than one gram.**
   How many scruples does it weigh?

   _____

3. **Peter has something that weighs more than one scruple.**
   How many grams does it weigh?

   _____

E Read the argument and write the conclusion.

He barely graduated from high school. I can't imagine why he applied to college.

What does the writer of this argument want us to conclude?

_____

_____

ERRORS W B T

A Read each argument and write the conclusion.

1. **I hear the new student is from France. Maybe I can pick up some extra money tutoring her in English.**

What does the writer of this argument want us to conclude?

_____

_____

2. **I don't think we should hire Mr. Smith. Ten years ago he was such a lazy worker that he was fired from his job. We don't want to hire a lazy person.**

What does the writer of this argument want us to conclude?

_____

_____

3. **I saw Jim running down the street right after the bank was robbed. I'd better go tell the police that Jim's the one they want.**

What does the writer of this argument want us to conclude?

_____

_____

B Read the facts and the information. If the information is relevant to fact A, write **relevant to fact A.** If the information is relevant to fact B, write **relevant to fact B.** If the information is irrelevant to both facts, write **irrelevant.**

Fact A. **Brenda can't tell time.**

Fact B. **Brenda spends all her time outdoors.**

1. Brenda is often late for class.

_____

2. Brenda plans to go to college.

_____

3. Brenda is sunburned in the summer.

_____

4. Brenda doesn't wear a watch.

_____

C There are no underlined statements in the passage below. Read the passage. Find a statement that contradicts an earlier statement.

- Underline the statement you assume to be true.
- Circle the contradiction.
- Make up an if-then statement that explains the contradiction.

> I really care about my health. Every morning, I take two vitamin C tablets and one multivitamin tablet. A lot of people don't like to take pills. I'll admit it's difficult to choke down five vitamin pills every morning, but I think it's worth it.

_____

_____

_____

_____

D Use the rule in the box and the evidence to answer the questions.

A rod is equal to 5.03 meters.

1. **Freda has something that is 5.03 meters long.**
   How many rods long is it?

   _____

2. **Karen has something that is more than one rod long.**
   How many meters long is it?

   _____

3. **Gina has something that is less than one meter long.**
   How many rods long is it?

   _____

E Here are the rules for using the verbs **has** and **have.**

- If you name one thing, use the verb **has.**
- If you name more than one thing, use the verb **have.**
- If you use the word **you** or **I,** use the verb **have.**

Write the verb **has** or **have** in each blank.

1. His family _____ moved three times this year.

2. You _____ my car keys.

3. Most dogs _____ long tails.

4. I _____ run five miles today.

5. A ram _____ long, curly horns.

6. The class _____ lots of library books.

F For each item, write a sentence that means the same thing by changing the underlined word or words.

1. By <u>pausing</u>, she lost her <u>chance</u>.

   _____

   _____

2. There should be <u>rules</u> against using <u>unclear</u> language in contracts.

   _____

   _____

   _____

3. <u>Changing</u> to gas heat was <u>limited</u> to a small area.

   _____

   _____

   _____

4. Some parts of these <u>rules</u> are <u>repetitive</u>.

   _____

   _____

LESSON 39

A Read the passage below.

> In 1979, British oddsmakers reported that there was only 1 chance in 250 that Earth would receive visitors from another planet. Most scientists agree that the chances of such an occurrence are slim. It is true that many strange events in the universe remain unexplained. However, there is no good evidence that those events are actually caused by visitors from outer space.

1. Here is a conclusion based on this passage:

> **There are no good explanations for some of the things that happen in the universe.**

The evidence that supports this conclusion is in one of the sentences. Which one?

_____

_____

_____

2. Here is another conclusion:

> **In general, scientists doubt that we will be visited by beings from outer space.**

The evidence that supports this conclusion is in one of the sentences. Which one?

_____

_____

_____

B Write the verb **has** or **have** in each blank.

1. He _____ finished his term paper.

2. Some houses _____ brick fireplaces.

3. I _____ to earn more money next year.

4. Three women _____ stopped the bus.

5. This jacket _____ a hood.

6. You _____ too many clothes.

C Look at this diagram:

The diagram contradicts part of these instructions:

1. Draw a horizontal line.
2. Make a line that slants down to the left from the right end of the horizontal line.
3. Make an **M** above the right end of the horizontal line.

Circle the instruction that the diagram contradicts.
Draw a new diagram that follows the instructions.

D There are no underlined statements in the passage below. Read the passage. Find a statement that contradicts an earlier statement.

• Underline the statement you assume to be true.
• Circle the contradiction.
• Make up an if-then statement that explains the contradiction.

"I'm eight and Kevin's only six," whined Rachel. "That means I'm bigger and I need more food to keep me going. That's why I should get the last piece of pie."

"But, mom," countered Kevin, "she's already had two pieces today and I haven't had any!"

"Rachel," said their mother calmly, "if you don't want to share the last piece with your older brother, then I don't think either of you should have any."

_____

_____

_____

E Read each argument and write the conclusion.

1. **Every time I get in the shower the phone rings. My girl friend hasn't called me all day and I'd like to hear from her. I guess I'll go get in the shower.**

What does the writer of this argument want us to conclude?

_____

_____

2. **I'm not going home for Christmas this year. Last year all my parents did was yell about what I should do with my life.**

What does the writer of this argument want us to conclude?

_____

_____

_____

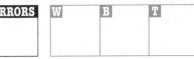
A There are no underlined statements in the passages below. Read each passage. Find a statement that contradicts an earlier statement.

• Underline the statement you assume to be true.
• Circle the contradiction.
• Make up an if-then statement that explains the contradiction.

1. A newspaper reporter stopped a woman on the street. "Excuse me," he said. "I'm conducting a survey. What do you do for a living?"

"I'm a fashion model for a magazine here in New York."

"Do you enjoy your work?"

"Yes, I do, very much."

"Thank you for your cooperation. Now I'd like to take a picture of you."

"No, please put your camera away. I haven't let anyone photograph me in four years."

_____

_____

_____

_____

_____

2. Plants and herbs can be used to cure many illnesses. Many years ago, people drank herb teas to help them sleep. They knew that the snake plant was good for burns, and that the cabbage leaf could draw infection from a wound. Today, not many people know much about what herbs can do. Herbal medicine is useful for only a few things, but it is worthy of study. In many cases, it can be a lot less expensive than going to a doctor.

_____

_____

_____

_____

_____

B Use the rule in the box and the evidence to answer the questions.

> **Regular gasoline is cheaper than premium gasoline.**

- **Five gallons of regular gasoline cost five dollars.**

1. How much do five gallons of premium gasoline cost?

_____

- **Jack bought forty gallons of regular gasoline. Jolene bought forty gallons of premium gasoline.**

2. What's the conclusion?

_____

_____

3. How do you know?

_____

_____

_____

- **A gallon of premium gasoline costs two dollars.**

4. How much does a gallon of regular gasoline cost?

_____

C Write the verb **has** or **have** in each blank.

1. The team _____ a game today.

2. Many trees _____ no leaves in the winter.

3. Their uncle _____ a long beard.

4. She _____ played in every game.

5. All birds _____ feathers.

6. I _____ too much homework.

Read the passage below.

> The Epic of Gilgamesh is one of the oldest written stories in the world. It is about a hero named Gilgamesh who traveled all over the world in search of the Tree of Life. Many fables from the Epic of Gilgamesh were retold in the stories of later civilizations. Some stories from Gilgamesh are presented in Greek myths. The biblical story of Noah and the flood was probably based on part of the Epic of Gilgamesh.

1. Here is a conclusion based on the passage:

   The Epic of Gilgamesh is older than most of the stories we know.

   The evidence that supports this conclusion is in one of the sentences. Which one?

   _____

   _____

   _____

2. Here is another conclusion:

   The early Greeks used materials from earlier legends.

   The evidence that supports this conclusion is in one of the sentences. Which one?

   _____

   _____

   _____

 Read each argument and write the conclusion.

1. **I asked my roommate to take out the garbage once a week, and the next day he moved to California. Some people really hate housework.**

   What does the writer of this argument want us to conclude?

   _____

   _____

   _____

2. **I'm sure that guy is a crook. He doesn't make enough money to afford that fancy car he drives.**

   What does the writer of this argument want us to conclude?

   _____

   _____

3. **Lenny started getting bad grades when he became friends with Mike. Mike is a bad influence on Lenny.**

   What does the writer of this argument want us to conclude?

   _____

   _____

F This lesson presented a fact that you will be tested on. The fact is:

> **A robot is a machine that looks and does some things like a human.**

Study this fact. Repeat it to yourself. Writing the fact may help you to remember it.

ERRORS | W | B | T

★ **A** Read the passage below.

The kiwi is a small bird that is native to New Zealand. It has hairy feathers and no wings. These timid birds, which have no tails, are now nearly extinct.

- Here's a conclusion:

There are few kiwis left in the world.

1. Does the passage contain evidence to support the conclusion or evidence to contradict the conclusion?

_____

_____

2. Which sentence contains the evidence?

_____

_____

_____

- Here's another conclusion:

The kiwi originally came from Hawaii.

3. Does the passage contain evidence to support the conclusion or evidence to contradict the conclusion?

_____

_____

4. Which sentence contains the evidence?

_____

_____

_____

B There are no underlined statements in the passages that follow. Read each passage. Find a statement that contradicts an earlier statement.

- Underline the statement you assume to be true.
- Circle the contradiction.
- Make up an if-then statement that explains the contradiction.

1. When settlers first came to America, they didn't have many of the foods that we now grow. For instance, there were almost no apple trees. One of America's favorite folk heroes changed that. Johnny Appleseed, whose real name was John Chapman, traveled the country on foot, planting apple seeds wherever he went. He was a kind, gentle man who loved nature and animals and people. He drove from the East Coast all the way to Indiana, where he is buried. His tombstone reads: "John Chapman. He lived for others."

_____

_____

_____

_____

2. I have to be alone. I need time to think about what I've done and what I should do next. I wish I had known how this thing was going to turn out. I have nothing to say for myself. I wish Meg were here with me. She'd understand.

_____

_____

_____

_____

 In the passage below, the verbs **has** and **have** are used incorrectly five times. Cross out each incorrect word. Write the correct word above it.

I has lots of jeans because jeans are my favorite choice of clothing. I'm lucky because the girls at my school don't has to wear dresses. I has some dresses that I wear to dances, but I usually wear jeans and a sweater to class. Most of my friends also wear jeans to school. The faculty have to dress more formally. One thing worries me. Many companies has regulations that require employees to get dressed up every day. I hope that when I graduate, I will get a job that does not have this regulation.

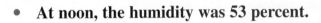 Use the rule in the box and the evidence to answer the questions.

> **When the dew point is reached, the humidity is 100 percent.**

- **During most summer nights, the dew point is reached.**
1. What's the conclusion?

_____

2. How do you know?

_____

- **At noon, the humidity was 53 percent.**
3. What's the conclusion?

_____

4. How do you know?

_____

- **The dew point was not reached today.**
5. What's the conclusion?

_____

6. How do you know?

_____

LESSON 41

 Here's what we know:

June has eight siblings.

For each item, combine one of the sentences below with the sentence in the box.

- **She's trying to get financial aid for college.**
- **Her family lives in a small house.**

1. Make a combined sentence with **therefore.**

_____

_____

_____

_____

2. Make a combined sentence with **however.**

_____

_____

_____

3. Make a combined sentence with **so.**

_____

_____

_____

4. Make a combined sentence with **but.**

_____

_____

_____

★ A In the passage below, the verbs **has** and **have** are used incorrectly five times. Cross out each incorrect word. Write the correct word above it.

The family next door have many pet animals, and I play with them every afternoon. Each animal have its own favorite toy. The guinea pigs have a wheel to run in. The cat have a catnip mouse. The dogs play with rubber bones, and the monkey have a teddy bear. The family even owns a horse, which I ride in the summer. My mother won't let me have any animals. When I grow up, I want to live on a farm. Then I will has all the animals I want.

B Read the passage below.

> You may hear the expression "the pain killer that many doctors recommend" in TV commercials. This pain killer is nothing more than plain aspirin. These commercials are trying to convince you that you are getting something special when you buy the product that contains "the pain killer that many doctors recommend." But the commercials may be using tricky language to hide the fact that you are paying more for what is actually only aspirin.

● Here's a conclusion:

The pain killer that many doctors recommend is nitrous oxide.

1. Does the passage contain evidence to support the conclusion or evidence to contradict the conclusion?

_____

_____

2. Which sentence contains the evidence?

_____

_____

● Here's another conclusion:

You may pay more for something if you think it contains something special.

3. Does the passage contain evidence to support the conclusion or evidence to contradict the conclusion?

_____

_____

4. Which sentence contains the evidence?

_____

_____

_____

_____

_____

There are no underlined statements in the passages below. Read each passage. Find a statement that contradicts an earlier statement.

- Underline the statement you assume to be true.
- Circle the contradiction.
- Make up an if-then statement that explains the contradiction.

1. I think war is terrible. I am a nonviolent person, and I think more people should try to be the same way. People have developed a high level of intelligence over thousands of years. It's a shame that we cannot find a more constructive way of dealing with others. I was telling this to a friend of mine yesterday, and he said I was stupid. I was so mad I hit him. That shut him up. He's an okay guy, but he's not too bright sometimes.

2. All of us dream in our sleep. Dreams are our way of explaining life to ourselves. Some people don't dream. Other people make a habit of remembering their dreams. Once you can remember your dreams, you can work at figuring them out. Dreams often offer important insights into ourselves— sometimes they even warn us of danger.

D Use the rule in the box and the evidence to answer the questions.

> **The farther north you go, the closer to the North Pole you get.**

- **Canada is farther north than Mexico.**

1. What's the conclusion?

_____

_____

2. How do you know?

_____

_____

- **Lou is ten miles from the North Pole.**
  Sally is ninety miles from the North Pole.

3. What's the conclusion?

_____

_____

4. How do you know?

_____

_____

- **A ship did not go any farther north.**

5. What's the conclusion?

_____

_____

6. How do you know?

_____

_____

E For each item, write a sentence that means the same thing by changing the underlined word or words.

1. He paused before grabbing the money from the cash drawer.

_____

_____

2. When Nora had the chance, she changed her dollars into German marks.

_____

_____

_____

3. The law limited the amount of money the old man could invest.

_____

_____

4. His directions were unclear and repetitive.

_____

_____

ERRORS | W | B | T

★ **A** Write the verb **has** or **have** in each blank.

1. Everybody _____ finished the final exam.

2. I _____ already eaten four meals today.

3. Her house _____ six bedrooms.

4. Those trucks _____ big cabs.

5. You _____ to go to the store.

6. Jacob _____ to cook dinner tonight.

B Use the rule in the box and the evidence to answer the questions.

| A dram is equal to 1.77 grams. |

- **Jolene has something that weighs one dram.**

1. How many grams does it weigh?

   _____

- **Jackson has something that weighs 1.77 drams.**

2. How many grams does it weigh?

   _____

- **Jana has something that weighs 1.77 grams.**

3. How many drams does it weigh?

   _____

C Read the passage below.

> The world's first space traveler wasn't a person. It was a dog named Laika. The word **laika** means **barker** in Russian. Russia sent the animal up into space on November 3, 1957. Laika orbited Earth in a satellite named *Sputnik II*.

- Here's a conclusion:

   The first space traveler was named after the sound it made.

1. Does the passage contain evidence to support the conclusion or evidence to contradict the conclusion?

   _____

   _____

2. Which sentence contains the evidence?

   _____

   _____

- Here's another conclusion:

   The first space traveler was American.

3. Does the passage contain evidence to support the conclusion or evidence to contradict the conclusion?

   _____

   _____

4. Which sentence contains the evidence?

   _____

   _____

   _____

D There are no underlined statements in the passages below. Read each passage. Find a statement that contradicts an earlier statement.

- Underline the statement you assume to be true.
- Circle the contradiction.
- Make up an if-then statement that explains the contradiction.

1. People have always loved to play sports. Some of the oldest sports are running and handball. Some of the newest sports are football and basketball. Baseball was developed from the English game of rounders in 1839. People argue over which is the most popular game in America. Although baseball has been played for less than a hundred years, some people say it is the best-loved game of all.

_____

_____

_____

_____

2. In some places in the world, people live to be very old. Some people in Peru have been reported to live to be 130 years old. These people live high in the mountains. Because the air there contains little oxygen, the heart works hard. These people get a lot of exercise and eat mostly vegetables and grains. Maybe they live so long because of what they eat. But their long life is probably caused by a combination of many things—their diet, their habits of exercise, and the large amount of oxygen in the air.

_____

_____

_____

_____

_____

E What kind of reference book would you use to find each of the following pieces of information?

1. What kinds of products Japan sells to other countries

_____

2. Which ocean surrounds Australia

_____

3. Another word that means **random**

_____

4. How to spell the plural of the word **octopus**

_____

5. How long Queen Victoria lived

_____

6. The names of the Canadian provinces

_____

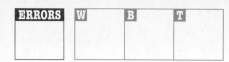

★ **A** What kind of reference book would you use to find each of the following pieces of information?

1. Which states you'd drive through to get from Florida to Michigan

_____

2. When the Russian Revolution took place

_____

3. How many states in the United States border the Pacific Ocean

_____

4. How many inventions Thomas Edison made

_____

5. What kinds of trees are cut for lumber in Alabama

_____

6. How many words begin with the letters **zu**

_____

 B Read the passage below.

Some people find the sight of an octopus absolutely terrifying. If these people knew more about the octopus, they would probably react in a different way, because the octopus is actually a timid animal. An octopus will blanch when it is frightened, which means that it will turn white with fear. In cases of extreme fear, it will simply die. Although the octopus is shy, it will become angry when teased. When you poke an octopus, it may turn red or purple, but it will not attack you. Some octopuses, besides being able to change color, can make colors ripple across their bodies to imitate the rippling of the ocean's surface.

• Here's a conclusion:

You can scare an octopus to death.

1. Does the passage contain evidence to support the conclusion or evidence to contradict the conclusion?

_____

_____

2. Which sentence contains the evidence?

_____

_____

• Here's another conclusion:

Whether or not you know anything about the octopus makes no difference in your attitude towards it.

3. Does the passage contain evidence to support the conclusion or evidence to contradict the conclusion?

_____

_____

4. Which sentence contains the evidence?

_____

_____

_____

_____

Write the word **who** or **which** for each item below. Remember, if the item refers to a human, use **who.** If the item refers to something that is not human, use **which.**

1. An idea _____

2. A doctor _____

3. A doctor's office _____

4. Tomatoes _____

5. Parents _____

6. A pig _____

7. A pig farmer _____

8. The dishes _____

 Read the argument below and answer the questions.

> **Herman found a puppy. Later that day, Herman had an auto accident. If Herman wants to avoid auto accidents, he should stay away from puppies.**

1. What does the writer want us to conclude?

_____

_____

2. Why does the writer think that if Herman wants to avoid auto accidents, he should stay away from puppies?

_____

_____

_____

3. What rule does the argument break?

_____

_____

_____

_____

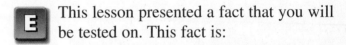 This lesson presented a fact that you will be tested on. This fact is:

> **A maverick can be a person who isn't part of the group.**

Study this fact. Repeat it to yourself. Writing this fact may help you to remember it.

ERRORS W B T

★ **A** Read the argument below and answer the questions.

> While Isabel was in the grocery store, her car was stolen. She says she'll never go to a grocery store again.

1. What does Isabel conclude?

_____

_____

_____

2. Why does Isabel think that going to the grocery store caused her car to be stolen?

_____

_____

_____

3. What rule does the argument break?

_____

_____

_____

_____

_____

B Read the passage below.

> More Americans have been killed in traffic accidents over the past fifty years than have been killed in all the wars our country fought in from 1700 to 1950. Every hour, five people are killed in automobile accidents in the United States. Every nine seconds, someone is injured by a car.

• Here's a conclusion:

> **Every day, over a hundred people die in automobile accidents in the United States.**

1. Does the passage contain evidence to support the conclusion or evidence to contradict the conclusion?

_____

_____

2. Which sentence contains the evidence?

_____

_____

_____

_____

• Here's another conclusion:

> **Cars are a fairly safe means of transportation.**

3. Does the passage contain evidence to support the conclusion or evidence to contradict the conclusion?

_____

_____

4. Which sentence contains the evidence?

_____

_____

_____

_____

_____

Write the word **who** or **which** for each item. Remember, if the item refers to a human, use **who.** If the item refers to something that is not human, use **which.**

1. The trees _____

2. A cattle rancher _____

3. The cattle _____

4. A clerk _____

5. Siblings _____

6. The rooms _____

7. A girl _____

8. A girl's bike _____

 This lesson presented some facts that you will be tested on. These facts are:

1. **Arabian stallions are bred with other kinds of horses to produce more intelligent horses.**
2. **Arabian horses performed well in battle because they were light and fast.**

Study these facts. Repeat them to yourself. Writing these facts may help you to remember them.

ERRORS | W | B | T

★ **A** Cross out the irrelevant words in the second piece of evidence and write the conclusion for each item.

1. **Carpenters work with wood.**
   Calvin is a carpenter with red hair.

   _____

2. **Some mammals live in the sea.**
   The sea lion is a mammal that makes a barking sound.

   _____

   _____

3. **All of Jupiter's moons circle around it.**
   Titan is one of Jupiter's sixteen known moons.

   _____

   _____

 B Read the argument below and answer the questions.

> **I took Grandma's Remedy for my cold and went to bed. Four days later, my cold was gone. Grandma's Remedy sure does work. If I hadn't taken it, I'd still have that cold.**

1. What does the writer want us to conclude?

   _____

   _____

2. Why does the writer think that taking Grandma's Remedy gets rid of a cold?

   _____

   _____

   _____

3. What rule does the argument break?

   _____

   _____

   _____

C Read the passage below.

> A number of years ago, farmers in central California decided to get rid of the coyotes in the area. They proceeded to poison coyotes. Soon they had reduced the coyote population almost to extinction. Their problems were not over, however. As the coyote population decreased, there was an increase in other life forms. The most notable change was in the population of mice. Within two years, mice swept across the California countryside, destroying millions of dollars worth of grain and other farm products.

- Here's a conclusion:

   Coyotes eat mice.

1. Does the passage contain evidence to support the conclusion or evidence to contradict the conclusion?

   _____

   _____

2. Which sentence contains the evidence?

   _____

   _____

   _____

- Here's another conclusion:

  The population of mice cannot change much in less than a decade.

3. Does the passage contain evidence to support the conclusion or evidence to contradict the conclusion?

   _____

   _____

4. Which sentence contains the evidence?

   _____

   _____

   _____

   _____

   _____

D Write the word **who** or **which** for each item. Remember, use **which** to refer to any whole that is made up of humans.

1. The family _____
2. The family members _____
3. The chorus _____
4. The singers _____
5. The workers _____
6. The crew _____
7. The band _____
8. The players in the band _____

E Read the rule and each piece of evidence. Answer the questions.

Here's the rule:

> **Green plants get their energy from the sun.**

Here are some pieces of evidence:

- **Kelp is a green plant.**

  1. Is this evidence relevant or irrelevant?

     _____

  2. What's the conclusion?

     _____

     _____

- **When it's winter at the North Pole, it's summer at the South Pole.**

  3. Is this evidence relevant or irrelevant?

     _____

  4. What's the conclusion?

     _____

     _____

- **Some living things are neither plants nor animals.**

  5. Is this evidence relevant or irrelevant?

     _____

  6. What's the conclusion?

     _____

     _____

- **Algae are green plants.**

  7. Is this evidence relevant or irrelevant?

  _____

  8. What's the conclusion?

  _____

  _____

- **Omnivores are animals that eat plants and other animals.**

  9. Is this evidence relevant or irrelevant?

  _____

  10. What's the conclusion?

  _____

  _____

- **Agriculture is a science.**

  11. Is this evidence relevant or irrelevant?

  _____

  12. What's the conclusion?

  _____

  _____

A Read the facts and the information. If the information is relevant to fact A, write **relevant to fact A.** If the information is relevant to fact B, write **relevant to fact B.** If the information is irrelevant to both facts, write **irrelevant.**

> Fact A. **Lois is a newspaper reporter.**
>
> Fact B. **Lois is afraid of heights.**

1. Lois meets a lot of people.

_____

2. Lois is a terrible cook.

_____

3. Lois prefers not to fly.

_____

4. Lois refuses to wear fur clothing.

_____

 B Read the passage below. Find a statement that contradicts an earlier statement.

• Underline the statement you assume to be true.
• Circle the contradiction.
• Make up an if-then statement that explains the contradiction.

> When the United States was being settled, most people didn't live or work in towns. They worked on their farms and grew or made many of the same kinds of things we buy today. Women had a big job at home—preparing meals and making soap, candles, and clothes for the family. If a woman wanted to work outside the home, there were very few jobs open to her. Some women taught school. But most women stayed home because they liked the long hours of leisure they had every day.

_____

_____

_____

_____

C Read the rule and each piece of evidence. Answer the questions.

Here's the rule:

> **All rivers flow to the sea.**

Here are some pieces of evidence:

- **Water skiing is a sport.**

1. Is this evidence relevant or irrelevant?

_____

2. What's the conclusion?

_____

_____

- **The Nile is a river.**

3. Is this evidence relevant or irrelevant?

_____

4. What's the conclusion?

_____

_____

- **Most Oregon forests are made up of evergreen trees.**

5. Is this evidence relevant or irrelevant?

_____

6. What's the conclusion?

_____

_____

- **Whales are mammals.**

7. Is this evidence relevant or irrelevant?

_____

8. What's the conclusion?

_____

_____

- **The Amazon is a river.**

9. Is this evidence relevant or irrelevant?

_____

10. What's the conclusion?

_____

_____

- **The first submarine was invented in 1620.**

11. Is this evidence relevant or irrelevant?

_____

12. What's the conclusion?

_____

_____

D For each item, write a sentence that means the same thing by changing the underlined word or words.

1. Claude had several <u>chances</u> to get rid of the <u>repetitive</u> sentences.

_____

_____

_____

_____

2. They <u>changed</u> their Swiss <u>money</u> into Canadian <u>money</u>.

_____

_____

_____

3. I would <u>pause</u> before signing the contract because it's too <u>unclear</u>.

_____

_____

_____

4. Discussing <u>repetitive rules</u> is a waste of time.

_____

_____

_____

E Read the argument below and answer the questions.

> We have a rooster that makes the sun come up every morning. Here's how it happens. The rooster starts crowing when it's dark out. That crowing must call the sun, because a few minutes later, the sky brightens and the sun comes up.

1. What does the writer want us to conclude?

_____

_____

2. Why does the writer think that the rooster's crowing makes the sun rise?

_____

_____

_____

3. What rule does the argument break?

_____

_____

_____

F Write the word **who** or **which** for each item. Use **which** to refer to any whole thing that is made up of humans.

1. The club members _____

2. The club _____

3. The faculty _____

4. The members of the faculty _____

5. The dance group _____

6. The dancers _____

7. The cooking staff _____

8. The cooks _____

ERRORS | W | B | T

★ **A** Use the facts to fill out the form.

Facts: **Your name is Stella Trinton. You are applying for a scholarship to beauty college. You like to fix hair and are interested in makeup. You are a senior at Elm High School in Duluth, Minnesota. You have a B average in school. Your favorite subjects are art and physical education. You play on the girls' basketball team. You belong to Pep Club and a Youth Club. Your hobbies are cooking, sports, and styling your girl friends' hair. You have been a camp counselor for three summers at a local camp. Your parents make $40,000 a year and have four children younger than you. Your father fishes for a living, and your mother runs a preschool.**

1. Name _____

2. Why do you want to be a beautician? _____

_____

3. What high school do you attend? _____

4. List all school activities you are involved in.

    a. _____

    b. _____

    c. _____

    d. _____

5. What is your grade average? _____

6. Have you ever held a summer job?   YES   NO

7. If the answer to question 6 is yes, list the job(s).

    a. _____

    b. _____

    c. _____

8. State your parents' total annual income. _____

9. Number of siblings your parents will be supporting this year _____

10. List your favorite subjects in school. _____

11. List your hobbies. _____

_____

B Read the argument below and answer the questions.

> The capital of Arizona has a greater population than the capital of California. Therefore, the state of Arizona must have a greater population than the state of California.

1. What does the writer want us to conclude?

_____

_____

2. The conclusion is based on information about a part. Name that part.

_____

_____

3. What rule does the argument break?

_____

_____

_____

 C Read the rule and each piece of evidence. Answer the questions.

Here's the rule:

> **All mammals have backbones.**

Here are some pieces of evidence:

- **A wallaby is a mammal.**

1. Is this evidence relevant or irrelevant?

_____

2. What's the conclusion?

_____

- **Humans and rats are mammals.**

3. Is this evidence relevant or irrelevant?

_____

4. What's the conclusion?

_____

- **Some animals can change color.**

5. Is this evidence relevant or irrelevant?

_____

6. What's the conclusion?

_____

- **Most of northern Africa is covered by desert.**

7. Is this evidence relevant or irrelevant?

_____

8. What's the conclusion?

_____

- **Whooping cranes are birds.**

9. Is this evidence relevant or irrelevant?

_____

10. What's the conclusion?

_____

- **Whales, dolphins, and porpoises are mammals.**

11. Is this evidence relevant or irrelevant?

_____

12. What's the conclusion?

_____

_____

D Read the facts and the information. If the information is relevant to fact A, write **relevant to fact A.** If the information is relevant to fact B, write **relevant to fact B.** If the information is irrelevant to both facts, write **irrelevant.**

Fact A. **Eric is an auto mechanic.**

Fact B. **Eric lives on the Atlantic coast.**

1. Eric often has grease under his fingernails.

_____

2. Eric will not drink alcohol.

_____

3. Eric goes deep-sea fishing at least twice a week.

_____

4. Both of Eric's cars run perfectly.

_____

E Each sentence below contains the word **who** or **which.** For each sentence, write what's referred to by **who** or **which.**

1. My sister, who lives in New York, owns a restaurant. _____

2. The book has a red cover, which is torn.

_____

3. Those trees, which were planted last year, are dying. _____

4. She works for Ana Crespo, who owns a bike shop. _____

5. His car, which is brand-new, has a flat tire.

_____

F Read the passage below. Find a statement that contradicts an earlier statement.

- Underline the statement you assume to be true.
- Circle the contradiction.
- Make up an if-then statement that explains the contradiction.

About ninety years ago, many people worked long hours in factories for as little as one dollar a day. Often, they worked seven days a week. There were no safety regulations. In garment factories, workers were crammed together in tiny, stuffy rooms. Fire drills were required once a week. People got angry about these terrible working conditions, and so they got together to organize unions. They went on strike until the factories agreed to provide more pay and better working conditions. Sometimes there were terrible fights between bosses and workers, and people were killed.

_____

_____

_____

_____

Read the argument below and answer the questions.

> **Most summer auto accidents occur on the hottest days. If we want the weather to cool off, we should cut down the number of auto accidents.**

1. What does the writer want us to conclude?

_____

_____

2. Why does the writer think that cutting down on auto accidents will make the weather cool off?

_____

_____

_____

3. What rule does the argument break?

_____

_____

_____

_____

 Here's what we know:

> **Sharon saw flames coming out of the house.**

For each item, combine one of the sentences below with the sentence in the box.

- **She went into the house anyway.**
- **She called the fire department.**

1. Make a combined sentence with **so.**

_____

_____

_____

2. Make a combined sentence with **but.**

_____

_____

_____

3. Make a combined sentence with **therefore.**

_____

_____

_____

4. Make a combined sentence with **however.**

_____

_____

_____

ERRORS	W	B	T

★ **A** Read the argument below and answer the questions.

> **Polio always broke out where there were a lot of flies. Polio could have been eliminated by getting rid of the flies.**

1. What does the writer want us to conclude?

   _____

   _____

2. Why does the writer think that getting rid of flies would have eliminated polio?

   _____

   _____

   _____

3. What rule does the argument break?

   _____

   _____

   _____

B Use the rule in the box and the evidence to answer the questions.

> **Exercise improves your circulation.**

- **In 1990, Mr. Jones worked at a desk every day, drove home, read the paper, and went to bed.**
  In 1998, Mr. Jones played handball every day, worked at his desk, walked home, read the paper, and went to bed.

1. What's the conclusion?

   _____

   _____

2. How do you know?

   _____

   _____

- **Fran exercises four times as much as her identical twin.**

3. What's the conclusion?

   _____

   _____

4. How do you know?

   _____

   _____

- **Linda loves to swim and play basketball. Ann would rather sew and read.**

5. Who probably has better circulation?

   _____

6. How do you know?

   _____

   _____

 C Read the passage below. Find a statement that contradicts an earlier statement.

- Underline the statement you assume to be true.
- Circle the contradiction.
- Make up an if-then statement that explains the contradiction.

Christopher Columbus was talking with the queen of Spain. "But, Your Majesty," he said, "I'm absolutely certain that the world is round."

"My advisor says you are a fool, Chris."

"But I can prove it."

"My advisor says "Hogwash,' Chris."

"Your Majesty, all I need is the money to buy a couple of ships and some supplies."

"My advisor says that we can't afford to support ridiculous projects like yours, Chris."

"Your Majesty, can I tell you something, just between you and me?"

"As you like, Chris."

"I'd like to put your advisor in a boat and sail him over the edge of the world."

"So would I, Chris. Here's your money. Now will you get out of my castle?"

"Thanks a lot, Your Majesty. You're a real swell queen."

 D You will be tested on some facts presented in this lesson. These facts are:

1. **Braille is the system of reading and writing that blind people use.**
2. **Braille is read by running your fingers across patterns of bumps.**

Study these facts. Repeat them to yourself. Writing these facts may help you to remember them.

E Read the passage below.

In ancient Egypt, anyone who killed a cat was immediately put to death. Egyptians worshipped cats as gods. When a cat died, its body was buried in the same way that an important person was buried. It was wrapped in cloth strips, covered with secret oils, and made into a mummy. It was then buried in a tomb. When a cat died, its owner would shave his eyebrows in mourning. Occasionally, mummified mice were buried with a cat so that the cat would not go hungry in its next life.

• Here's a conclusion:

In ancient Egypt, cats were not important.

1. Does the passage contain evidence to support the conclusion or evidence to contradict the conclusion?

_____

_____

2. Which sentence contains the evidence?

_____

_____

_____

• Here's another conclusion:

Ancient Egyptians believed in life after death.

3. Does the passage contain evidence to support the conclusion or evidence to contradict the conclusion?

_____

_____

4. Which sentence contains the evidence?

_____

_____

_____

_____

_____

F Each sentence below contains the word **who** or **which.** For each sentence, write what's referred to by **who** or **which.**

1. He raises jonquils, which have fragrant blossoms.

_____

2. He wrote a paper about Susan B. Anthony, who fought for women's right to vote.

_____

3. Her mother, who just moved to town, is looking for a job.

_____

4. She bought that car from her neighbor, who owns many old cars.

_____

5. These books, which are required for my class, are hard to read.

_____

G Read the argument below and answer the questions.

> **I'll never vote for a Democrat again. The last one I voted for turned out to be a crook.**

1. What does the writer want us to conclude?

_____

_____

2. The conclusion is based on information about a part. Name that part.

_____

_____

3. What rule does the argument break?

_____

_____

_____

H Read the rule and each piece of evidence. Answer the questions.

Here's the rule:

> **Islands are surrounded by water.**

Here are some pieces of evidence:

- **Australia is an island.**

1. Is this evidence relevant or irrelevant?

_____

2. What's the conclusion?

_____

_____

- **Canada has many bodies of water.**

3. Is this evidence relevant or irrelevant?

_____

4. What's the conclusion?

_____

- **Hawaii is an island.**

5. Is this evidence relevant or irrelevant?

_____

6. What's the conclusion?

_____

_____

- **London is a city.**

7. Is this evidence relevant or irrelevant?

_____

8. What's the conclusion?

_____

- **North America is a continent.**

9. Is this evidence relevant or irrelevant?

_____

10. What's the conclusion?

_____

- **Japan is an island.**

11. Is this evidence relevant or irrelevant?

_____

12. What's the conclusion?

_____

_____

LESSON 49

Tomorrow you will be tested on facts you have learned. The test will include all of the facts presented in Lessons 45–49 and some of the facts from earlier lessons. These facts are:

1. A boar is a wild pig with large tusks.
2. A nook is a small place.
3. Some types of equus became large and others became slender, depending on what climate they lived in.
4. When you haze people, you torment them.
5. When you tantalize someone, you tease that person by putting something just out of reach.
6. A clue is a hint that helps you find your way out of a puzzle.
7. In Middle English, the word for thread was **clewe.**
8. Donkeys and zebras descended from equus.
9. Two other names for a donkey are a burro and an ass.
10. A robot is a machine that looks and does some things like a human.
11. The Greek word **paragraphos** means **by the side of writing.**
12. A maverick can be a person who isn't part of the group.
13. Arabian stallions are bred with other kinds of horses to produce more intelligent horses.
14. Arabian horses performed well in battle because they were light and fast.
15. Braille is the system of reading and writing that blind people use.
16. Braille is read by running your fingers across patterns of bumps.

★ Look at this diagram:

restrict

The diagram contradicts part of these instructions:

1. Draw a vertical line.
2. Draw a horizontal line below the vertical line.
3. Make a line that slants down to the right from the right end of the horizontal line.
4. Write the word **restrict** above the vertical line.

Circle the instruction that the diagram contradicts.
Draw a new diagram that follows the instructions.

B You will be tested on some facts presented in this lesson. These facts are:

1. Before the Pony Express, mail delivery from St. Joseph, Missouri, to Sacramento, California, took twenty days.
2. The Pony Express delivered mail from St. Joseph to Sacramento in eight days.
3. The Pony Express was faster than regular mail delivery because the Pony Express stationed fresh horses along the route.

Study these facts. Repeat them to yourself. Writing these facts may help you to remember them.

C Read the rule and each piece of evidence. Answer the questions.

Here's the rule:

> **The steeper the slope of the land, the faster a stream flows.**

Here are some pieces of evidence:

● **The Rogue River is on a steeper slope than the Mississippi.**

1. Is this evidence relevant or irrelevant?

_____

2. What's the conclusion?

_____

_____

● **Crater Lake is high in the mountains of Oregon.**

3. Is this evidence relevant or irrelevant?

_____

4. What's the conclusion?

_____

● **The Willamette River flows through mountains and into the valley.**

5. Is this evidence relevant or irrelevant?

_____

6. What's the conclusion?

_____

_____

_____

- **Mountain goats are not bothered by steep climbs.**

7. Is this evidence relevant or irrelevant?

_____

8. What's the conclusion?

_____

_____

- **Bicycles are a great way to get around town.**

9. Is this evidence relevant or irrelevant?

_____

10. What's the conclusion?

_____

_____

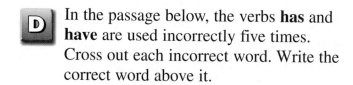 In the passage below, the verbs **has** and **have** are used incorrectly five times. Cross out each incorrect word. Write the correct word above it.

This year, our Christmas tree have only handmade decorations. We baked cookies and strung them on the tree. Some of the cookies has glitter and frosting. Other cookies has funny faces. We also strung popcorn and cranberries for the tree. This kind of decoration have three benefits:

1. It is fun to do.

2. It is an inexpensive form of decoration.

3. After Christmas, we will put the tree outside. Then we will watch the birds has a good time eating the cookies and the popcorn.

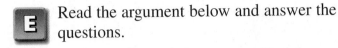 Read the argument below and answer the questions.

> **I'll never go to that lousy library again. The last book I got there was terrible.**

1. What does the writer want us to conclude?

   _____

   _____

2. The conclusion is based on information about a part. Name that part.

   _____

   _____

3. What rule does the argument break?

   _____

   _____

   _____

 Read the passage below.

> An adult rhinoceros can weigh up to five tons. In spite of its huge size, a rhino can gallop along at a speed of about twenty-eight miles per hour. Rhinos seem to have bad tempers and will attack almost anything, including trains. African hunters do not fear the rhinoceros, despite its size. The reason is that the rhino closes its eyes when it charges and is easy to dodge.

● Here's a conclusion:

   Rhinos are cowardly.

1. Does the passage contain evidence to support the conclusion or evidence to contradict the conclusion?

   _____

   _____

2. Which sentence contains the evidence?

   _____

   _____

   _____

● Here's another conclusion:

   Because of their weight, rhinos are slow movers.

3. Does the passage contain evidence to support the conclusion or evidence to contradict the conclusion?

   _____

   _____

4. Which sentence contains the evidence?

   _____

   _____

   _____

ERRORS | W | B | T

A Cross out the irrelevant words in the second piece of evidence and write the conclusion for each item below.

1. **All water towers are used to store water. Salem's water tower is the second-largest in the state.**

   _____

   _____

2. **All the houses on Fog Island are made of stone.**
   Burt owns the largest house on Fog Island.

   _____

   _____

3. **All stars need fuel to make them shine. Our sun is the closest star to us.**

   _____

   _____

B Read the argument below and answer the questions. Assume that the Ale is a real car.

> **The Ale must be the best car in automotive history, because the Ale has the best kind of carburetor.**

1. What does the writer want us to conclude?

   _____

   _____

2. The conclusion is based on information about a part. Name that part.

   _____

3. What rule does the argument break?

   _____

   _____

   _____

   _____

C Each sentence below contains the word **who** or **which**. For each sentence, write what's referred to by **who** or **which**.

1. Milk, which is high in calcium, prevents rickets.

   _____

2. She spent her vacation in Athens, which is the capital of Greece.

   _____

3. The macaw, which is a type of parrot, has brightly colored feathers.

   _____

4. She has many books by Agatha Christie, who was a mystery writer.

   _____

5. His siblings, who live in Ohio, are very rich.

   _____

D Read the rule and each piece of evidence. Answer the questions. Here's the rule:

The closer something is to the sun, the hotter that thing is.

Here are some pieces of evidence:

- **Mars is closer to the sun than Neptune.**

1. Is this evidence relevant or irrelevant?

_____

2. What's the conclusion?

_____

_____

- **All green plants need sunlight.**

3. Is this evidence relevant or irrelevant?

_____

4. What's the conclusion?

_____

_____

- **As far as we know, Earth is the only planet that has air conditioners.**

5. Is this evidence relevant or irrelevant?

_____

6. What's the conclusion?

_____

_____

- **Mercury is the planet nearest to the sun.**

7. Is this evidence relevant or irrelevant?

_____

8. What's the conclusion?

_____

_____

- **People often behave strangely when there is a full moon.**

9. Is this evidence relevant or irrelevant?

_____

10. What's the conclusion?

_____

_____

E Look at diagram 1.

Diagram 1

You can't see the boxes in this diagram, but **some boxes are in the triangle.**

1. We're looking for a box. What's the conclusion about where that box is?

_____

_____

2. Draw boxes in diagram 1.

- Look at diagram 2.

Diagram 2

You can see the dots and the oval in this diagram, but you can't see the rectangle.

3. Complete the deduction.

All the dots are in the oval.
Part of the oval is in the rectangle.

So, _____

_____

ERRORS | W | B | T

★ **A** Read the facts and the information below. If the information is relevant to fact A, write **relevant to fact A.** If the information is relevant to fact B, write **relevant to fact B.** If the information is irrelevant to both facts, write **irrelevant.**

Fact A. **Lisa doesn't have a job.**

Fact B. **Lisa is going to medical school.**

1. Lisa plays the clarinet.

_____

2. Lisa knows nearly everything about the human digestive system.

_____

3. Lisa does not receive regular paychecks.

_____

4. Lisa spends a lot of time studying.

_____

B For each item, write a sentence that means the same thing by changing the underlined word or words.

1. Lana <u>paused</u> while explaining where they got all the <u>money</u>.

_____

_____

2. They lost the <u>chance</u> to reach a decision because the situation remained <u>unclear</u>.

_____

_____

_____

3. The <u>rule</u> <u>limited</u> their parking.

_____

_____

4. Greta <u>changed</u> the <u>154</u> passage into one that was much more interesting.

_____

_____

_____

C Write the verb **has** or **have** in each blank.

1. They _____ been sick for two weeks.

2. This chair _____ a broken leg.

3. You _____ lots of books.

4. I _____ to swim every day.

5. Nobody _____ run three races today.

6. Many people _____ middle names.

Read the argument below and answer the questions.

I picked up a beautiful agate at the bottom of Pike's Peak. Do you realize that the entire mountain must be made of agate?

1. What does the writer want us to conclude?

_____

_____

2. The conclusion is based on information about a part. Name that part.

_____

3. What rule does the argument break?

_____

_____

_____

 Read the evidence and write the conclusion for each item below.

1. Here's the evidence:

   Bananas are fruit.
   Fruit contains seeds.

What's the conclusion?

_____

2. Here's the evidence:

   Gazelles are mammals.
   Some mammals are herbivorous.

What's the conclusion?

_____

3. Here's the evidence:

   Every horse is an animal.
   An Arabian is a horse.

What's the conclusion?

_____

 Rosalie sometimes has trouble using the words **who** and **which.** Below are some sentences that she wrote. Cross out **who** or **which** if it is used incorrectly.

1. The truck, who was red, was covered with dirt.
2. The general gave orders to the platoon, who was in uniform.
3. The general gave orders to the soldiers, who were in uniform.
4. Spinach, which is an excellent source of iron, is my favorite vegetable.
5. The football team, who was the best in the state, won a trophy.
6. The driver had an older brother, which was friendly.
7. My uncle, who has a beard, plays bassoon in the orchestra.
8. She is president of that club, who fights for women's rights.

You will be tested on some facts presented in this lesson. These facts are:

1. **A boycott takes place when people stop buying from a business or selling to a business.**
2. **When a business is successfully boycotted, it can either change its practices or go out of business.**

Study these facts. Repeat them to yourself. Writing these facts may help you to remember them.

ERRORS | W | B | T

★ **A** Write the instructions for the diagram.

② currency

③ ambiguous (①) ④ redundant

1. (what) _____

_____

2. (what and where) _____

_____

_____

3. (what and where) _____

_____

_____

4. (what and where) _____

_____

_____

B In the passage in the next column, there are eight places where model-sentence words could be used. Read the passage carefully. To replace a word with a model-sentence word, first cross out the word. Then write the model-sentence word above it. Make sure the words **a** and **an** are used correctly.

The rules were clear enough: no smoking in the train station. Mr. Jefferson's problem was that he couldn't go five minutes without smoking. So he looked around, and when he felt that he had a chance, he grabbed his cigarettes from his pocket. When he pulled them out, however, he also pulled out an envelope containing $12,000 in large bills. The money was for an insurance settlement that Mr. Jefferson was supposed to make later that day. The envelope fell to the floor. As Mr. Jefferson puffed on his cigarette, a policeman approached him. He said something, but Mr. Jefferson couldn't hear him above the repetitive announcements echoing over the loudspeaker. Although Mr. Jefferson couldn't hear the officer, the situation did not seem unclear. Mr. Jefferson was sure the officer was reminding him about the rule that limited smoking. So, without pausing, Mr. Jefferson ground out his cigarette and was about ready to leave when the officer walked over, picked up the envelope, and handed it to him. "You dropped this," he said.

Read the argument below and answer the questions.

It must rain year-round in Oregon. I was just there for three days and it rained the whole time.

1. What does the writer want us to conclude?

   _____

   _____

2. The conclusion is based on information about a part. Name that part.

   _____

3. What rule does the argument break?

   _____

   _____

   _____

   _____

D In the story below, the verbs **is** and **are** and the verbs **was** and **were** are used incorrectly five times. Cross out each incorrect word. Write the correct word above it.

Sometimes it seems like cooking is becoming a "lost art." Anybody who are in a hurry can buy a frozen TV dinner or pick up a hamburger at a fast-food restaurant. People who work is not always in the mood to make a meal from scratch. In some places, it are cheaper to eat at drive-ins than to eat home-cooked food. A hundred years ago, most people was spending half the day cooking food for their families. Today, cooking a meal is as easy as opening a can of spaghetti. The only problem are to decide how many cans to open.

E Here's what we know:

> **I have to buy some new clothes.**

For each item, combine one of the sentences below with the sentence in the box.

- **I'm going to the shopping mall.**
- **I don't have any money.**

1. Make a combined sentence with **and.**

_____

_____

2. Make a combined sentence with **therefore.**

_____

_____

_____

3. Make a combined sentence with **however.**

_____

_____

_____

4. Make a combined sentence with **but.**

_____

_____

_____

F Read the passage. Find a statement that contradicts an earlier statement.

- Underline the statement you assume to be true.
- Circle the contradiction.
- Make up an if-then statement that explains the contradiction.

Gardens are a good way to save money. Just a tiny garden can produce enough vegetables to feed a family of four all summer. If you can the vegetables, you will have vegetables all winter long. The most important step toward a good garden is preparing the soil before you plant. If you want the garden to feed more than three people, you must prepare a very large plot of ground. Then just plant the seeds and watch them grow.

_____

_____

_____

_____

G Charles sometimes has trouble using the words **who** and **which.** Below are some sentences that he wrote. Cross out **who** or **which** if it is used incorrectly.

1. The teacher praised the class, which behaved well at the assembly.
2. Her spouse, which works downtown, drives a sports car.
3. She rooms with Libby Levine, who is my sister.
4. The impala, who is an antelope, is native to Africa.
5. The coach talked to the team, who was in low spirits.
6. The moon, who is far away, has been visited by humans.
7. Julia is going to the party, who starts at nine.
8. The dancer, who was six feet tall, received a standing ovation.

A Look at this diagram:

This diagram contradicts part of these instructions:

1. Draw a horizontal line.
2. Make a circle to the right of the line.
3. Draw a vertical line below the circle.
4. Write the word **convert** above the horizontal line.

Circle the instruction that the diagram contradicts.
Draw a new diagram that follows the instructions.

 B Use the rule in the box and the evidence to answer the questions.

> **The better the soil, the better the plants will grow.**

- **Jim and Joe used the same garden. Jim put lots of fertilizer in the soil before he planted his seeds. Joe just dug up the soil a little bit before he planted his seeds.**

1. What's the conclusion?

_____

_____

2. How do you know?

_____

_____

- **Mike's garden has much better soil than Sarah's garden.**

3. What is the conclusion?

_____

- **The soil in the valley is rich and black. The soil in the hills is mostly clay.**

4. What's the conclusion?

_____

_____

5. How do you know?

_____

_____

C Read the arguments below and answer the questions.

- **That basketball star eats Tootles for breakfast every day. I think I'll eat Tootles when I start playing basketball next winter.**

1. What does the writer want us to conclude?

_____

_____

_____

2. Why does the writer think that eating Tootles will make him a better basketball player?

_____

_____

3. What rule does the argument break?

_____

_____

_____

4. How would you prove that eating Tootles does not make you a better basketball player?

_____

_____

_____

_____

● **The plants in New Mexico must grow very well. Albuquerque has some of the most beautiful lawns and gardens I've ever seen.**

5. What does the writer want us to conclude?

_____

_____

_____

6. Why does the writer think that plants in New Mexico must grow very well?

_____

_____

_____

7. What rule does the writer's argument break?

_____

_____

_____

8. How would you find out if the plants in New Mexico grow very well?

_____

_____

_____

D Read the passage below.

> Ostriches are the world's largest birds, often reaching a height of more than two meters. They have extremely strong legs that enable them to kick with the force of a mule and to run forty kilometers an hour. Ostriches have small wings that extend when they are running, but they cannot fly. They can hiss like a snake and roar like a lion. Contrary to popular belief, ostriches do not bury their heads in the sand when they are scared.
>
> Although ostriches are native to Africa, ostriches were raised in several countries during the 1800s. Their feathers were used a lot in hatmaking and dressmaking. Today, fashions have changed, so few people raise ostriches anymore.

● Here's a conclusion:

> **Things that many people believe are not necessarily true.**

1. Does the passage contain evidence to support this conclusion or evidence to refute this conclusion?

_____

_____

2. Which sentence contains the evidence?

_____

_____

_____

- Here's another conclusion:

  Ostriches do not build nests in trees.

3. Does the passage contain evidence to support this conclusion or evidence to refute this conclusion?

_____

4. Which sentence contains the evidence?

_____

_____

_____

_____

- Here's another conclusion:

  Eagles are larger than ostriches.

5. Does the passage contain evidence to support this conclusion or evidence to refute this conclusion?

_____

6. Which sentence contains the evidence?

_____

_____

_____

- Here's another conclusion:

  Many people continue to raise ostriches.

7. Does the passage contain evidence to support this conclusion or evidence to refute this conclusion?

_____

8. Which sentence contains the evidence?

_____

_____

_____

_____

E Read the rule and each piece of evidence. Answer the questions. Here's the rule:

> **Every gas engine pollutes the air.**

Here are some pieces of evidence:

- **Many trains in Europe run on electricity.**

1. Is this evidence relevant or irrelevant?

_____

2. What's the conclusion?

_____

_____

- **Most cars have gas engines.**

3. Is this evidence relevant or irrelevant?

_____

4. What's the conclusion?

_____

_____

- **A person who rides a bicycle works like an engine.**

5. Is this evidence relevant or irrelevant?

_____

6. What's the conclusion?

_____

_____

- **Irving's lawn mower has a gas engine.**

7. Is this evidence relevant or irrelevant?

_____

8. What's the conclusion?

_____

_____

- **Early trains were powered by steam engines.**

9. Is this evidence relevant or irrelevant?

_____

10. What's the conclusion?

_____

_____

- **Most chain saws have gas engines.**

11. Is this evidence relevant or irrelevant?

_____

12. What's the conclusion?

_____

_____

F In the passage below, there are ten places where model-sentence words could be used. Read the passage carefully. To replace a word with a model-sentence word, first cross out the word. Then write the model-sentence word above it. Make sure the words **a** and **an** are used correctly.

Doris had a chance to buy the old Taylor house. Without pausing for five seconds, she did it. She didn't have enough money for the down payment, but a bank agreed to make her a loan. She found some of the rules in the mortgage unclear, but she purchased the old house anyway. Her dream was to change it into a showplace; however, she didn't know how much it would cost. She also didn't know that there were rules that limited how much remodeling one could do without a building permit. Four months after she bought the old place, she had a much better understanding of old houses. She had a better understanding of the seemingly repetitive passages in the mortgage. Now her goal was different. She wanted to fix up the old place and sell it at the first chance.

G Tomorrow you will be tested on facts you have learned. The test will include all of the facts presented in Lessons 50–54 and some of the facts from earlier lessons. These facts are:

1. The Greek word **paragraphos** means **by the side of writing.**
2. Eohippus was the earliest-known close relative of the modern horse.
3. We know that eohippus was related to the horse because its skeleton resembles the skeleton of a modern horse.
4. Eohippus defended itself by outrunning its enemies.
5. The feet of eohippus changed over the centuries to make it a better runner.
6. Modern horses and other similar animals belong to a group called equus.
7. A robot is a machine that looks and does some things like a human.
8. Some types of equus became large and others became slender, depending on what climate they lived in.
9. A maverick can be a person who isn't part of the group.
10. Arabian stallions are bred with other kinds of horses to produce more intelligent horses.

11. Arabian horses performed well in battle because they were light and fast.
12. Braille is the system of reading and writing that blind people use.
13. Braille is read by running your fingers across patterns of bumps.
14. Before the Pony Express, mail delivery from St. Joseph, Missouri, to Sacramento, California, took twenty days.
15. The Pony Express delivered mail from St. Joseph to Sacramento in eight days.
16. The Pony Express was faster than regular mail delivery because the Pony Express stationed fresh horses along the route.
17. A boycott takes place when people stop buying from a business or selling to a business.
18. When a business is successfully boycotted, it can either change its practices or go out of business.

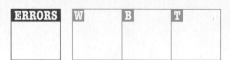

ERRORS W B T

★ **A** For each item, write a sentence that means the same thing by changing the underlined word or words.

1. The last <u>rule</u> requires them to <u>change</u> to diesel-powered engines.

_____

_____

2. Her <u>unclear</u> statement about the recovery of the <u>money</u> left many questions.

_____

_____

_____

3. The essay contest's <u>rules</u> <u>limited</u> the students' use of <u>repetitive</u> sentences.

_____

_____

_____

4. By <u>pausing</u>, she lost her <u>chance</u>.

_____

_____

B In the passage below, the verbs **has** and **have** are used incorrectly five times. Cross out each incorrect word. Write the correct word above it.

Everybody in my gym class have to jog a mile every day. Some of the kids have special running clothes. I run in my gym shorts because I don't has jogging shorts. You don't has to wear special clothes to run as long as the clothes you wear are comfortable. Nobody have trouble jogging a mile now, but at first some people couldn't even run half a mile. Next week we have to start running two miles. It will be interesting to see who have trouble with that extra mile.

Read the rule and each piece of evidence. Answer the questions. Here's the rule:

> **Every bone needs calcium.**

Here are some pieces of evidence:

- **The vena cava is a vein.**

1. Is this evidence relevant or irrelevant?

   _____

2. What's the conclusion?

   _____

   _____

- **The mandible is the lower jawbone.**

3. Is this evidence relevant or irrelevant?

   _____

4. What's the conclusion?

   _____

   _____

- **The pituitary is a gland that controls your growth.**

5. Is this evidence relevant or irrelevant?

   _____

6. What's the conclusion?

   _____

   _____

- **The femur is the longest bone in the human body.**

7. Is this evidence relevant or irrelevant?

   _____

8. What's the conclusion?

   _____

   _____

- **The stirrup bone in the ear is the smallest bone in the human body.**

9. Is this evidence relevant or irrelevant?

   _____

10. What's the conclusion?

   _____

   _____

- **The average adult brain weighs three pounds.**

11. Is this evidence relevant or irrelevant?

   _____

12. What's the conclusion?

   _____

   _____

D Read the arguments and answer the questions.

- **He started taking Grandma's Cold Remedy, and five days later his cold went away. That stuff really works.**

1. What does the writer want us to conclude?

   _____

   _____

   _____

2. Why does the writer think that Grandma's Cold Remedy really works?

   _____

   _____

3. What rule does the argument break?

   _____

   _____

   _____

4. How would you prove that taking Grandma's Cold Remedy doesn't make colds go away?

   _____

   _____

   _____

   _____

- **One of the largest lakes in the United States is in the state of Utah. Utah must be one of the largest states.**

5. What does the writer want us to conclude?

   _____

   _____

6. Why does the writer think that Utah is one of the largest states?

   _____

   _____

7. What rule does the argument break?

   _____

   _____

   _____

8. How would you find out if Utah is one of the largest states?

   _____

   _____

   _____

A Read the facts and the information below. If the information is relevant to fact A, write **relevant to fact A.** If the information is relevant to fact B, write **relevant to fact B.** If the information is irrelevant to both facts, write **irrelevant.**

Fact A. **The sawmill is the only industry in Brownsville.**

Fact B. **The sawmill is over a hundred years old.**

1. Square dancing is very popular in Brownsville.

_____

2. Nearly everyone in Brownsville works at the sawmill.

_____

3. Much of the original machinery in the mill has been replaced.

_____

4. The Brownsville mill is the only mill in Blair County.

_____

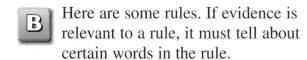 **B** Here are some rules. If evidence is relevant to a rule, it must tell about certain words in the rule.

- Read each rule.
- Underline the right word or words.
- Then fill in the blank.

1. **Muscles pull like rubber bands when they work.**

Relevant evidence must tell that something

is _____.

2. **All reptiles are cold-blooded.**

Relevant evidence must tell that something

is _____.

3. **Every gaff is a flerb.**

Relevant evidence must tell that something

is _____.

4. **Insects do not have bones.**

Relevant evidence must tell that something

is _____.

C For each item, write a sentence that means the same thing by changing the underlined word or words.

1. Her answer was filled with irrelevant details.

_____

_____

2. Lee's answer was filled with irrelevant details.

_____

_____

3. The teacher's irrelevant answers confused me.

_____

_____

4. His movements were filled with nervous jerks.

_____

_____

D Read the arguments and answer the questions.

- **Sugar-Frosted Bounders have real wheat in them. Everybody knows that wheat is good for you. So run out and buy some Bounders today.**

1. What does the writer want us to conclude?

_____

_____

2. Why does the writer think that Sugar-Frosted Bounders are good for you?

_____

_____

3. What rule does the argument break?

_____

_____

_____

4. How would you prove that Sugar-Frosted Bounders are not good for you?

_____

_____

_____

- **The day Don asked me for a date, I won $10,000. I wish he'd ask me out again because I'd sure like to win some more money.**

5. What does the writer want us to conclude?

_____

_____

6. Why does the writer think she will win more money if Don asks her out again?

_____

_____

7. What rule does the argument break?

_____

_____

_____

8. How would you prove that the writer won't win more money if Don asks her out again?

_____

_____

_____

_____

E You will be tested on a fact presented in this lesson. This fact is:

> **A spoonerism is made by exchanging the first parts of words.**

Study this fact. Repeat it to yourself. Writing this fact may help you to remember it.

A Below are some rules. If evidence is relevant to a rule, it must tell about certain words in the rule.

- Read each rule.
- Underline the right word or words.
- Then fill in the blank.

1. **All birds are warm-blooded.**

   Relevant evidence must tell that something

   is _____ .

2. **Many insects eat plants.**

   Relevant evidence must tell that something

   is _____ .

3. **Diddlers are doozy.**

   Relevant evidence must tell that something

   is _____ .

4. **Some substances are transparent.**

   Relevant evidence must tell that something

   is _____ .

B For each item, write a sentence that means the same thing by changing the underlined word or words.

1. Her answer was filled with irrelevant details.

   _____

   _____

2. His answers were filled with irrelevant details.

   _____

   _____

3. Our conversation was filled with long pauses.

   _____

   _____

4. The professor often yelled at students who gave irrelevant answers.

   _____

   _____

   _____

C Read the passage below. Find a statement that contradicts an earlier statement.

- Underline the statement you assume to be true.
- Circle the contradiction.
- Make up an if-then statement that explains the contradiction.

"Come on down to Joe's Recreational Vehicle Emporium, home of the new Bowman Model. The Bowman has a garbage disposal, microwave oven, color television, dishwasher, and sliding glass doors. The Bowman is unlike any camper you have ever seen. Take it to your favorite spot in the mountains or at the lake. Find out what roughing it is all about. See the amazing Bowman Camper at Joe's, on Fifth Avenue."

_____

_____

_____

_____

LESSON 57

D Select the right word for combining each pair of sentences below. Then write the combined sentence. Remember to punctuate each sentence correctly.

1. He stubbed his toe. He is in a bad mood.
and   however

_____

2. She has no money. She never buys anything.
so   but

_____

3. Johnny Appleseed loved apples. He planted apple seeds all over the United States.
so   but

_____

_____

4. Huskies are very strong dogs. They are used to pull sleds.   **therefore   but**

_____

_____

5. She walked home in the rain. Her hat is ruined.   **and   but**

_____

_____

6. Bill smashed up my car. I'm not speaking to him.   **therefore   however**

_____

_____

_____

E Read the arguments and answer the questions.

• **The sun always rises right after that rooster crows. I don't know how we'll get the sun to rise if the rooster dies.**

1. What does the writer want us to conclude?

_____

_____

2. Why does the writer think that the rooster's crowing makes the sun rise?

_____

_____

3. What rule does the argument break?

_____

_____

_____

_____

4. How would you prove that the rooster doesn't make the sun rise?

_____

_____

_____

_____

- **If Sheila eats ice cream every day, she doesn't catch colds. She's been eating ice cream daily for a month now, and she hasn't had a single cold.**

5. What does the writer want us to conclude?

_____

_____

6. Why does the writer think that if Sheila eats ice cream daily she won't catch colds?

_____

_____

_____

7. What rule does the argument break?

_____

_____

_____

8. How would you prove that eating ice cream every day doesn't keep Sheila from catching colds?

_____

_____

_____

_____

 You will be tested on a fact presented in this lesson. This fact is:

> **Two things that stimulated Houston's growth were (1) a railroad that connected Houston with cities to the north and east, and (2) a canal that made Houston into an inland seaport.**

Study this fact. Repeat it to yourself. Writing this fact may help you to remember it.

ERRORS | W | B | T

★ **A**   Use the facts to fill out the form.

Facts: **Your name is Eric Vacek. Your father is a lawyer, and you think he does interesting work. You don't want to be a lawyer yourself, but you think it would be fun to work in a lawyer's office. You want to start out as a secretary and maybe work into a position as a legal assistant. You have a degree in history from the University of Florida, which you attended from 1990 to 1994. You worked part-time as a waiter at Pete's Greek Food from 1991 to 1993. From 1993 to 1994, you worked as a secretary in the office of the chairman of the history department, scheduling meetings and lectures and typing correspondence. You are applying for a secretarial position at Brown & Gaylord, Attorneys at Law. You are single, twenty-five years old, and your social security number is 922-34-5397. Your address is P.O. Box 194, Gainesville, FL. Your phone number is 538-2674.**

1. Print your name, last name first: _____

2. State your present address: _____

_____

3. Age _____   4. Social security number _____   5. Phone _____

6. Do you have any typing experience?   Yes   No

7. List all jobs you have held, beginning with the most recent one.

   a. Employer _____

     Position _____ Date _____

     Duties _____

   b. Employer _____

     Position _____ Date _____

     Duties _____

8. Print any additional information about yourself that may be relevant to this job.

_____

_____

B Select the right word for combining each pair of sentences below. Then write the combined sentence. Remember to punctuate each sentence correctly.

1. I stopped to watch a squirrel. I missed my bus.   **and   but**

_____

_____

2. Sharon saw smoke pouring out of her neighbor's house. She called the fire department.   **so   however**

_____

_____

3. Elmer is sleepy. He won't take a nap. **therefore   but**

_____

_____

4. She wants to be on the track team. She hasn't run for three weeks. **therefore   however**

_____

_____

_____

5. They blindfolded me. I couldn't tell where I was taken.   **so   but**

_____

_____

6. This cat showed up yesterday. It was still on my doorstep this morning.   **and   but**

_____

_____

_____

C Below are some rules. If evidence is relevant to a rule, it must tell about certain words in the rule.

- Read each rule.
- Underline the right word or words.
- Then fill in the blank.

1. **Most cars waste a lot of gasoline.**

   Relevant evidence must tell that something

   is _____.

2. **Carnivorous animals eat meat.**

   Relevant evidence must tell that something

   is _____.

3. **Some plants are too small to be seen without a microscope.**

   Relevant evidence must tell that something

   is _____.

4. **All amphibians are cold-blooded.**

   Relevant evidence must tell that something

   is _____.

LESSON 58

D For each item, write a sentence that means the same thing by changing the underlined word or words.

1. Her <u>answer</u> was <u>filled</u> with <u>irrelevant</u> details.

_____

_____

2. Jo's <u>answer</u> was <u>filled</u> with <u>irrelevant</u> comments.

_____

_____

3. Including <u>irrelevant</u> facts will make an <u>answer</u> longer than it needs to be.

_____

_____

_____

4. Rita's cupboards were <u>filled</u> with all kinds of food.

_____

_____

E Read the passage below.

> In 1613, an Italian astronomer named Galileo Galilei published a book confirming the Copernican theory that the sun is the center of the solar system and that Earth travels around the sun. Galileo had improved the newly invented telescope, and he used it to gather data about the motions of the planets and sunspots. This information gave the evidence he needed to support the new theory of the solar system.
>
> Unfortunately, this new theory directly contradicted the accepted belief that Earth was the center of the solar system. Galileo's second book on the theory was published in 1630. Church leaders strongly disapproved of the work, and its sale was forbidden. In 1633, Galileo was brought to trial, where he was forced to kneel and say that he no longer believed the sun was the center of the solar system.

• Here's a conclusion:

   The publishing of Galileo's books was encouraged.

1. Does the passage contain evidence to support this conclusion or evidence to contradict this conclusion?

_____

_____

2. Which sentence contains the evidence?

_____

_____

_____

- Here's another conclusion:

   The church did not agree with Galileo.

3. Does the passage contain evidence to support this conclusion or evidence to contradict this conclusion?

   _____

   _____

4. Which sentence contains the evidence?

   _____

   _____

   _____

- Here's another conclusion:

   Galileo did not agree with the general public about the solar system.

5. Does the passage contain evidence to support this conclusion or evidence to contradict this conclusion?

   _____

   _____

6. Which sentence contains the evidence?

   _____

   _____

   _____

   _____

 You will be tested on some facts presented in this lesson. These facts are:

1. **Millard Fillmore was moderate in his views, which means he didn't take a strong stand on anything.**
2. **Millard Fillmore became president of the United States when President Taylor died.**

Study these facts. Repeat them to yourself. Writing these facts may help you to remember them.

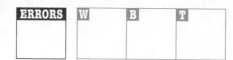

ERRORS | W | B | T

★ **A** Write the verb **has** or **have** in each blank.

1. This water _____ a bad taste.

2. You _____ cut lots of firewood.

3. Six big planes _____ crashed this year.

4. I _____ been drinking lots of juice.

5. Their friends _____ left for New York.

6. It _____ floppy ears and a bushy tail.

B For each item, write a sentence that means the same thing by changing the underlined word or words.

1. Her <u>answer</u> was <u>filled</u> with <u>irrelevant</u> details.

_____

_____

2. That author's books are <u>filled</u> with <u>irrelevant</u> and redundant passages.

_____

_____

3. After <u>pausing</u>, she gave an ambiguous <u>answer</u>.

_____

_____

4. The senator's <u>answers</u> were <u>irrelevant</u> to the point being discussed.

_____

_____

C Read the arguments and answer the questions.

• **We saw three fish near the shore of the Mississippi River, but we saw only one fish near the shore of the Columbia River. There's no doubt about it. The Mississippi is better for fishing than the Columbia.**

1. What does the writer want us to conclude?

_____

_____

_____

2. Why does the writer think that the Mississippi is better for fishing than the Columbia?

_____

_____

_____

3. What rule does the argument break?

_____

_____

_____

4. How would you find out if the Mississippi is better for fishing than the Columbia?

_____

_____

_____

- **She must be good in math. Look at how well she does in social studies and reading.**

5. What does the writer want us to conclude?

_____

_____

_____

6. Why does the writer think that the other person must be good in math?

_____

_____

7. What rule does the argument break?

_____

_____

_____

_____

8. How would you find out if the other person is good in math?

_____

_____

_____

D Read the passage below.

> You may think that rockets are a modern invention. Actually, there is evidence that the Chinese used rockets in warfare almost 800 years ago. Rockets were used primarily for war or fireworks during the next 600 years. In 1807, Henry Tengrouse converted the destructive power of rockets to a peaceful use. He invented a method of rocketing lifelines to sinking ships.
>
> Since 1807, rockets have been put to helpful as well as destructive uses. Rockets are used to put satellites in orbit. These satellites make communication by telephone, radio, and television easier and easier across long distances. Military rockets have been improved as well. Rockets that once could fly only a few hundred yards and then make a small explosion can now travel thousands of miles and demolish a medium-sized city. Some countries in the word have hundreds of these rockets, enough to destroy the entire world many times over. How do you think Henry Tengrouse would feel about that?

- Here's a conclusion:
  Americans were not the first to use rockets.

1. Does the passage contain evidence to support this conclusion or evidence to contradict this conclusion?

_____

2. Which sentence contains the evidence?

_____

_____

_____

- Here's another conclusion:

    China has never been involved in a war.

3. Does the passage contain evidence to support this conclusion or evidence to contradict this conclusion?

    _____

    _____

4. Which sentence contains the evidence?

    _____

    _____

    _____

- Here's another conclusion:

    The destructive power of military rockets has increased.

5. Does the passage contain evidence to support this conclusion or evidence to contradict this conclusion?

    _____

    _____

6. Which sentence contains the evidence?

    _____

    _____

    _____

    _____

    _____

E Below are some rules. If evidence is relevant to a rule, it must tell about certain words in the rule.

- Read each rule.
- Underline the right word or words.
- Then fill in the blank.

1. **Many of the dinosaurs were plant eaters.**

    Relevant evidence must tell that something

    is _____.

2. **All reptiles are born on land.**

    Relevant evidence must tell that something

    is _____.

3. **Birds lay eggs.**

    Relevant evidence must tell that something

    is _____.

4. **Some adults are over six feet tall.**

    Relevant evidence must tell that something

    is _____.

F Tomorrow you will be tested on facts you have learned. The test will include all of the facts presented in Lessons 55–59 and some of the facts from earlier lessons. These facts are:

1. Donkeys and zebras descended from equus.
2. Two other names for a donkey are a burro and an ass.
3. A robot is a machine that looks and does some things like a human.
4. When you haze people, you torment them.
5. A maverick can be a person who isn't part of the group.
6. Arabian stallions are bred with other kinds of horses to produce more intelligent horses.
7. Arabian horses performed well in battle because they were light and fast.
8. Braille is the system of reading and writing that blind people use.
9. Braille is read by running your fingers across patterns of bumps.
10. Before the Pony Express, mail delivery from St. Joseph, Missouri, to Sacramento, California, took twenty days.
11. The Pony Express delivered mail from St. Joseph to Sacramento in eight days.
12. The Pony Express was faster than regular mail delivery because the Pony Express stationed fresh horses along the route.
13. A boycott takes place when people stop buying from a business or selling to a business.
14. When a business is successfully boycotted, it can either change its practices or go out of business.
15. A spoonerism is made by exchanging the first parts of words.
16. Two things that stimulated Houston's growth were (1) a railroad that connected Houston with cities to the north and east, and (2) a canal that made Houston into an inland seaport.
17. Millard Fillmore was moderate in his views, which means he didn't take a strong stand on anything.
18. Millard Fillmore became president of the United States when President Taylor died.

ERRORS | W | B | T

A   Here's what we know:

> The store on the corner was robbed last night.

For each item, combine one of the sentences below with the sentence in the box.

- **The police were here asking questions.**
- **The owner won't install a burglar alarm.**

1. Make a combined sentence with **but**.

_____

_____

_____

2. Make a combined sentence with **so**.

_____

_____

_____

3. Make a combined sentence with **and**.

_____

_____

_____

4. Make a combined sentence with **therefore**.

_____

_____

_____

_____

B   For each item, write a sentence that means the same thing by changing the underlined word or words.

1. His directions were <u>unclear</u> and <u>repetitive</u>.

_____

_____

2. Lucia gave an <u>unclear</u> <u>answer</u>.

_____

_____

3. That company has many <u>irrelevant</u> <u>rules</u>.

_____

_____

4. This book is <u>filled</u> with <u>repetitive</u> descriptions.

_____

_____

C Read the facts and the information below. If the information is relevant to fact A, write **relevant to fact A.** If the information is relevant to fact B, write **relevant to fact B.** If the information is irrelevant to both facts, write **irrelevant.**

Fact A. **An adult whooping crane is two meters tall.**

Fact B. **Whooping cranes are nearly extinct.**

1. Like most birds, whooping cranes migrate every year.

_____

2. The whooping crane is protected by federal law.

_____

3. Until recently, hundreds of whooping cranes were shot each year by hunters.

_____

4. Whooping cranes get their name from the whooping sound of their call.

_____

D Read the arguments and answer the questions.

• **The Albany Bears have a catcher who is the best home-run hitter in the league. I'll bet the Bears are the best team in the league.**

1. What does the writer want us to conclude?

_____

_____

2. Why does the writer think the Bears are the best team in the league?

_____

_____

_____

3. What rule does the argument break?

_____

_____

_____

4. How would you find out if the Bears are the best team in the league?

_____

_____

_____

• **If I breathe deeply before I go to bed at night, I can keep elephants out of the park. I've been breathing deeply at night ever since I moved to this city, and during that time there have been no elephants in the park.**

5. What does the writer want us to conclude?

_____

_____

_____

6. Why does the writer think that breathing deeply at night keeps elephants out of the park?

_____

_____

_____

_____

7. What rule does the argument break?

_____

_____

_____

8. How would you prove that breathing deeply does not keep elephants out of the park?

_____

_____

_____

_____

E Below are some rules. If evidence is relevant to a rule, it must tell about certain words in the rule.

• Read each rule.
• Underline the right word or words.
• Then fill in the blank.

1. **Insects do not have backbones.**

    Relevant evidence must tell that something

    is _____.

2. **Burning things need oxygen.**

    Relevant evidence must tell that something

    is _____.

3. **Herbivorous animals eat nothing but plants.**

    Relevant evidence must tell that something

    is _____.

4. **All mammals have hair.**

    Relevant evidence must tell that something

    is _____.

A Each sentence below contains the word **who** or **which**. For each sentence, write what's referred to by **who** or **which.**

1. Seattle, which was built on seven hills, is a seaport.

_____

2. The judge spoke to the jury, which had just returned to the courtroom.

_____

3. Linda McCall, who is my neighbor, is taking a vacation next week.

_____

B For each item, write a sentence that means the same thing by changing the underlined word or words.

1. His answer to that question is <u>unclear</u>.

_____

_____

2. I took the <u>chance</u> to suggest a change in the <u>rule</u>.

_____

_____

_____

3. The major's speech was <u>filled</u> with <u>irrelevant</u> and <u>repetitive</u> details.

_____

_____

_____

4. They <u>changed</u> their Swiss <u>money</u> into Canadian <u>money</u>.

_____

_____

_____

C Each argument that follows breaks one of these rules:

- Just because you know about a part doesn't mean you know about the whole thing.
- Just because you know about a part doesn't mean you know about another part.
- Just because you know about a whole thing doesn't mean you know about every part.

Read each argument that follows. Write the rule that each argument breaks.

1. The painting in his living room is an original, so the painting upstairs must be an original also.

_____

_____

_____

2. I read today that the Shazzam is the best car to come out this year. So, it must have the best tires and the best windshield of any car on the road.

_____

_____

_____

3. She won't buy clothes in that store anymore. The last dress she bought there fell apart the first time she washed it.

_____

_____

_____

_____

D Read the passage below. Find a statement that contradicts an earlier statement.

- Underline the statement you assume to be true.
- Circle the contradiction.
- Make up an if-then statement that explains the contradiction.

> "Frank, I'm lonely. My girl friend has been gone for two weeks."
>
> "Don't worry, Alan. Absence makes the heart grow fonder."
>
> "But she hasn't written. What if she's met another guy?"
>
> "Alan, maybe she's forgotten all about you. You've heard the expression, 'out of sight, out of mind.' Well, it's true."

_____

_____

_____

E If evidence is relevant to a rule, it must tell about certain words in the rule. Read the rule and underline the right words. Then answer the questions about each piece of evidence.
Remember, if the evidence is irrelevant, there is no conclusion.

Rule. **All paper is made from wood fiber.**

- Evidence A. **Cardboard is made of wood fiber.**

1. Is evidence A relevant or irrelevant?

_____

2. What's the conclusion?

_____

_____

- Evidence B. **Particle board is made of wood fiber.**

3. Is evidence B relevant or irrelevant?

_____

4. What's the conclusion?

_____

_____

- Evidence C. **Pasteboard is paper.**

5. Is evidence C relevant or irrelevant?

_____

6. What's the conclusion?

_____

_____

- Evidence D. **Playing cards are paper.**

7. Is evidence D relevant or irrelevant?

_____

8. What's the conclusion?

_____

_____

F | Read the passage below.

Levi Hutchins was a clockmaker in New Hampshire in the eighteenth century. He firmly believed in getting to his job on time, but he found that he would occasionally sleep late. What he needed was a device to wake him up at the time he wanted to get up.

One day, while looking at the shelves of clocks in his shop, he was inspired to make the first alarm clock. He later said that once he finally came up with the idea of an alarm clock, making it was quite easy. Today, many people all over the world rely on Hutchins's invention to start their day on time.

- Here's a conclusion:

Hutchins did not find the first alarm clock difficult to build.

1. Does the passage contain evidence to support this conclusion or evidence to refute this conclusion?

_____

_____

2. Which sentence contains the evidence?

_____

_____

_____

_____

- Here's another conclusion:

Before he invented the alarm clock, Hutchins was a dependable employee.

3. Does the passage contain evidence to support this conclusion or evidence to refute this conclusion?

_____

_____

4. Which sentence contains the evidence?

_____

_____

_____

_____

_____

- Here's another conclusion:

    **If there were no alarm clocks, many
    people would probably wake up late
    every day.**

5. Does the passage contain evidence to
   support this conclusion or evidence to refute
   this conclusion?

   _____
   _____

6. Which sentence contains the evidence?

   _____
   _____
   _____
   _____

- Here's another conclusion:

    Hutchins was always punctual.

7. Does the passage contain evidence to
   support this conclusion or evidence to refute
   this conclusion?

   _____
   _____

8. Which sentence contains the evidence?

   _____
   _____
   _____
   _____

G Lola sometimes has trouble using the
words **who** and **which.** Below are some
sentences that she wrote. Cross out **who**
or **which** if it is used incorrectly.

1. Franklin Roosevelt, which was confined to a
   wheelchair, was elected president four times
   in a row.

2. Her family, who lived next door for ten
   years, just moved to Idaho.

3. That band, which plays jazz, has become
   very popular.

4. The *Iliad*, who is a very old book, is about
   the Trojan War.

A Each argument below breaks one of these rules:

- Just because you know about a part doesn't mean you know about the whole thing.
- Just because you know about a part doesn't mean you know about another part.
- Just because you know about a whole thing doesn't mean you know about every part.

Read each argument below. Write the rule that each argument breaks.

1. The tag on a jacket I looked at said the jacket was made of 100 percent wool. Who's ever heard of a wool zipper?

_____

_____

_____

2. Becky belongs to the same club that Molly belongs to. Molly is a really selfish person, so I guess Becky must be selfish, too.

_____

_____

_____

3. Cheetahs have good eyes and a very good sense of hearing, so they must have a good sense of smell, too.

_____

_____

_____

B Noreen sometimes has trouble using the words **who** and **which.** Below are some sentences that she wrote. Cross out **who** or **which** if it is used incorrectly.

1. She plants lots of squash, which grows well in this area.
2. That building was designed by Frank Lloyd Wright, which was a great architect.
3. France, who is one of the largest countries in Europe, is famous for its excellent wine.
4. Reba, who lives next door, is taking flying lessons.

C Each sentence below contains the word **who** or **which.** For each sentence, write what's referred to by **who** or **which.**

1. Jolene works at Business Industries, which makes business machines.

_____

2. Kangaroos, which are related to opossums, are native to Australia.

_____

3. He loves to read books by Robert Heinlein, who is a science-fiction writer.

_____

D Read the passage below. Find a statement that contradicts an earlier statement.

- Underline the statement you assume to be true.
- Circle the contradiction.
- Make up an if-then statement that explains the contradiction.

"Dad, I have something I want to talk to you about, but I'm afraid you won't want to hear it."

"Nonsense. A father should always listen to whatever his daughter has to say."

"It's about school, Dad. It's been so sunny out, and classes are so boring that I've skipped school a couple times to go swimming and—"

"WHAT?"

"Let me explain—"

"I don't want to hear another word. Go to your room and stay there until dinner."

_____

_____

_____

_____

E If evidence is relevant to a rule, it must tell about certain words in the rule. Read the rule below and underline the right words. Then answer the questions about each piece of evidence.
Remember, if the evidence is irrelevant, there is no conclusion.

Rule. **Large felines are carnivorous.**

- Evidence A. **A lion is carnivorous.**

1. Is evidence A relevant or irrelevant?

_____

2. What's the conclusion?

_____

_____

- Evidence B. **Jaguars and tigers are large felines.**

3. Is evidence B relevant or irrelevant?

_____

4. What's the conclusion?

_____

_____

- Evidence C. **A snow leopard is carnivorous.**

5. Is evidence C relevant or irrelevant?

_____

6. What's the conclusion?

_____

_____

- Evidence D. **A leopard is carnivorous.**

7. Is evidence D relevant or irrelevant?

_____

8. What's the conclusion?

_____

_____

F Here's the main-idea sentence for a paragraph:

> **"The world is facing a serious fuel shortage.**

Read each sentence below. Write **yes** if the sentence provides more information about the main idea. Write **no** if the sentence does not provide more information about the main idea.

1. In Europe, gasoline costs as much as four dollars a gallon. _____

2. Part of the world faced a serious shortage of food during the famine of 1877. _____

3. The world is 38,400 kilometers around at the equator. _____

4. Scientists suggest the use of solar energy for heating homes. _____

5. Some new houses use wind power to produce electricity for heat. _____

6. The world faces a serious problem because the population continues to increase. _____

G For each item, write a sentence that means the same thing by changing the underlined word or words.

1. They made up a fitting plan.

_____

_____

2. The committee made up a fitting schedule.

_____

_____

3. The plan that we are using was made up by the director.

_____

_____

_____

4. Army generals should be good at making up defense plans.

_____

_____

_____

★ **A**   Here's the main-idea sentence for a paragraph:

> **Susan worked hard to become a good artist.**

Read each sentence below. Write **yes** if the sentence provides more information about the main idea. Write **no** if the sentence does not provide more information about the main idea.

1. Her hobbies were horseback riding and rock collecting. _____

2. She applied to art school when she graduated. _____

3. All her friends were going to the football game. _____

4. She spent a lot of money on paints and pencils. _____

5. Susan visited a lot of art museums. _____

6. Susan's mother was a newspaper reporter. _____

B   If evidence is relevant to a rule, it must tell about certain words in the rule. Read the rule below and underline the right words. Then answer the questions about each piece of evidence.
Remember, if the evidence is irrelevant, there is no conclusion.

> Rule. **Joggers exercise their heart and lungs.**

• Evidence A. **Mom and Dad exercise their heart and lungs.**

1. Is evidence A relevant or irrelevant?

   _____

2. What's the conclusion?

   _____

   _____

• Evidence B. **The members of the swimming team are joggers.**

3. Is evidence B relevant or irrelevant?

   _____

4. What's the conclusion?

   _____

   _____

   _____

• Evidence C. **My dad is a jogger.**

5. Is evidence C relevant or irrelevant?

   _____

6. What's the conclusion?

   _____

   _____

• Evidence D. **Soccer players exercise their heart and lungs.**

7. Is evidence D relevant or irrelevant?

   _____

8. What's the conclusion?

   _____

   _____

C For each item, write a sentence that means the same thing by changing the underlined word or words.

1. They made up a fitting plan.

_____

_____

2. The club discussed a fitting plan for the bake sale.

_____

_____

3. This new ad was made up by a child.

_____

_____

4. The team's plans are not working out well.

_____

_____

D Change each sentence by using **who** or **which** for the underlined part.

1. Our class is going to an assembly.

_____

_____

2. Maple trees lose their leaves in the fall.

_____

_____

3. These students are going to graduate.

_____

_____

4. His sister plays the clarinet.

_____

_____

5. That dog howls every night.

_____

_____

E Each argument below breaks one of these rules:

- Just because you know about a part doesn't mean you know about the whole thing.
- Just because you know about a part doesn't mean you know about another part.
- Just because you know about a whole thing doesn't mean you know about every part.

Read each argument below. Write the rule that each argument breaks.

1. He went to Mexico on his vacation, so he must be a world traveler.

_____

_____

_____

2. I've got to meet that girl. Her voice on the phone is gorgeous.

_____

_____

_____

3. This cereal is supposed to be really good for you, so the chemicals in it must be good for you too.

_____

_____

_____

F Read the evidence and write the conclusion for each item.

1. Here's the evidence:

   **Some desks are made of wood.
   A rolltop is a desk.**

   What's the conclusion?

   _____

   _____

2. Here's the evidence:

   **Desks are furniture.
   A rolltop is a desk.**

   What's the conclusion?

   _____

   _____

3. Here's the evidence:

   **All banks are closed on Sunday.
   The First National is a bank.**

   What's the conclusion?

   _____

   _____

Answers to some questions are based on words in a passage. Answers to other questions are based on deductions. Read this passage.

"Over the past forty years, people have become increasingly interested in a subject called ecology. The word **ecology** comes from a Greek word that means **house.** The house that is referred to by the word **ecology** is our Earth, the world we live in. The study of ecology is the study of living things in the world and how the life of one thing affects the lives of other things. The more we study ecology, the more we discover that the life of a beetle in a faraway place may affect the lives of birds near us. And the lives of these birds may affect the lives of worms and insects. We are finding that a change in any plant or animal affects many other plants and animals.

People weren't always interested in ecology. They used to believe they could kill plants and animals if they didn't like them, or if they wanted something that plants and animals had. When humans wanted leopard-skin coats, hunters went into Africa and shot hundreds of thousands of leopards. When some people who called themselves sportsmen wanted to have a good time, they shot thousands of buffaloes from train windows—killing for the sport of watching the buffaloes fall to the ground. When humans wanted oil for lamps, thousands of whales were killed for their oil.

Today, many people are beginning to recognize that our house is our world and that all the living things in the house affect each other. The buffaloes affect the grass, and the grass affects the insects. When there are no buffaloes, our house changes in many ways.

- Here's a question that is answered by words in the passage:

  When you study ecology, what do you study?

Underline the words in the passage that answer the question.

- Here's a question that is not answered by words in the passage:

  Would other living things be affected if all eagles were killed?

That question is answered by a deduction. Here's the deduction:

  **A change in any living thing affects other living things.
  Eagles are living things.
  So, a change in eagles affects other living things.**

- Here's another question:

  If people wanted beaver-skin hats a hundred years ago, what would they have done?

What's the answer to that question?
If that question is answered by words in the passage, you can find the words in the passage. Can you find the words?
So, is the question answered by words or by a deduction?

- Here's another question:

  The word *ecology* comes from a Greek word meaning what?

What's the answer to that question?
If that question is answered by words in the passage, you can find the words in the passage. Can you find the words?
So, is the question answered by words or by a deduction?

Write the answer to each question. For some items, you circle either **words** or **deduction.** If you circle **words,** underline the words in the passage that answer the item.

1. When you study ecology, what do you study?

   _____

   _____

   _____

   _____

   _____

   Circle how the question is answered:

   words   deduction

2. Would other living things be affected if all eagles were killed? _____

   Circle how the question is answered:

   words   deduction

3. If people wanted beaver-skin hats a hundred years ago, what would they have done?

   _____

   _____

   Circle how the question is answered:

   words   deduction

4. The word **ecology** comes from a Greek word meaning what?

   _____

   Circle how the question is answered:

   words   deduction

5. Why is the study of ecology important to humans?

   _____

   _____

   _____

   _____

6. How did the average person who lived in 1850 feel about the study of ecology?

   _____

   _____

   _____

7. What attitude did people used to have about the plants and animals around them?

_____

_____

_____

_____

_____

_____

★ **B** Read the facts and the items below. If an item is relevant to fact A, write **relevant to fact A.** If an item is relevant to fact B, write **relevant to fact B.** If an item is irrelevant to both facts, write **irrelevant.**

Fact A. **Cynthia works as a secretary in an insurance company.**

Fact B. **Cynthia is taking dancing lessons.**

1. Cynthia won first prize in a dance contest.

_____

2. Cynthia can type over 100 words per minute.

_____

3. Cynthia reads and speaks Spanish, French, and Russian.

_____

4. Cynthia goes bowling every Thursday night.

_____

C If evidence is relevant to a rule, it must tell about certain words in the rule. Read the rule below and underline the right words. Then answer the questions about each piece of evidence.
Remember, if the evidence is irrelevant, there is no conclusion.

> Rule. **Merchandise is something that is bought and sold.**

- Evidence A. **The winter coat in the store is merchandise.**

1. Is evidence A relevant or irrelevant?

_____

2. What's the conclusion?

_____

_____

_____

- Evidence B. **My new sweater was bought and sold.**

3. Is evidence B relevant or irrelevant?

_____

4. What's the conclusion?

_____

_____

- Evidence C. **That down-filled jacket is merchandise.**

5. Is evidence C relevant or irrelevant?

_____

6. What's the conclusion?

_____

_____

• Evidence D. **Her shoes are merchandise.**

7. Is evidence D relevant or irrelevant?

_____

8. What's the conclusion?

_____

_____

D For each item, write a sentence that means the same thing by changing the underlined word or words.

1. They made up a fitting plan.

_____

_____

2. A fitting schedule must be made up if we want to meet our deadline.

_____

_____

_____

3. My friend will make up the senator's election plans.

_____

_____

4. His color choice was not fitting for an office.

_____

_____

E Here's the main-idea sentence for a paragraph:

> **The coconut can be used for many different things.**

Read each sentence below. Write **yes** if the sentence provides more information about the main idea. Write **no** if the sentence does not provide more information about the main idea.

1. People in tropical areas greatly depend on coconut trees. _____

2. Some rubber, brake fluid, and hand lotion are made from coconut. _____

3. Although corn is mostly used to feed livestock, it is also used to make cooking oil, food products for humans, and some kinds of paper. _____

4. Coconuts provide food for people and animals. _____

5. George Washington Carver discovered many uses for the peanut. _____

6. Coconut can be eaten in desserts, salads, and main dishes. _____

F Each argument that follows breaks one of these rules:

• Just because you know about a part doesn't mean you know about the whole thing.
• Just because you know about a part doesn't mean you know about another part.
• Just because you know about a whole thing doesn't mean you know about every part.

Read each argument below. Write the rule that each argument breaks.

1. Florida is supposed to be the Sunshine State. I'm sure that I'll have sunny weather when I go to Miami next week.

_____

_____

_____

_____

2. Tony's Italian Restaurant makes terrible hamburgers. I don't think I'd like to try their spaghetti.

_____

_____

_____

3. Gina told me once that her family is very large. I'll bet that her house is crowded.

_____

_____

_____

_____

G Change each sentence by using **who** or **which** for the underlined part.

1. Fir trees are green all year long.

_____

_____

2. That chorus is going on tour.

_____

_____

3. The men will be back soon.

_____

_____

4. Dolphins are sea mammals.

_____

_____

5. My uncle has three beagles.

_____

_____

6. This dance group is famous in Europe.

_____

_____

H You will be tested on some facts presented in this lesson. These facts are:

1. **The word underlined ecology comes from a Greek word that means house.**

2. **The study of ecology is the study of the living things in the world and how they affect each other.**

Study these facts. Repeat them to yourself. Writing these facts may help you to remember them.

ERRORS | W | B | T |

A Answers to some questions are based on words in a passage. Answers to other questions are based on deductions.

If a question is answered by words in a passage, you can find those words.
If a question is answered by a deduction, you cannot find the words. You must make up a deduction.
Read this passage.

A hundred years ago, people were not concerned with ecology. They believed that there was no end to different types of wildlife. It seemed to them that it was impossible to kill all the ducks or all the buffaloes or all the leopards. So they killed ducks and leopards and buffaloes by the hundreds of thousands. When we look back on this killing, we may feel shocked. But for the people who lived a hundred years ago, wild animals seemed to be as plentiful as weeds. Nobody worried about killing these animals.

The killing led to some animals' becoming extinct. A type of animal becomes extinct when there are no more animals of that type. At one time, the passenger pigeon was a common bird. Today, the passenger pigeon is extinct. At one time, the Labrador duck was plentiful.

Today, this type of duck is extinct. Since the year 1800, over 100 species of animals have become extinct. This situation is very sad, because once an animal becomes extinct, it will never be seen on Earth again. Think of that. Although the passenger pigeon lived on Earth for over one hundred thousand years, you will never see a living passenger pigeon, nor will your children or grandchildren. The only type of passenger pigeon you will see is in a picture or in a museum.

- Here's a question:

   Why didn't people a hundred years ago worry about killing thousands of buffaloes?

What's the answer to that question?
If that question is answered by words in the passage, you can find those words.
Can you find the words?
So, is the question answered by words or by a deduction?

- Here's another question:

   What does it mean when we say that an animal is extinct?

What's the answer to that question?
If that question is answered by words in the passage, you can find those words.
Can you find the words?
So, is the question answered by words or by a deduction?

Write the answer to each question. For some items, you circle either **words** or **deduction.** If you circle **words,** underline the words in the passage that answer the item.

1. Why didn't people a hundred years ago worry about killing thousands of buffaloes?

   _____

   _____

   _____

   _____

   Circle how the question is answered:

           words   deduction

2. What does it mean when we say that an animal is extinct?

   _____

   _____

   _____

   Circle how the question is answered:

           words   deduction

3. Why weren't people concerned with ecology a hundred years ago?

   _____

   _____

   _____

   Circle how the question is answered:

           words   deduction

4. Name two animals that have become extinct.

   _____

   _____

5. Will you ever see a live Labrador duck?

   _____

   Circle how the question is answered:

           words   deduction

6. Why not?

   _____

   _____

7. Will you ever see a live passenger pigeon?

   _____

   Circle how the question is answered:

           words   deduction

★ **B** Combine the sentences in each item below by using the word **who** or the word **which**. In each new sentence, put a comma before **who** or **which**.

1. I bought a birthday present for my father. My father will be fifty-two next week.

_____

_____

_____

2. She bought that coat. That coat was on sale for fifty dollars.

_____

_____

3. The detective followed the mysterious woman. The mysterious woman got on a train.

_____

_____

_____

4. Sailors used to get scurvy. Scurvy is a disease of the mouth and gums.

_____

_____

_____

5. Rachel made a peach tart. A peach tart is her favorite dessert.

_____

_____

_____

C Each argument below breaks one of these rules:

Rule 1. Just because two things happen around the same time doesn't mean one thing causes the other thing.

Rule 2. Just because you know about a part doesn't mean you know about the whole thing.

Rule 3. Just because you know about a part doesn't mean you know about another part.

Rule 4. Just because you know about a whole thing doesn't mean you know about every part.

After each argument below, write the number of the rule the argument breaks.

1. I played some classical music and she fell asleep on my couch. Next time she comes over, I'll remember not to play classical

music. _____

2. He does very well in math classes. I'm sure he could help me write my biology paper.

_____

3. Of course she's stupid. She flunked

chemistry last term. _____

4. Pete was in the room when the money disappeared. I wouldn't hang around with

that guy if I were you. _____

5. Everyone says that New York is an unfriendly place. When I go there, I'm sure

that no one will be nice to me. _____

D For each item, write a sentence that means the same thing by changing the underlined word or words.

1. They <u>made up</u> a <u>fitting plan</u>.

_____

_____

2. The class will <u>make up</u> a <u>plan</u> for winning the attendance award.

_____

_____

3. <u>Plans</u> for gas rationing may be <u>fitting</u> in the near future.

_____

_____

4. She <u>made up</u> a <u>fitting</u> menu for the occasion.

_____

_____

E You will be tested on some facts presented in this lesson. These facts are:

1. **A type of animal becomes extinct when there are no more animals of that type.**
2. **A hundred years ago, people were not concerned with ecology because they believed there was no end to different types of wildlife.**

Study these facts. Repeat them to yourself. Writing these facts may help you to remember them.

ERRORS | W | B | T

A Answers to some questions are based on words in a passage. Answers to other questions are based on deductions.

If a question is answered by words in a passage, you can find those words.
If a question is answered by a deduction, you cannot find the words. You must make up a deduction.
Read this passage.

Once a type of animal becomes extinct, it is gone forever. As you read in the last selection, over 100 species of animals have become extinct since the year 1800. In addition to these animals, there are over one thousand species that are endangered. An endangered species is one that is nearly extinct. Species become endangered when only a few of the species are alive. When the number of new babies born each year becomes smaller than the number of animals that die each year, the population of the species becomes very small. Each year, the population gets smaller and smaller until the species is extinct.

The prairie chicken is a large, wild bird that looks something like a grouse or pheasant. At one time, prairie chickens were nearly as common on the Midwest prairie as stones. Today, the prairie chicken is an endangered species, even though some people are working hard to prevent it from becoming extinct. Other endangered species include the grizzly bear, the Alaskan brown bear, the African elephant, the Alaskan fur seal, many types of whales, some types of rhinoceros, sea turtles, and many species of birds, such as the whooping crane.

The list of endangered and extinct animals will continue to grow until humans decide that the world should be a place for all living things, not just those living things that get along well with humans. The African elephant may be a pest and may not get along well with farmers in Africa; however, if we get rid of African elephants, we won't be able to change our minds later and get them back. Once an animal is extinct, it is extinct forever.

- Here's a question:

  What is an endangered species?

What's the answer to that question?
If that question is answered by words in the passage, you can find those words.
Can you find the words?
So, is the question answered by words or by a deduction?

- Here's another question:

  If the number of peacocks born each year is smaller than the number that die each year, what will happen to peacocks?

What's the answer to that question?
If that question is answered by words in the passage, you can find those words.
Can you find the words?
So, is the question answered by words or by a deduction?

Write the answer to each question. Circle **W** if the question is answered by words in the passage. Circle **D** if the question is answered by a deduction. If you circle **W** for an item, underline the words in the passage that give the answer.

1. What is an endangered species?

   _____

   _____

   _____ **W**   **D**

2. If the number of peacocks born each year is smaller than the number that die each year, what will happen to peacocks?

   _____ **W**   **D**

3. How many species of animals are currently endangered?

   _____

4. What does it mean when we say that an animal is extinct?

   _____

5. Name five species that are endangered.

   _____

   _____

   _____

   _____

   _____

6. How can humans limit the number of species that become endangered or extinct?

   _____

   _____

   _____

   _____

7. What will happen to grizzly bears if their population keeps getting smaller?

   _____ **W**   **D**

★ **B** For each item, write a sentence that means the same thing by changing the underlined word or words.

1. She <u>paused</u> before presenting her <u>answers</u>.

_____

_____

_____

2. They <u>made up</u> a <u>fitting plan</u>.

_____

_____

3. The <u>rule</u> called for <u>changing</u> from nuclear power to solar power.

_____

_____

_____

4. The chairperson had a <u>chance</u> to <u>change</u> the <u>unclear plan</u> into one that would work.

_____

_____

_____

C Here are two main ideas.

Main idea for paragraph 1:

The teacher was giving a test.

Main idea for paragraph 2:

Nancy forgot to study.

Each sentence below belongs to either paragraph 1 or paragraph 2. Read each sentence. Write **1** in the blank if the sentence belongs to paragraph 1. Write **2** in the blank if the sentence belongs to paragraph 2.

1. She wrote three questions on the board for everyone to answer. _____

2. She couldn't answer any test questions.

_____

3. She watched the class to make sure that no one cheated. _____

4. She handed out the second part of the test, which was a true-false test.

_____

5. She thought about peeking at her neighbor's paper, but she decided not to. _____

6. She graded the papers and returned them to the class the next day. _____

7. She stared at her test paper, waiting for the period to end. _____

8. She told herself that she would study for the next test. _____

D Read the rules.

Rule 1. Just because two things happen around the same time doesn't mean one thing causes the other thing.

Rule 2. Just because you know about a part doesn't mean you know about the whole thing.

Rule 3. Just because you know about a part doesn't mean you know about another part.

Rule 4. Just because you know about a whole thing doesn't mean you know about every part.

After each argument below, write the number of the rule the argument breaks.

1. I heard that Mexico is a very poor country. I guess nobody there has any money. _____

2. Martha must cook everything well. She makes the best cookies I've ever eaten. _____

3. When I asked Linda out for a date, she fainted. If I'd known it meant that much to her, I would have asked her out sooner. _____

4. I wouldn't buy a thing from that store. The last pair of shoes that I bought there fell apart in a week. _____

5. The used cars we sell have Pave-O-Puncher tires. Pave-O-Punchers last for 500,000 miles, so you know that our used cars must last forever. _____

E If evidence is relevant to a rule, it must tell about certain words in the rule. Read the rule and underline the right words. Then answer the questions about each piece of evidence.
Remember, if the evidence is irrelevant, there is no conclusion.

> Rule. **Centaurs have the torso and legs of a horse.**

- Evidence A. **Ixion is a centaur.**

1. Is evidence A relevant or irrelevant?

_____

2. What's the conclusion?

_____

_____

- Evidence B. **Chiron was a centaur.**

3. Is evidence B relevant or irrelevant?

_____

4. What's the conclusion?

_____

_____

- Evidence C. **Criptus has the torso and legs of a horse.**

5. Is evidence C relevant or irrelevant?

_____

6. What's the conclusion?

_____

_____

- Evidence D. **Trigger has the torso and legs of a horse.**

7. Is evidence D relevant or irrelevant?

_____

8. What's the conclusion?

_____

_____

F Combine the sentences in each item by using the word **who** or the word **which**. In each new sentence, put a comma before **who** or **which**.

1. We saw a play by Noel Coward. Noel Coward was an English writer.

_____

_____

_____

2. Mr. Mendez makes many sandals. The sandals are sold at the Saturday Market.

_____

_____

3. She drove to school with Pete. Pete is her boy friend.

_____

_____

4. Maya gets along well with her siblings. Her siblings are older than she is.

_____

_____

_____

5. We cheered for our team. Our team was winning its final game of the year.

_____

_____

_____

G You will be tested on some facts presented in this lesson. These facts are:

1. **An endangered species is one that is nearly extinct.**

2. **There are over one thousand species of animals that are currently endangered.**

Study these facts. Repeat them to yourself. Writing these facts may help you to remember them.

To read a graph, you use two sets of numbers. One set is up and down, and the other set is across the bottom. Look at the graph below.

The up-and-down numbers on this graph stand for years. Circle the word **years** at the top of the graph.

The letter **D** is on the graph. That letter is next to the year 1982. Put the letter **A** next to the year 1988.
Put the letter **B** next to the year 1994.
Put the letter **C** where the year 1985 would be. That's halfway between 1984 and 1986.

The numbers at the bottom of the graph tell about the number of fish caught. Circle the words **number of fish caught** at the bottom of the graph.

The letter **F** is on the graph. That letter is right above 3000 fish. Put the letter **M** right above 7000 fish.

Put the letter **P** right above 1000 fish.
Put the letter **R** right above 8000 fish.

Find the letter **H.**
H shows the number of fish caught in one year.
To find the year for **H,** go this way: ←.
What year is **H** next to?
To find the number of fish caught for **H,** go this way: ↓ .
How many fish is **H** above?
So, **H** shows 4000 fish caught in 1988.

Find the letter **G.**
G shows the number of fish caught in one year.
To find the year for **G,** which way do you go?
What year is **G** next to?
To find the number of fish caught for **G,** which way do you go?
How many fish is **G** above?
So, **G** shows 6000 fish caught in 1984.

Find the letter **J.**
J shows the number of fish caught in one year.
To find the year for **J,** which way do you go?
What year is **J** next to?
To find the number of fish caught for **J,** which way do you go?
How many fish is **J** above?
So, **J** shows 10,000 fish caught in 1992.

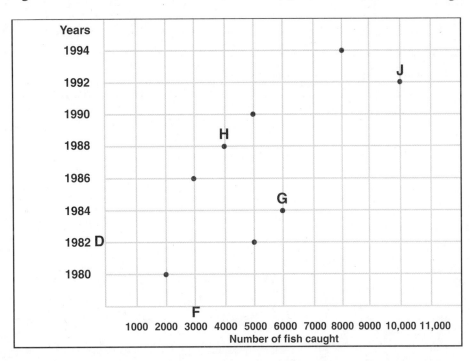

★ **B** Look at diagram 1.

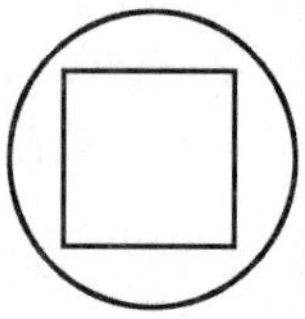

Diagram 1

You can't see the dots in the diagram, but **all the dots are in the square.**

1. Complete the deduction.

> **All the dots are in the square.**
> **The square is in the circle.**

So, _____

_____

• Look at diagram 2.

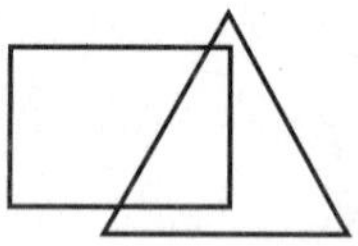

Diagram 2

You can't see the dots, but **all the dots are in the rectangle.**

2. Complete the deduction.

> **All the dots are in the rectangle.**
> **Part of the rectangle is in the triangle.**

So, _____

_____

3. Draw dots in diagram 2.

C Here are two main ideas.

Main idea for paragraph 1:

> **The forest was on fire.**

Main idea for paragraph 2:

> **Firefighters were trying to stop the blaze.**

Each sentence below belongs to either paragraph 1 or paragraph 2. Read each sentence. Write **1** in the blank if the sentence belongs to paragraph 1. Write **2** in the blank if the sentence belongs to paragraph 2.

1. Hundreds of animals were running to the river for safety. _____

2. Many of the animals' homes were destroyed.

   _____

3. Smoke jumpers were trying to surround the fire. _____

4. Helicopters sprayed the blaze with huge fire extinguishers. _____

5. People with axes tried to clear brush out of the fire's path. _____

6. No one was hurt trying to put the fire out.

   _____

7. Smoke from the fire spread for miles.

   _____

8. Some rangers were cutting a fire gap.

   _____

Read the passage below and answer the questions. Circle **W** if the question is answered by words in the passage. Circle **D** if the question is answered by a deduction. If you circle **W** for an item, underline the words in the passage that give the answer.

Living things are designed to keep living, or survive. If you were suddenly underwater with your air supply cut off, you wouldn't have to think about surviving. Your heart would speed up, your body would produce a chemical called adrenalin to give you additional strength, and all your body's power would focus on one goal—getting air.

Cats, dogs, frogs, and other animals are designed to survive. If you tried to prevent a house cat from breathing, the animal would instantly change from a peaceful house pet to a very vicious animal with one goal—surviving.

Air is not the only thing that animals need to survive. They also need water and food. Animals are designed to survive; therefore, they seek the food and water they need. Some animals eat vegetation and others eat animals. All animals have one thing in common: they do not manufacture their own food. They hunt it, one way or another.

Green plants are different. Green plants are the only living things that actually manufacture their own food. The recipe they use is very simple and very important. They take three ingredients (sunlight, water, and carbon dioxide) and

convert them into green vegetation—stems and leaves. Plants don't have to hunt for food. As long as a plant has sunshine, water, and enough soil to support its roots, the plant will manufacture its own food. This process is called photosynthesis.

1. What is the only type of living thing that produces its own food?

_____ W   D

2. For this thing to manufacture food, three ingredients must be present. What are they?

_____

_____ W   D

3. What is a basic goal of all living things?

_____

4. Can a kangaroo manufacture its own food?

_____ W   D

How do you know?

_____

_____

5. Can a rosebush manufacture its own food?

_____ W   D

How do you know?

_____

6. What do we call the process that plants use to make food?

_____ W   D

LESSON 67

E Combine the sentences in each item that follows by using the word **who** or the word **which.** In each new sentence, put a comma before **who** or **which.**

1. He spent the summer with his grandfather. His grandfather lives in Canada.

   _____

   _____

   _____

2. Frank captured a giant bird-wing butterfly. A giant bird-wing butterfly is the rarest butterfly in the world.

   _____

   _____

   _____

3. My friend has a sister named Lisa. Lisa wants to be a cowgirl.

   _____

   _____

   _____

4. We complained to the faculty. The faculty was angry with us.

   _____

   _____

   _____

5. This court case will go to the Supreme Court. The Supreme Court is the highest court in the United States.

   _____

   _____

   _____

F For each item, write a sentence that means the same thing by changing the underlined word or words.

1. The defendant's answer conflicts with his first story and makes the case unclear.

   _____

   _____

2. He is taking the chance to make up a way to buy that island.

   _____

   _____

3. The rule limited their parking.

   _____

   _____

4. The robbers made up a plan for stealing the money.

   _____

   _____

You will be tested on some facts presented in this lesson. These facts are:

1. **Living things are designed to keep living.**
2. **Green plants are the only living things that manufacture their own food.**
3. **For plants to manufacture food, they must have sunlight, water, and carbon dioxide.**

Study these facts. Repeat them to yourself. Writing these facts may help you to remember them.

LESSON 68

ERRORS	W	B	T

★ **A** Write the verb **has** or the verb **have** in each blank.

1. You _____ always been a good student.

2. The sugar in these jars _____ ants in it.

3. Many families _____ two cars.

4. I _____ run in three marathons.

5. The gate to his yard _____ a lock on it.

6. Mr. Demos _____ four ice-cream shops.

B Combine the sentences in each item that follows by using the word **who** or the word **which.** In each new sentence, put a comma before **who** or **which.**

1. They hired Tom. Tom had lots of experience.

_____

_____

2. Mr. Stevens bought her car. The car was very expensive.

_____

_____

_____

3. We went to the racetrack. The racetrack was closed.

_____

_____

4. The new regulation will be discussed by the committee. The committee meets on Monday.

_____

_____

_____

_____

5. She waved to her mother. Her mother was fishing off the dock.

_____

_____

_____

6. I worry about Milly. Milly is in the hospital.

_____

_____

Read the passage below and answer the questions. Circle **W** if the question is answered by words in the passage. Circle **D** if the question is answered by deduction. If you circle **W** for an item, underline the words in the passage that give the answer.

> Plants make their own food through a process called photosynthesis. This process involves changing water, sunlight, and carbon dioxide into green vegetation. Animals do not make their own food. They must hunt for food.
>
> Different kinds of animals eat different things. Animals that eat other animals are called carnivorous. Animals that eat plants are called herbivorous. We can see that herbivorous animals could not survive without plants. If there were no plants, herbivorous animals would have nothing to eat, and they would soon become extinct.
>
> But herbivorous animals are not the only type of animal that needs plants. Carnivorous animals need plants as much as herbivorous animals do. We know that if there were no plants, herbivorous animals would soon be extinct; therefore, the carnivorous animals could not eat them. Carnivorous animals would have to eat other carnivorous animals. But before long, there would be no more animals for carnivorous animals to eat, and they would become extinct.
>
> Herbivorous animals feed directly on green plants. Carnivorous animals feed indirectly on green plants. This means that they feed on things that feed on plants. If a monkey did not eat green plants, the monkey could not survive to become dinner for a hungry leopard.

1. What do we mean when we say that an antelope is herbivorous?

_____

_____ **W** **D**

2. What is the only type of living thing that manufactures its own food?

_____

_____

3. What is photosynthesis?

_____

_____

_____

4. What do we mean when we say that an otter is carnivorous?

_____

_____

_____ **W** **D**

5. What would happen to herbivorous animals if there were no plants?

_____

_____

_____

_____ **W** **D**

6. What would happen to carnivorous animals if there were no herbivorous animals?

_____

_____

_____ **W** **D**

7. What do we mean when we say that a lion feeds indirectly on green plants?

_____

_____

_____ **W**   **D**

D Here are two main ideas.

Main idea for paragraph 1:

A dragon captured a girl from the kingdom.

Main idea for paragraph 2:

A knight was sent to free the girl.

Each sentence that follows belongs to either paragraph 1 or paragraph 2. Read each sentence. Write **1** in the blank if the sentence belongs to paragraph 1. Write **2** in the blank if the sentence belongs to paragraph 2.

1. He lured her into his cave with gold and jewels. _____

2. He blocked the entrance to his cave with his huge, scaly body. _____

3. He had a new suit of shining armor. _____

4. When the girl screamed for help, he blew fire in her face, scorching her golden hair.

_____

5. Hearing her calls for help, he galloped toward the dragon's cave. _____

6. His sword and lance had been newly sharpened by the blacksmith. _____

7. He tore the girl's coat with his huge claws.

_____

8. He killed the beast with one thrust of his sword. _____

E Here are the rules for using the verbs **was** and **were.**

- If you name one thing, use the verb **was.**
- If you name more than one thing, use the verb **were.**
- If you use the word **you,** use the verb **were.**

Write the verb **was** or **were** i each blank.

1. You _____ a big baby.

2. We _____ in Greeley, Colorado, last summer.

3. She _____ a terrific speaker at the meeting.

4. Those girls _____ watching too much television.

5. I _____ going to bake a cake for your birthday.

6. You _____ going to meet me at the game.

7. Mr. Dennis _____ the girls' volleyball coach.

8. They _____ on their way when they heard the news.

9. Sand _____ blowing into my eyes.

10. You _____ just in time to catch the bus.

F You will be tested on some facts presented in this lesson. These facts are:

1. **Herbivorous animals eat plants.**
2. **Carnivorous animals eat other animals.**
3. **If there were no plants, herbivorous animals would become extinct.**
4. **If there were no herbivorous animals, carnivorous animals would become extinct.**

Study these facts. Repeat them to yourself. Writing these facts may help you to remember them.

LESSON 69

★ **A** Here are two main ideas.

Main idea for paragraph 1:

A robber was running from the scene of a crime.

Main idea for paragraph 2:

A police officer arrived in two minutes.

Each sentence below belongs to either paragraph 1 or paragraph 2. Read each sentence. Write **1** in the blank if the sentence belongs to paragraph 1. Write **2** in the blank if the sentence belongs to paragraph 2.

1. He had a mask on so no one could recognize him. _____

2. He had a bagful of money. _____

3. He was blowing a whistle to alert other officers. _____

4. He ducked into an alley, hoping that no one would see him. _____

5. He shouted, "Stop that man!" _____

6. He set a couple of bloodhounds loose to track him down. _____

7. He hid the money under a large rock. _____

B Read the argument below and answer the questions.

> **Tom must be a magician. Susan said she saw him walk down the hall and turn into a bathroom.**

1. What does the writer want us to conclude?

_____

2. What evidence does the writer use to support this conclusion?

_____

3. To show that the argument is faulty, you point out something about the evidence. What is that?

_____

_____

4. What meaning of **turn into** does the writer use?

_____

5. What's another meaning?

_____

_____

6. If the evidence has two meanings, the writer's conclusion is not the only conclusion that is possible. What's another conclusion?

_____

_____

7. What rule does the argument break?

_____

_____

_____

C Here are the rules for using the verbs **is** and **are.**

- If you name one thing, use the verb **is.**
- If you name more than one thing, use the verb **are.**
- If you use the word **you,** use the verb **are.**

Write the verb **is** or **are** in each blank.

1. It _____ my turn to pick up the girls.

2. You _____ in charge of the concession stand.

3. My teammates _____ the best in our district.

4. You _____ not going to drive my car.

5. The bags of rice _____ in the cupboard.

6. You _____ scheduled for an 8 A.M. English class.

7. We _____ going to the museum on Tuesday.

8. His club _____ going to the swim meet.

9. You _____ needed in the principal's office.

10. He _____ my choice for the basketball team.

D Combine the sentences in each item below by using the word **who** or the word **which.** In each new sentence, put a comma before **who** or **which.**

1. I yelled at Jack. Jack fell in the water.

   _____

   _____

2. We dug up the treasure chest. The treasure chest was full of gold.

   _____

   _____

3. She will speak to our club. Our club is interested in women's rights.

   _____

   _____

4. Donna bought a horse. The horse is a strawberry roan.

   _____

   _____

5. I ate some peanut butter. The peanut butter stuck to the roof of my mouth.

   _____

   _____

6. I told Susy. Susy told Michael.

   _____

   _____

E In the next lesson, you will be tested on facts you have learned. The test will include all of the facts presented in Lessons 64–68, and some of the facts from earlier lessons. These facts are:

1. Modern horses and other similar animals belong to a group called equus.
2. Some types of equus became large and others became slender, depending on what climate they lived in.
3. A clue is a hint that helps you find your way out of a puzzle.
4. The word **ecology** comes from a Greek word that means **house.**
5. The study of ecology is the study of the living things in the world and how they affect each other.
6. A type of animal becomes extinct when there are no more animals of that type.
7. A hundred years ago, people were not concerned with ecology because they believed there was no end to different types of wildlife.

8. An endangered species is one that is nearly extinct.
9. There are over one thousand species of animals that are currently endangered.
10. Living things are designed to keep living.
11. Green plants are the only living things that manufacture their own food.
12. For plants to manufacture food, they must have sunlight, water, and carbon dioxide.
13. Herbivorous animals eat plants.
14. Carnivorous animals eat other animals.
15. If there were no plants, herbivorous animals would become extinct.
16. If there were no herbivorous animals, carnivorous animals would become extinct.
17. When you haze people, you torment them.
18. When you tantalize someone, you tease that person by putting something just out of reach.

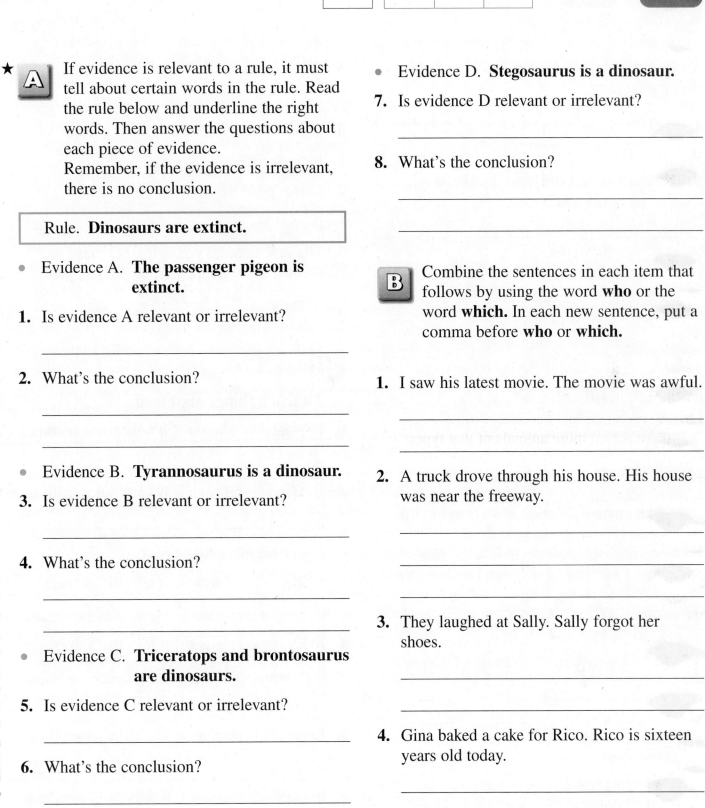

A If evidence is relevant to a rule, it must tell about certain words in the rule. Read the rule below and underline the right words. Then answer the questions about each piece of evidence.
Remember, if the evidence is irrelevant, there is no conclusion.

Rule. **Dinosaurs are extinct.**

• Evidence A. **The passenger pigeon is extinct.**

1. Is evidence A relevant or irrelevant?

_____

2. What's the conclusion?

_____

_____

• Evidence B. **Tyrannosaurus is a dinosaur.**

3. Is evidence B relevant or irrelevant?

_____

4. What's the conclusion?

_____

_____

• Evidence C. **Triceratops and brontosaurus are dinosaurs.**

5. Is evidence C relevant or irrelevant?

_____

6. What's the conclusion?

_____

_____

• Evidence D. **Stegosaurus is a dinosaur.**

7. Is evidence D relevant or irrelevant?

_____

8. What's the conclusion?

_____

_____

B Combine the sentences in each item that follows by using the word **who** or the word **which.** In each new sentence, put a comma before **who** or **which.**

1. I saw his latest movie. The movie was awful.

_____

2. A truck drove through his house. His house was near the freeway.

_____

_____

3. They laughed at Sally. Sally forgot her shoes.

_____

_____

4. Gina baked a cake for Rico. Rico is sixteen years old today.

_____

_____

_____

5. Everyone watched the priest. The priest was lighting candles.

_____

_____

6. We went to hear the band. The band was playing at the hotel.

_____

_____

_____

C Here are two main ideas.

Main idea for paragraph 1:

We use too much gasoline.

Main idea for paragraph 2:

The price of cars is always going up.

Each sentence that follows belongs to either paragraph 1 or paragraph 2. Read each sentence. Write **1** in the blank if the sentence belongs to paragraph 1. Write **2** in the blank if the sentence belongs to paragraph 2.

1. We drive nearly twice as much as we need to. _____

2. Our cities are choked with fumes from automobile exhaust. _____

3. A particular model of car can go up two hundred dollars or more in a single year.

_____

4. Every year, we pay billions of dollars to foreign countries for their crude oil. _____

5. The price of steel is always going up.

_____

6. Some people think that the car makers want bigger profits. _____

7. Large, powerful cars have engines that get poor mileage. _____

8. The raw material that is used to make the product is very expensive to process in a refinery. _____

D Read each rule below and fill in the blanks.

● **All living things need food.**

1. Evidence is relevant if it tells that something is _____.

2. Evidence is relevant if it tells that something does not _____.

● **Every building has a roof.**

3. Evidence is relevant if it tells that something is _____.

4. Evidence is relevant if it tells that something does not _____.

● **All fish have gills.**

5. Evidence is relevant if it tells that something is _____.

6. Evidence is relevant if it tells that something does not _____.

A Write the verb **was** or the verb **were** in each blank.

1. You _____ too late to register for the class.

2. I _____ going to go grocery shopping today.

3. Gina Romero _____ at last night's game.

4. You _____ late for work yesterday.

5. The trees in our yard _____ shading the house.

Write the verb **has** or the verb **have** in each blank.

1. I _____ no money in my checking account.

2. They _____ to win one more game to be the champs.

3. You _____ too many pets.

4. Our faculty _____ a superior reputation.

5. One meter of snow _____ fallen today.

B Read each rule and fill in the blanks.

• **Liquids expand when they are heated.**

1. Evidence is relevant if it tells that something

   is _____.

2. Evidence is relevant if it tells that something

   does not _____.

• **Vehicles take you places.**

3. Evidence is relevant if it tells that something

   is _____.

4. Evidence is relevant if it tells that something

   does not _____.

• **All engines need fuel.**

5. Evidence is relevant if it tells that something

   is _____.

6. Evidence is relevant if it tells that something

   does not _____.

C Combine the sentences in each item that follows by using the word **who** or the word **which**. In each new sentence, put a comma before **who** or **which**.

1. I like to read Yeats. Yeats was an Irish poet.

   _____

   _____

2. The principal gave free movie tickets to that class. That class had the best attendance record in the school.

   _____

   _____

   _____

   _____

   _____

3. They lived on a farm. The farm was twenty kilometers from town.

_____

_____

_____

4. Let me talk to Rosa. Rosa knows the answers to your questions.

_____

_____

_____

5. We gave a party for Von. Von is moving to California.

_____

_____

6. She lost her ring. Her ring was a present from her mother.

_____

_____

_____

D Read the argument below and answer the questions.

Sam said his tree had a lovely bark. I had no idea that trees could make sounds like dogs.

1. What does the writer want us to conclude?

_____

_____

2. What do you point out to show that the argument is faulty?

_____

_____

3. What evidence has more than one meaning?

_____

4. Write a conclusion that is based on the other meaning of that evidence.

_____

_____

_____

E Here are two main ideas.

Main idea for paragraph 1:

Millions of Americans are out of shape.

Main idea for paragraph 2:

Poor nutrition is a common problem in the United States.

Each sentence that follows belongs to either paragraph 1 or paragraph 2. Read each sentence. Write **1** in the blank if the sentence belongs to paragraph 1. Write **2** in the blank if the sentence belongs to paragraph 2.

1. Most people do not get enough exercise.

_____

2. Many common packaged foods have very little nutritional value. _____

3. Automobiles make it easy for people to avoid walking. _____

4. Millions of Americans do nothing but sit at a desk all day. _____

5. Advertising and packaging often mislead people about the quality of the food they buy. _____

6. Watching television is the most popular form of recreation in America, but it involves no physical exercise. _____

7. A survey of one community showed that nearly half of the teenagers were not getting enough iron in their diets. _____

F If evidence is relevant to a rule, it must tell about certain words in the rule. Read the rule below and underline the right words. Then answer the questions about each piece of evidence.
Remember, if the evidence is irrelevant, there is no conclusion.

Rule. **Mollusks have shells.**

- Evidence A. **Oysters have shells.**

1. Is evidence A relevant or irrelevant?

   _____

2. What's the conclusion?

   _____

   _____

- Evidence B. **Crabs and crayfish are mollusks.**

3. Is evidence B relevant or irrelevant?

   _____

4. What's the conclusion?

   _____

   _____

- Evidence C. **Sea turtles have shells.**

5. Is evidence C relevant or irrelevant?

   _____

6. What's the conclusion?

   _____

   _____

- Evidence D. **Snails have shells.**

7. Is evidence D relevant or irrelevant?

   _____

8. What's the conclusion?

   _____

   _____

ERRORS | W | B | T

★ **A** Here's what we know:

| She wants to lose a lot of weight. |

For each item, combine one of the sentences below with the sentence in the box.

- **She hasn't eaten for three days.**
- **She plans to eat a dozen cookies tonight.**

1. Make a combined sentence with **but.**

_____

_____

_____

2. Make a combined sentence with **however.**

_____

_____

_____

_____

3. Make a combined sentence with **so.**

_____

_____

_____

4. Make a combined sentence with **and.**

_____

_____

_____

B Write the verb **is** or the verb **are** in each blank.

1. You _____ very difficult to work with sometimes.

2. The hail _____ beating on the windows.

3. You _____ a terrific poet.

4. Whales _____ becoming extinct.

5. We _____ going cross-country skiing in the Sierras.

Write the verb **has** or the verb **have** in each blank.

1. She _____ taken several trips to New Zealand.

2. I _____ to go to a conference in Atlanta on Tuesday.

3. Some house cats _____ no claws.

4. You _____ the oddest sense of humor.

5. The concrete _____ footprints in it.

C Read the argument below and answer the questions.

> **The description of the robber said he was armed. Since most people have arms, I don't think it was a very good description.**

1. What does the writer want us to conclude?

_____

_____

2. What do you point out to show that the argument is faulty?

_____

_____

3. Write a conclusion that is based on the other meaning of that evidence.

_____

_____

_____

D Read the passage below and answer the questions. Circle **W** if the question is answered by words in the passage. Circle **D** if the question is answered by a deduction. If you circle **W** for an item, underline the words in the passage that give the answer.

> Animals that feed directly on plants are called herbivorous. Animals that feed on other animals are called carnivorous. These animals feed indirectly on plants by eating animals that eat plants.
>
> Most farm animals are herbivorous. Cows, goats, sheep, and horses eat no meat.

By eating grass and other types of plants, they receive all the nourishment they need.

These mammals are well designed for grazing (eating grass and other vegetation). Their teeth are flat, which is helpful for grinding grass, leaves, and seeds.

Not only are their teeth well designed for grazing, but their eyes are, too. Many herbivorous mammals do not see the same image with both eyes. Both of your eyes point straight ahead. When you focus on an object, both eyes see almost the same thing. Many herbivorous mammals are different. The left eye of a cow sees everything that is on the left side, while the right eye sees everything that is on the right side. When the cow's head is facing straight ahead, the cow is not really looking straight ahead. The cow is looking mostly to the right side and to the left side. Both eyes can see only a little bit of what is straight ahead. But most of what the left eye sees is different from what the right eye sees.

How do these strange eyes help these herbivorous mammals? The eyes allow the animal to eat and to watch out for its enemies at the same time. When the animal eats grass, its head is down, facing the ground. If the animal had the same kind of eyes that you have, it would be looking at the ground. A carnivorous animal could sneak up and have it for dinner. If the animal has eyes that look to the sides, the animal is actually looking at everything on both sides as it eats. When a cow is eating, it can actually see somebody standing next to its rear end. No animal could easily sneak up on a grazing cow.

1. What do we call animals that feed directly on plants?

   _____ **W   D**

2. What do we mean when we say that a cougar is carnivorous?

   _____

   _____

   _____ **W   D**

3. Name three herbivorous animals.

   _____

   _____

4. Tell about the two parts of a horse that are well designed for grazing.

   _____

   _____

   _____

   _____

5. How do your eyes differ from the eyes of a sheep?

   _____

   _____

   _____

   _____ **W   D**

6. Why is it important for a horse to have the kind of eyes it has?

   _____

   _____

   _____

   _____ **W   D**

7. Do both eyes of a person see almost the same thing?

   _____

8. Do both eyes of a goat see almost the same thing?

   _____

E Select the right word for combining each pair of sentences that follows. Then write the combined sentence. Remember to punctuate each sentence correctly.

1. Jill felt very tired. She went to bed two hours early.

   therefore   however

   _____

   _____

2. We threw out the glue. The glue was no good.

   who   which

   _____

   _____

3. Susan and her husband like to travel. They went on a vacation to Greece.

and **but**

_____

_____

_____

4. Angela almost never eats meat. She ate a hamburger for lunch.

so **however**

_____

_____

_____

5. We watched the team. The team was practicing in the gym.

who **which**

_____

_____

_____

6. Julian and Carla went to a movie after school. They were late for dinner.

and **however**

_____

_____

_____

_____

F Read each rule below and fill in the blanks.

- **All soil has nutrients.**

1. Evidence is relevant if it tells that something

is _____.

2. Evidence is relevant if it tells that something

does not _____.

- **Ores must be mined.**

3. Evidence is relevant if it tells that something

is _____.

4. Evidence is relevant if it tells that something

is not _____.

- **Evergreen trees have needles.**

5. Evidence is relevant if it tells that something

is _____.

6. Evidence is relevant if it tells that something

does not _____.

7. Make up a deduction that tells that something does not have needles.

_____

_____

_____

_____

LESSON 72

 You will be tested on some facts presented in this lesson. These facts are:

---

1. **The teeth and the eyes of many herbivorous mammals are well designed for grazing.**
2. **The eyes of many herbivorous mammals allow them to eat and to watch out for enemies at the same time.**
3. **The right and the left eye of many herbivorous mammals see different things.**

Study these facts. Repeat them to yourself. Writing these facts may help you to remember them.

A Read each rule below and fill in the blanks.

- **All adhesives hold things together.**

1. Evidence is relevant if it tells that something

   is _____.

2. Evidence is relevant if it tells that something

   does not _____.

- **Looms produce cloth.**

3. Evidence is relevant if it tells that something

   is _____.

4. Evidence is relevant if it tells that something

   does not _____.

- **Seeds produce new growth.**

5. Evidence is relevant if it tells that something

   is _____.

6. Evidence is relevant if it tells that something

   does not _____.

7. Make up a deduction that tells that
   something does not produce new growth.

   _____

   _____

   _____

   _____

B Write the instructions for this diagram.

③ extraneous

② restrict

① converted

④ regulation

1. (what) _____

   _____

   _____

2. (what and where) _____

   _____

   _____

3. (what and where) _____

   _____

   _____

4. (what and where) _____

   _____

Read the argument below and answer the questions.

Rod said he hurt a muscle in his calf. I had no idea he had a cow.

1. What does the writer want us to conclude?

   _____

   _____

2. What do you point out to show that the argument is faulty?

   _____

   _____

3. Write a conclusion that is based on the other meaning of that evidence.

   _____

   _____

   _____

4. What rule does the argument break?

   _____

   _____

   _____

 In the passage below, the verbs **is** and **are** and the verbs **has** and **have** are used incorrectly seven times. Cross out each incorrect word. Write the correct word above it.

> Cars, once regarded as expensive toys, is now a way of life for millions of families. We are only beginning to realize how much trouble our love for cars have gotten us into. The air in our larger cities have lots of chemical garbage in it, much of it from cars. Because we love to drive so much, the demand for gasoline products are always increasing. As our demand rises, oil companies has to produce more gas at a faster rate. Large oil spills from drilling rigs and sinking tankers is becoming more and more frequent. It is possible that our love for cars are gradually destroying the world's oceans.

E Select the right word for combining each pair of sentences that follows. Then write the combined sentence. Remember to punctuate each sentence correctly.

1. Both brothers like to play tennis. Neither of them played in the tournament yesterday.

therefore **but**

_____

_____

_____

_____

2. The traffic was unusually heavy. Hilda was almost two hours late for work.

therefore **but**

_____

_____

_____

_____

3. Tom joined the club. The club was for tennis players only.

who **which**

_____

_____

_____

4. The gas station attendant's directions were ambiguous. We got lost trying to find your house.

so **however**

_____

_____

_____

_____

5. Howard never practices playing his violin. He sounded excellent in the concert.

however **therefore**

_____

_____

_____

_____

6. A teacher yelled at the class. The class was rowdy.

who **which**

_____

_____

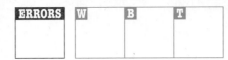
★ **A** Read each rule below and fill in the blanks.

- **Hot air is lighter than cold air.**

1. Evidence is relevant if it tells that something is _____.

2. Evidence is relevant if it tells that something is not _____.

- **Reptiles are cold-blooded.**

3. Evidence is relevant if it tells that something is _____.

4. Evidence is relevant if it tells that something is not _____.

5. Make up a deduction that tells that something is not cold-blooded.

_____

_____

_____

_____

B In the passage below, there are seven places where model-sentence words could be used. Read the passage carefully. To replace a word with a model-sentence word, first cross out the word. Then write the model-sentence word above it.

> There is a storage room on the bottom floor of the reactor plant. Entrance to this room is limited to those people who have been cleared and display the fitting passes and badges. You may wonder why somebody made up such strict rules about entering a storage room. When you go inside the room, you can't see the reason. You notice that the walls are nearly a meter thick and that they are lined with lead. The room is lined with heavy cabinets. The reason for the design of the room and for the security rules is inside the cabinets. The cabinets house the plutonium that is used in the reactor. When used in a fitting way, this material can be changed into useful energy. When used inappropriately, however, it can kill.

C Read the argument below and answer the questions.

When we went to the seashore, Mom said, "Look at those waves." I looked around but I couldn't see anybody who was waving.

1. What does the writer want us to conclude?

_____

_____

2. What do you point out to show that the argument is faulty?

_____

_____

3. Write a conclusion that is based on the other meaning of that evidence.

_____

_____

_____

4. What rule does the argument break?

_____

_____

_____

_____

 D In the passage below, the verbs **has** and **have** and the verbs **is** and **are** are used incorrectly six times. Cross out each incorrect word. Write the correct word above it.

Everybody in my physical education class have to jog a mile every day. Some of the kids have special running clothes. I run in my tennis shorts, because I don't has jogging shorts. You don't has to wear special clothes as long as your clothes for running is comfortable. Nobody have trouble jogging a mile now, but at first some people couldn't even run half a mile. Next week we is going to start running two miles. It will be interesting to see who has trouble with that extra mile.

ERRORS | W | B | T

★ **A** Read the rule and each piece of evidence. Write a conclusion after each piece of evidence.

Rule. **Every muscle pulls.**

Evidence	**Conclusion**
1. The femur does not pull.	_____
2. The deltoid is a muscle.	_____
3. The masseter is a muscle.	_____
4. The cranium does not pull.	_____

B Each argument below breaks one of these rules:

Rule 1. Just because two things happen around the same time doesn't mean one thing causes another thing.

Rule 2. Just because you know about a part doesn't mean you know about the whole thing.

Rule 3. Just because you know about a part doesn't mean you know about another part.

Rule 4. Just because you know about the whole thing doesn't mean you know about every part.

Rule 5. Just because words are the same doesn't mean they have the same meaning.

After each argument below, write the number of the rule the argument breaks.

1. He plants his garden during the new moon and he always has the best vegetables in town. This year, I'm going to plant during the new moon. _____

2. I heard that living in Alaska is very expensive. All the people up there must make a lot of money. _____

3. The kitchen at Pete's Pizza must be very dirty, because I got sick the last time I ate there. _____

4. I'm sure they're vegetarians. They invited us to dinner and all they served was three different kinds of vegetables. _____

5. He is so far in debt that he even has a bill on his cap. _____

C Use the rule in the box and the evidence below to answer the questions.

> **Smaller mammals eat more for their size than larger mammals.**

• **A human baby is always smaller than its mother.**

1. What's the conclusion?

_____

_____

2. How do you know?

_____

_____

• **An ocelot is only about one-fourth the size of a lion.**

3. What's the conclusion?

_____

_____

4. How do you know?

_____

_____

• **A blue whale is not smaller than a bear.**

5. What's the conclusion?

_____

_____

_____

6. How do you know?

_____

_____

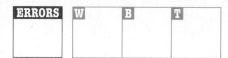

ERRORS | W | B | T

A Some sentences have redundant parts. A part is redundant if it repeats something that has already been said. In the following sentences, the redundant part is underlined.

The man, <u>who was an adult male</u>, stood on the street corner.

Here's why the underlined part is redundant. If you know that it was a man, you already know that it was an adult male. The underlined words repeat something that has already been said.

• Here's another sentence:

"I will purchase the dress," she said, <u>deciding to buy it</u>.

Here's why the underlined part is redundant. If you know that she will purchase the dress, you already know that she has decided to buy it. The underlined words repeat something that has already been said.

• Here's another sentence:

The man, <u>who was an adult male</u>, stood on the street corner.

Explain why the underlined part in the sentence is redundant. Do this by completing the sentence below.

If you know that it was a man, you already

know that _____.

• Here's another sentence:

He presented his inquiries <u>in the form of questions</u>.

Explain why the underlined part is redundant. Do this by completing the sentence below.

If you know that he made inquiries, you already know that

_____.

• Here's another sentence:

The Great Pyramids of Egypt are made of huge stone blocks <u>that are very big</u>.

Explain why the underlined part is redundant. Do this by completing the sentence below.

If you know that the stone blocks are huge, you already know that

_____.

Read each sentence that follows. Explain why the underlined part is redundant by filling in the blanks.

1. In the middle of his speech, he paused <u>by hesitating</u>.

   If you know that he paused, you already know that

   _____.

2. He decided to convert his car engine <u>by changing it</u>.

   If you know that he converted his car engine, you already know that

   _____.

3. The last time I saw Richard was in 1972, <u>and I haven't seen him since then</u>.

If you know that 1972 was the last time I saw Richard, you already know that

_____

_____.

4. She sleeps until noon, <u>never getting up before 12</u>.

If you know that she sleeps until noon, you already know that

_____.

★ **B** Read the rule and each piece of evidence.
Write a conclusion after each piece of evidence.

Rule. **All musical instruments make sound.**

Evidence   **Conclusion**

1. A violin is a musical instrument.   _____

_____

2. Asters do not make sounds.   _____

_____

3. Oboes are musical instruments.   _____

_____

4. A mandolin is a musical instrument.   _____

_____

LESSON 76

 Each argument below breaks one of these rules:

Rule 1. Just because two things happen around the same time doesn't mean one thing causes another thing.

Rule 2. Just because you know about a part doesn't mean you know about the whole thing.

Rule 3. Just because you know about a part doesn't mean you know about another part.

Rule 4. Just because you know about the whole thing doesn't mean you know about every part.

Rule 5. Just because words are the same doesn't mean they have the same meaning.

After each argument below, write the number of the rule the argument breaks.

1. Dan is so bright that he doesn't need a reading lamp in his room. _____

2. Jerry Thompson is the healthiest man I know. I'll bet his son never gets sick either.

   _____

3. I bought these cookies because they must be good for me. After all, they have whole wheat flour in them, and whole wheat flour is good for me. _____

4. "The reason you fell off the bike and broke your arm," Granny said, "is because you took her bike without asking." _____

5. Henry Brown is an intelligent, thoughtful government worker. I'll bet the government makes only intelligent, thoughtful decisions.

   _____

Use the facts to fill out the form.

Facts: Your name is John Woolfe, and you are single. You are applying for a position as a drafting technician. At night you are a second-year student in drafting at Trident College in Franklin Park, Illinois. You are twenty-one years old and have worked summers for the Village of River Grove, Illinois. You draw street improvement and storm sewer plans. Your grades at the college are all A's. Your favorite hobbies are tennis, soccer, and cross-country hiking. The Village of River Grove paid you $8 per hour for your summer work, and your total earnings were $3000 for the summer. Your father is chief engineer for the Village of River Grove, and your mother runs a dog-grooming business at home.

a. Print your name on line 5.
b. State your father's occupation on line 10.
c. Print your marital status on line 3.
d. On line 2, state what position you want with this company.
e. On line 9, print your age.
f. On line 7, state your qualifications for the job you want.
g. List two hobbies on line 8.
h. State name and address of most recent employer on line 1.
i. On line 6, state your hourly rate of pay and total income on most recent job.
j. On line 11, tell what year you are in college. Give name of college you are attending.
k. State occupation of your mother on line 4.

1. _____

2. _____

3. _____

4. _____

5. _____

6. _____

7. _____
   _____
   _____

8. _____

9. _____

10. _____

11. _____

LESSON 76

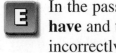

E In the passage below, the verbs **has** and **have** and the verbs **is** and **are** are used incorrectly six times. Cross out each incorrect word. Write the correct word above it.

Anybody that have enough money should visit Florida in the spring. The sand beaches in Florida is very white. Our class are going there again this spring, just as we have done for the last two years. We has terrific volleyball games on the beach. Our team has won almost every game. Anybody who have seen us play would agree that we is the best team.

A Each argument is faulty. Read the arguments and answer the questions.

• **Your new plant probably doesn't need much water because my new jade plant only needs to be watered once a week.**

1. What does the writer want us to conclude?

_____

_____

2. How could you show that the argument is faulty?

_____

_____

_____

• **Joe takes business classes, so I think I'll ask his advice about the stock market.**

3. What does the writer want us to conclude?

_____

_____

4. How could you show that the argument is faulty?

_____

_____

_____

• **Don't loan her anything that you want to get back. She borrowed a book of mine and lost it.**

5. What does the writer want us to conclude?

_____

_____

6. How could you show that the argument is faulty?

_____

_____

_____

B Read the rule and each piece of evidence.
Write a conclusion after each piece of evidence.

> Rule. **Carnivorous animals eat meat.**

Evidence	**Conclusion**
1. Horses do not eat meat.	_____
	_____
	_____
2. Cows do not eat meat.	_____
	_____
	_____
3. Felines are carnivorous animals.	_____
	_____
	_____
4. A deer does not eat meat.	_____
	_____

C Read each sentence below. Explain why the underlined part is redundant by filling in the blanks.

1. We'll send to you, without charge, this wonderful gadget <u>as a free gift</u>.

If you know that it will be sent without charge, you already know that

_____.

2. If you continue to drive like that, you will destroy your car and <u>ruin it completely</u>.

If you know that driving like that will destroy your car, you already know that

_____.

3. We are prepared to make a dramatic half-price offer—that is, <u>50 percent off</u> —when you buy our product.

If you know that the price will be cut in half, you already know that

_____.

4. "I . . . I . . . I . . . ," he said <u>again and again</u>.

If you know that he repeated **I** several times, you already know that

_____.

★ **A** Read each sentence below. Explain why the underlined part is redundant by filling in the blanks.

1. "Okay, everybody out. I don't go any farther," said the bus driver, <u>announcing the end of the journey</u>.

   If you know that the bus driver doesn't go any farther, you already know that

   _____.

2. In an unhurried manner, the astronaut stepped <u>slowly</u> onto the planet's surface.

   If you know that the astronaut moved in an unhurried manner, then you already know that

   _____.

3. I can't afford that car, <u>because I just don't have enough money</u>.

   If you know that the person can't afford that car, you already know that

   _____

   _____.

4. Her inquiries to the school board were very specific <u>questions</u>.

   If you know that she made inquiries to the school board, then you already know that

   _____.

B Read each item. Cross out the irrelevant words in the second piece of evidence, and write the conclusion for each item.

1. **Herb teas have no stimulants.**

   Mint tea is a sweet, flavorsome herb tea.

   _____

   _____

2. **Some birds lay blue eggs.**

   A robin is a common bird in America.

   _____

   _____

3. **Islands are surrounded by water.**

   Australia is a large island in the Pacific Ocean.

   _____

   _____

ERRORS	W	B	T

★ **A** Read the rule and each piece of evidence. Write a conclusion after each piece of evidence.

> **Rule. Cactus plants store large amounts of water.**

Evidence	**Conclusion**
1. A prickly pear is a cactus plant.	_____
	_____
2. Spider plants do not store large amounts of water.	_____
	_____
3. Mescal is a cactus plant.	_____
	_____

B Read each sentence below. Explain why the underlined part is redundant by filling in the blanks.

1. With all this extra corn, we've <u>got more than we can use</u>.

   If you know that the corn is extra, you already know that

   _____

   _____.

2. Last week's catastrophe was very <u>destructive</u>.

   If you know that what happened last week was a catastrophe, you already know that

   _____.

3. "There's absolutely nothing I can do for you," she said <u>helplessly</u>.

   If you know that there is nothing she can do, you already know that

   _____.

Read the passage below and answer the questions. Circle **W** if the question is answered by words in the passage. Circle **D** if the question is answered by a deduction. If you circle **W** for an item, underline the words in the passage that give the answer.

You have read about how herbivorous mammals are well designed for grazing. Their teeth are flat for grinding vegetation, and their eyes permit them to eat and watch for enemies at the same time.

Just as herbivorous mammals are well designed to graze, carnivorous mammals are well designed to hunt, to kill, and to eat the flesh of animals.

The feline family belongs to the group of carnivorous mammals. The house cat is a member of the feline family, along with the leopard, the lion, the tiger, and the jaguar. All are expert killers. The canine family is also carnivorous. The dog is a member of the canine family, which also includes foxes, wolves, and coyotes. These animals do not have the sharp claws of the felines, but the canines are also designed to hunt and kill.

The eyes of a herbivorous mammal permit the animal to see what's on both sides of it at once. A carnivorous mammal does not have to see both sides at once, but it must have a good image of the animal it is hunting. The eyes of a carnivorous mammal look straight ahead so that it can see what its mouth will bite into.

There are different theories about why a carnivorous mammal needs two eyes rather than one. The simplest explanation is that the animal may lose one eye in battle with another animal. Since a carnivorous

mammal has two eyes, it can survive the loss of one eye because it needs only one good eye for hunting.

Just as the teeth of herbivorous mammals are designed to grind food, the teeth of carnivorous mammals are designed to tear flesh. The teeth are pointed and sharp, not flat. These teeth do not grind the food into small pieces. Their goal is to tear it into chunks that are just small enough to be swallowed. These chunks are digested more slowly than small bits. Therefore, the carnivore doesn't have to eat as frequently as it would if it swallowed small bits.

1. Tell about two parts of a sheep that are well designed for grazing.

_____

_____

_____

2. Tell about two parts of a jaguar that are well designed for hunting.

_____

_____

_____

_____

_____ **W   D**

3. Name three felines.

_____

_____

4. Do both eyes of a steer see almost the same thing?

_____

5. Do both eyes of a wolf see almost the same thing?

_____

6. What is one theory about why carnivorous mammals have two eyes instead of one?

_____

_____

_____

_____ **W D**

7. How are the teeth of a goat different from the teeth of a tiger?

_____

_____

_____

_____

_____ **W D**

8. Why do carnivorous mammals swallow large chunks of food instead of small bits?

_____

_____

_____

 You will be tested on some facts presented in this lesson. These facts are:

1. **The teeth and the eyes of carnivorous mammals are well designed for hunting.**
2. **The right and the left eye of many carnivorous mammals see nearly the same thing.**
3. **The teeth of a herbivorous mammal are flat, and the teeth of a carnivorous mammal are pointed.**

Study these facts. Repeat them to yourself. Writing these facts may help you to remember them.

★ **A** Select the right word for combining each pair of sentences that follows. Then write the combined sentence. Remember to punctuate each sentence correctly.

1. Susan did not like her drawing of the horse. It won first prize in the art contest.

and **however**

_____

_____

_____

_____

2. Carol got very hungry while watching the movie on television. She made two egg-salad sandwiches.

and **but**

_____

_____

_____

_____

3. Alex loves riding on airplanes. He took a train to the meeting in San Francisco.

so **however**

_____

_____

_____

_____

4. I avoid that dog. That dog does crazy things.

who **which**

_____

_____

5. I spoke to Marta. Marta is always late for work.

who **which**

_____

_____

LESSON 80

B Read the rule and each piece of evidence.
Write a conclusion after each piece of evidence.

> Rule. **Predators kill the animals they eat.**

Evidence	Conclusion
1. Buzzards do not kill the animals they eat.	_____
	_____
2. Eagles are predators.	_____
	_____
3. A leopard is a predator.	_____
	_____
4. Carrion beetles do not kill the animals they eat.	_____
	_____

C Read each sentence that follows. Explain why the underlined part is redundant by filling in the blanks.

1. Before I got to the schoolroom, I stopped at the drugstore and then went to class.

If you know that I got to the schoolroom, you already know that

_____.

2. We are pleased to announce our first half-price sale—you get 50 percent off—when you buy anything in our store.

If you know that prices will be cut in half, you already know that

_____.

3. He got a temporary job that lasted a short time.

If you know that his job was temporary, you already know that

_____.

4. Those huge, overpopulated cities have too many people in them.

If you know that the cities are overpopulated, you already know that

_____.

_____.

Read the passage below.

The world's saltiest body of water is the Dead Sea, located between Israel and Jordan. The water of the Dead Sea is about seven times as salty as the water in the Atlantic or the Pacific Ocean. The reason that the Dead Sea is so salty is that it is shrinking. It was once much larger, but it is slowly drying up. The amount of salt that was once contained in a large body of water is now restricted to a very small body of water. There are no fish in the Dead Sea, and plants are very scarce. Salt water is heavier than fresh water. The water of the Dead Sea is so salty that a swimmer cannot sink in it.

- Here's a conclusion:

  The Dead Sea is a good name for this body of water.

1. Does the passage contain evidence to support this conclusion or evidence to refute this conclusion?

   _____

   _____

2. Which sentence contains the evidence?

   _____

   _____

   _____

   _____

- Here's another conclusion:

  Even if you're a poor swimmer, you're probably safe in the Dead Sea.

3. Does the passage contain evidence to support this conclusion or evidence to contradict this conclusion?

   _____

   _____

4. Which sentence contains the evidence?

   _____

   _____

   _____

   _____

A Look at diagram 1.

Diagram 1

You can't see the dots in the diagram, but you can see the circle and the square.
Here's a deduction based on the diagram:

All the dots are in the circle.
None of the circle is in the square.
So, none of the dots are in the square.

The diagram below shows that the conclusion is right.

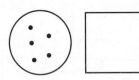

● Look at diagram 2.

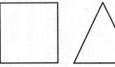

Diagram 2

You can't see the dots in the diagram, but you can see the triangle and the square. Complete the deduction:

All the dots are in the triangle.
None of the triangle is in the square.

So, _____

_____

Check your conclusion by drawing dots in diagram 2 so that all the dots are in the triangle.

● Look at diagram 3.

Diagram 3

You can see the dots and the circle, but you can't see the oval. Complete the deduction:

All the dots are in the circle.
None of the circle is in the oval.

So, _____

_____

Check your conclusion by drawing an oval in diagram 3 so that none of the circle is in the oval.

★ **B** Read the facts and the items below. If an item is relevant to fact A, write **relevant to fact A.** If an item is relevant to fact B, write **relevant to fact B.** If an item is irrelevant to both facts, write **irrelevant.**

Fact A. **Freddie is very tall.**

Fact B. **Freddie is studying landscape gardening.**

1. Freddie's mother is very short.

_____

2. On the weekends, Freddie works at a lawn and garden shop.

_____

3. Freddie plays on the school basketball team.

_____

4. Freddie reads 400 words per minute.

_____

C Read the passage below and answer the questions. Circle **W** if the question is answered by words in the passage. Circle **D** if the question is answered by a deduction. If you circle **W** for an item, underline the words in the passage that give the answer.

From what you have learned about herbivorous mammals and carnivorous mammals, you should be able to draw conclusions about the skulls of some mammals.

Picture 1   **Picture 2**

Look at picture 1. The flat teeth in picture 1 tell you that this may be the skull of a herbivorous mammal. So do the holes for the eyes. If the eyes look to the side, the mammal is probably herbivorous. If the eyes look straight ahead, the mammal is probably carnivorous.

The skull of the animal in picture 1 is thin and light. The mammal is probably a fast-running animal whose body is as light as possible. This mammal is not well designed to fight, but with its speed, it can probably outrun most predators.

Compare the skull of the herbivorous animal with the skull in picture 2. The skull in picture 2 belongs to a carnivorous mammal. The teeth are strong and sharp,

built to rip and eat flesh. The eye sockets are facing straight ahead, and the bones around the eyes and top of the skull are very heavy. Look at the thick ridge down the middle of the skull. The skull of this animal is a weapon used in battles with other animals, so it must be thick and strong.

The skull of the animal in picture 1 belongs to a horse. The skull of the animal in picture 2 belongs to a lion. Look at the skull in picture 3.

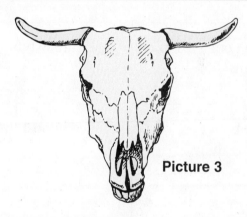

Picture 3

1. Are the eye sockets likely to be those of a carnivore or herbivore?

_____ **W   D**

2. Are the teeth those of a grazing animal or a meat-eating animal?

_____ **W   D**

3. Is the skull that of a light, fast-moving animal or a heavy animal?

_____

4. Can you figure out what animal the skull belongs to?

_____

5. Why do carnivorous mammals have thick, heavy skulls?

_____

_____

_____ W   D

6. How are the teeth of a sheep different from the teeth of a fox?

_____

_____

_____

7. Do both eyes of a horse see almost the same thing?

_____

8. Do both eyes of a coyote see almost the same thing?

_____

D Look at the diagram.

○   △

You can't see the dots in the diagram, but you can see the triangle and the circle.

1. Complete the deduction:

All the dots are in the triangle.
None of the triangle is in the circle.

So, _____

_____

2. Check your conclusion by drawing dots in the diagram so that all the dots are in the triangle.

E Read the evidence and write the conclusion for each item below.

1. Here's the evidence:

Some fish have teeth.
A barracuda is a fish.

What's the conclusion?

_____

_____

2. Here's the evidence:

Fish breathe in water.
Tadpoles breathe in water.

What's the conclusion?

_____

_____

3. Here's the evidence:

Fish breathe in water.
Sea lions do not breathe in water.

What's the conclusion?

_____

_____

F Read the argument below and answer the questions.

Here's your choice: sit at home watching television or get out on a Speed motorcycle. Just remember this: you'll have a lot more fun on a Speed.

1. What does the writer want us to conclude?

_____

_____

_____

2. What choices does the writer use as evidence for this conclusion?

_____

_____

_____

3. What rule does the argument break?

_____

_____

_____

4. To show that the argument is faulty, what do you do?

_____

_____

_____

5. Name one example.

_____

_____

_____

G You will be tested on some facts presented in this lesson. These facts are:

1. **A cold war happens when two countries are close to being in a shooting war with each other.**
2. **In 1969, the first person walked on the moon.**

Study these facts. Repeat them to yourself. Writing these facts may help you to remember them.

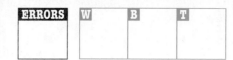

LESSON 82

ERRORS	W	B	T

A Look at diagram 1.

Diagram 1

You can't see the dots in the picture, but you can see the rectangle and the circle. Complete the deduction:

**All the dots are in the rectangle.
None of the rectangle is in the circle.**

So, _____

_____

Check your conclusion by drawing dots in diagram 1 so that all the dots are in the rectangle.

• Look at diagram 2.

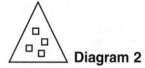

Diagram 2

You can see the boxes and the triangle, but you can't see the oval.

Complete the deduction:

**All the boxes are in the triangle.
None of the triangle is in the oval.**

So, _____

_____

Check your conclusion by drawing an oval in diagram 2 so that none of the triangle is in the oval.

B There is a redundant part in each sentence below. Tell why each part is redundant.

• **We want to preserve our wildlife and save our forest animals.**

What's the redundant part?
Complete the sentence below:

If _____

_____,

then _____

_____

_____.

• **The system, which is made up of parts, was put into operation.**

What's the redundant part?
Complete the sentence below:

If _____

_____,

then _____

_____.

252 LESSON 82

Copyright © SRA/McGraw-Hill

★ **C** For each item, write a sentence that means the same thing by changing the underlined word or words.

1. His directions were <u>unclear</u> and <u>repetitive</u>.

_____

_____

2. The cashier <u>paused</u> before accepting their French <u>money</u>.

_____

_____

_____

3. Her <u>fears</u> had no <u>fitting</u> outlet.

_____

_____

4. They argued that the <u>rule</u> was <u>irrelevant</u>.

_____

_____

_____

D Read the argument below and answer the questions.

"You must stop skipping classes. If you don't, you'll either flunk out of school or be expelled."

1. What does the writer want us to conclude?

_____

_____

2. What choices does the writer use as evidence for this conclusion?

_____

_____

_____

3. What rule does the argument break?

_____

_____

_____

4. To show that the argument is faulty, what do you do?

_____

_____

_____

5. Name one example.

_____

_____

_____

LESSON 82

E Underline the redundant part in the sentence below. Then explain why the underlined part is redundant by filling in the blanks.

"I will never give up," he said, <u>refusing to surrender</u>.

If _____

_____ ,

then _____

_____ .

F Look at diagram 1.

Diagram 1

You can see the rectangle and the triangle, but you can't see the boxes.

1. Complete the deduction:

    All the boxes are in the triangle.
    None of the triangle is in the rectangle.

So, _____

_____

2. Check your conclusion by drawing boxes in diagram 1 so that all of the boxes are in the triangle.

- Look at diagram 2.

Diagram 2

You can see the dots and the oval, but you can't see the square.

3. Complete the deduction:

    All the dots are in the oval.
    None of the oval is in the square.

So, _____

_____

4. Check your conclusion by drawing a square in diagram 2 so that none of the oval is in the square.

G Read the rule and each piece of evidence. Write a conclusion after each piece of evidence.

Rule. **All reptiles are cold-blooded.**

Evidence   Conclusion

1. A West Indian gecko is a reptile. _____

_____

2. The reticulated python is a reptile. _____

_____

3. A marten is not cold-blooded. _____

_____

4. The bee hummingbird is not cold-blooded. _____

_____

 H You will be tested on a fact presented in this lesson. This fact is:

Leonardo da Vinci was an inventor, a painter, a musician, and a scientist.

Study this fact. Repeat it to yourself. Writing the fact may help you remember it.

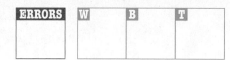

LESSON 83

 A There is a redundant part in each sentence below. Tell why each part is redundant.

● **These real diamonds are not imitation jewels!**

What's the redundant part?
Complete the sentence below:

If _____

_____,

then _____

_____.

● **"I don't doubt what you say because I believe you."**

What's the redundant part?
Complete the sentence below:

If _____

_____,

then _____

_____.

★ **B** Write the verb **is** or **are** in each blank.

1. The salt in the salt shaker _____ damp.

2. Special privileges _____ given to senators.

3. You _____ the one person I have been looking for.

4. Some of the members of the band _____ giving a party.

5. Everybody who runs in these races _____ capable of winning.

6. Members of the club _____ given a special discount.

 **C** Look at diagram 1.

Diagram 1

You can see the circle and the triangle, but you can't see the boxes.

1. Complete the deduction:

   All the boxes are in the circle.
   None of the circle is in the triangle.

   So, _____

   _____

2. Check your conclusion by drawing the boxes in diagram 1 so that all the boxes are in the circle.

● Look at diagram 2.

Diagram 2

You can see the dots and the square, but you can't see the oval.

3. Complete the deduction:

   All the dots are in the square.
   None of the square is in the oval.

   So, _____

   _____

4. Check your conclusion by drawing an oval in diagram 2 so that none of the square is in the oval.

D Read the argument below and answer the questions.

"We must either destroy Mars or be destroyed by the Martians. I'd rather destroy than be destroyed, wouldn't you?"

1. What does the writer want us to conclude?

_____

_____

_____

2. What choices does the writer use as evidence for this conclusion?

_____

_____

_____

3. What rule does the argument break?

_____

_____

_____

_____

4. To show that the argument is faulty, what do you do?

_____

_____

_____

5. Name one example.

_____

_____

_____

E Underline the redundant part in each sentence below. Then explain why the underlined part is redundant by filling in the blanks.

1. "Yes," she affirmed, pacing the floor.

If _____

_____,

then _____

_____.

2. The table was set with a huge variety of many foods.

If _____

_____,

then _____

_____.

F You will be tested on a fact presented in this lesson. This fact is:

In 1869, the first coast-to-coast railroad in the United States was completed.

Study this fact. Repeat it to yourself. Writing the fact may help you remember it.

G Each argument below breaks one of these rules:

Rule 1. Just because two things happen around the same time doesn't mean one thing causes the other thing.

Rule 2. Just because you know about a part doesn't mean you know about the whole thing.

Rule 3. Just because you know about a part doesn't mean you know about another part.

Rule 4. Just because you know about the whole thing doesn't mean you know about every part.

Rule 5. Just because words are the same doesn't mean they have the same meaning.

After each argument below, write the number of the rule the argument breaks.

1. I know Pat took my purse. She was the last one in the room before I noticed it was

   missing. _____

2. You can tell she's a real snob about everything. She doesn't speak to anyone at

   the office. _____

3. Sue said to meet her at the riverbank. When it came time to go meet her, I looked up banks in the phone directory and discovered there was no River Bank. She must have

   gotten her banks confused. _____

4. The record of this company is nearly perfect. Other large corporations have been sued for trying to control the market, for not complying with federal laws, and for using unfair sales tactics. Our company has never been guilty of any of these offenses. We enjoy the record of being a very honorable, honest organization. You know, therefore, that every employee in our company is

   completely honorable and honest. _____

H Write the instructions for this diagram.

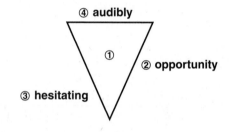

④ audibly
① ② opportunity
③ hesitating

1. (what) _____

   _____

2. (what and where) _____

   _____

   _____

3. (what and where) _____

   _____

   _____

4. (what and where) _____

   _____

   _____

A Look at diagram 1.

Diagram 1

You can't see the dots in the diagram, but **all the dots are in the triangle.**

1. Complete the deduction.

   All the dots are in the triangle.
   The triangle is in the circle.

So, _____

_____

2. Draw the dots in diagram 1.

• Look at diagram 2.

Diagram 2

You can't see the dots in the diagram, but **all the dots are in the triangle.**

3. Complete the deduction.

   All the dots are in the triangle.
   None of the triangle is in the circle.

So, _____

_____

4. Draw the dots in diagram 2.

B Read the argument below and answer the questions.

> **When you graduate from high school, you can either go to college or work at a job you hate for the rest of your life.**

1. What does the writer want us to conclude?

   _____

   _____

   _____

2. What choices does the writer use as evidence for this conclusion?

   _____

   _____

   _____

3. What rule does the argument break?

   _____

   _____

   _____

   _____

4. To show that the argument is faulty, what do you do?

   _____

   _____

   _____

5. Name one example.

   _____

   _____

   _____

Read the passage that follows and answer the questions. Circle **W** if the question is answered by words in the passage. Circle **D** if the question is answered by a deduction. If you circle **W** for an item, underline the words in the passage that give the answer.

Not every carnivorous animal kills. Those that kill are called predators. Wolves, lions, tigers, and sharks are fierce predators. Some other predators may not be as dangerous to people as a shark or a jaguar, but these animals are still predators, which means that they kill so they can eat. Frogs and robins are predators. Frogs eat flies; robins eat worms. The eagle is a predator with good eyesight and very strong claws, which are called talons.

Parasites and scavengers are two types of carnivorous animals that do not kill. Leeches and ticks are parasites. They attach themselves to another animal and suck nourishment from their "host," but they do not kill the host. The host does the work of hunting for food while the parasite feasts on the host.

Instead of killing animals, scavengers wait for animals to die or to be killed by predators. After the predators have eaten what they want, the scavengers eat the remains of the animals. Bears are scavengers. So are porcupines, crows, buzzards, hyenas, and jackals.

Remember that carnivorous animals include parasites and scavengers. A parasite attaches itself to a host, and a scavenger waits for an animal to die or be killed by a predator.

1. What do we call carnivores that kill?

_____ **W** **D**

2. How is a parasite different from a predator?

_____

_____

_____ **W** **D**

3. What do we call the plant or animal that a parasite lives on?

_____

4. What do scavengers eat?

_____

_____ **W** **D**

5. How are parasites and scavengers the same?

_____

_____

_____

6. How are parasites and scavengers different?

_____

_____

_____

_____

7. The passage names three types of carnivores. One type is the predator. Fill in the boxes below for the other two types.

- Below the box for predators, list six kinds of predators.

- Below the other two boxes, list two examples of each kind of animal.

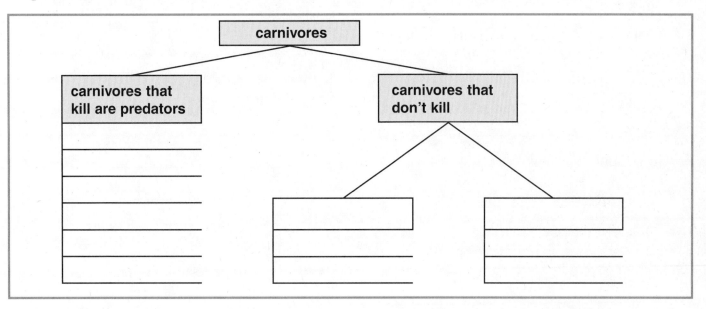

D Each argument below is faulty.

- **This club is well liked and it has many friends. Consider the facts. There are 100 members in the club. Each member in the club has at least five friends. Therefore, the club has at least 500 friends.**

1. What does the writer want us to conclude?

_____

_____

2. How could you show that the argument is faulty?

_____

_____

_____

- **I told the man at the cat hospital that I would give no more money to that hospital. He said, "All right. You can give just as much money as you gave before."**

3. What does the writer want us to conclude?

_____

_____

_____

4. How could you show that the argument is faulty?

_____

_____

_____

• **This ring contains one of the most precious metals in the world—gold. If it has gold in it, this ring must be one of the most precious rings in the world. Yet, believe it or not, it is yours for only $4.56 plus postage.**

5. What does the writer want us to conclude?

_____

_____

_____

6. How could you show that the argument is faulty?

_____

_____

_____

_____

_____

E Underline the redundant part in each sentence that follows. Then explain why the underlined part is redundant by filling in the blanks.

1. I found this toothbrush in a remote part of Africa, far from civilization.

If _____

_____,

then _____

_____.

2. Between 1934 and 1944, a full ten years passed.

If _____

_____,

then _____

_____.

3. Everyone could hear the professor, who spoke quite audibly.

If _____

_____,

then _____

_____.

F You will be tested on some facts presented in this lesson. These facts are:

1. **Scavengers and parasites are two kinds of carnivores that do not kill.**
2. **Ticks and leeches are two kinds of parasites.**
3. **Bears, porcupines, crows, and vultures are scavengers.**

Study these facts. Repeat them to yourself. Writing these facts may help you remember them.

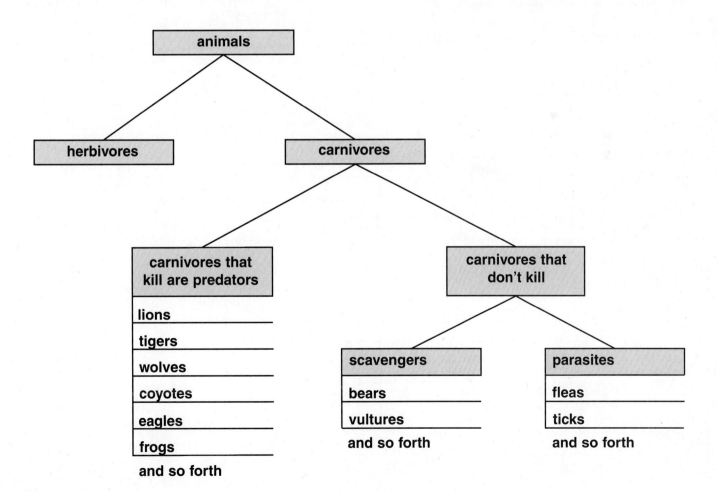

G Tomorrow you will be tested on facts you have learned. The test will include all the facts presented in Lessons 70–84 and some of the facts from earlier lessons. These facts are:

1. The teeth and the eyes of herbivorous mammals are well designed for grazing.
2. The eyes of herbivorous mammals allow them to eat and to watch out for enemies at the same time.
3. The right and the left eye of many herbivorous mammals see different things.
4. The teeth and the eyes of carnivorous mammals are well designed for hunting.
5. The right and the left eye of many carnivorous mammals see nearly the same thing.
6. The teeth of a herbivorous mammal are flat, and the teeth of a carnivorous mammal are pointed.
7. A cold war happens when two countries are close to being in a shooting war with each other.
8. In 1969, the first person walked on the moon.
9. Leonardo da Vinci was an inventor, a painter, a musician, and a scientist.
10. In 1869, the first coast-to-coast railroad in the United States was completed.
11. Study the chart below. Make sure that you could fill in this chart.

animals

herbivores

carnivores

carnivores that kill are predators
- lions
- tigers
- wolves
- coyotes
- eagles
- frogs

and so forth

carnivores that don't kill

scavengers
- bears
- vultures

and so forth

parasites
- fleas
- ticks

and so forth

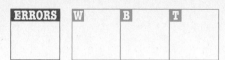

ERRORS	W	B	T

A **INFORMATION TEST.** Answer each item. You have eleven minutes.

1. Name the two parts of a herbivorous mammal that are well designed for grazing.

_____

_____

_____

2. Do both eyes of a herbivorous mammal see almost the same thing? _____

3. Name the two parts of a carnivorous mammal that are well designed for hunting.

_____

_____

_____

4. Do both eyes of a carnivorous mammal see almost the same thing? _____

5. What is a cold war?

_____

_____

_____

6. Name three different things that Leonardo da Vinci did.

_____

_____

7. Why do herbivorous mammals have the kind of eyes they have?

_____

_____

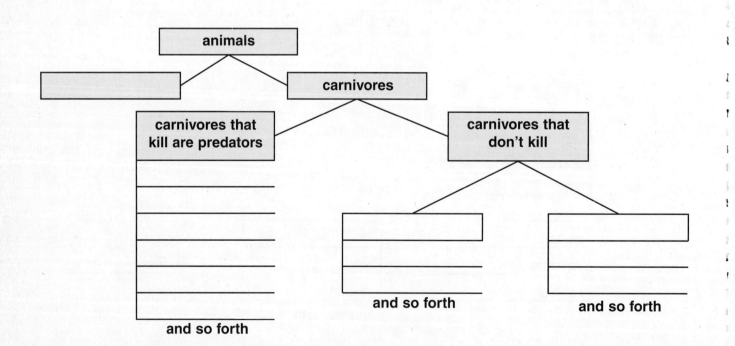

8. How are the teeth of a herbivorous mammal different from those of a carnivorous mammal?

_____

_____

_____

9. When did the first person walk on the moon? _____

10. When was the first coast-to-coast railroad in the United States completed? _____

11. Fill in the chart on page 264.

★ **B** Underline the redundant part in each sentence that follows. Then explain why the underlined part is redundant by filling in the blanks.

1. **This opportunity, which represents a real chance, was presented to Mr. Jones.**

   If _____

   _____,

   then _____

   _____

2. **"My, goodness," he said as he spoke.**

   If _____,

   then _____

   _____

3. **I had my car fixed by a mechanic, who does car work.**

   If _____

   _____,

   then _____

   _____

C Read the argument below and answer the questions.

If you don't cut your hair, you're going to get it caught in a machine someday. Or maybe you'll end up in a pool hall with a bunch of bums.

1. What does the writer want us to conclude?

   _____

   _____

2. What rule does the argument break?

   _____

   _____

   _____

3. Show that the argument is faulty.

   _____

   _____

LESSON 85

D For each item, write a sentence that means the same thing by changing the underlined word or words.

1. A strange <u>event</u> caused the <u>fear</u> that she <u>showed</u>.

   _____

   _____

   _____

2. None of the scientists could explain the <u>event</u>.

   _____

   _____

3. A total eclipse is an exciting <u>event</u> to see.

   _____

   _____

4. As the bear approached, Tom's face <u>showed</u> his <u>fear</u>.

   _____

   _____

   _____

E Look at this diagram:

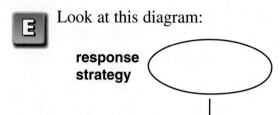

The diagram contradicts part of these instructions:

1. Draw an oval.
2. Draw a horizontal line below the oval.
3. Write the word **response** to the left of the oval.
4. Write the word **strategy** below the word **response.**

Circle the instruction that the diagram contradicts.

Draw a new diagram that follows the instructions.

★ **A** Underline the redundant part in each sentence below. Then explain why the underlined part is redundant by filling in the blanks.

1. **He purchased the bike for his son by buying it.**

If _____
_____ ,

then _____
_____ .

2. **"Yes, yes, yes," she said repeatedly.**

If _____
_____ ,

then _____
_____ .

3. **He encouraged his sister to buy the store by urging her to purchase it.**

If _____
_____
_____ ,

then _____
_____
_____ .

B Look at diagram 1.

Diagram 1

You can't see the rectangle, but **part of the oval is in the rectangle.**

1. Complete the deduction.

All the boxes are in the oval.
Part of the oval is in the rectangle.

So, _____
_____

2. Draw the rectangle in diagram 1.

Look at diagram 2.

Diagram 2

You can't see the rectangle. **None of the oval is in the rectangle.**

3. Complete the deduction.

All the boxes are in the oval.
None of the oval is in the rectangle.

So, _____
_____

4. Draw the rectangle in diagram 2.

LESSON 86

C Read the passage that follows and answer the questions. Circle **W** if the question is answered by words in the passage. Circle **D** if the question is answered by a deduction. If you circle **W** for an item, underline the words in the passage that give the answer.

Some parasites are plants and some parasites are animals. Mistletoe is a plant parasite that grows in the tops of trees. Mushrooms are also plant parasites. Still another plant parasite is a flowering plant called dodder, which grows on the stalks of other plants and sucks the sap from them.

Some animal parasites use plant hosts. The mealybug lives off the soft parts of plants. The animal parasites we are most familiar with, however, are animal parasites that use animal hosts. Ticks and mosquitoes are animal parasites that use animal hosts.

Everybody knows how mosquitoes work. They stick a tube into your skin and suck out blood. When they are filled, they fly off. What you may not know about mosquitoes is that only females bite in this manner and that they must get blood from a host before they can lay eggs.

Mosquito bites can be very harmful. In some areas, there are so many mosquitoes that a person could go crazy while trying unsuccessfully to escape from the swarming insects. In addition, some mosquitoes carry deadly diseases, such as malaria and yellow fever.

Just as mosquitoes bother humans, fleas and ticks bother dogs, cats, and other animals. Moose and elk will sometimes thunder through the forest, trying to run from fleas or stinging flies. Often, the animal that is under the attack of insects will not stop running until it reaches a lake or river. It will then dive in to find relief.

One of the most disgusting parasites is the leech, which looks like a large, flat worm, and is able to attach itself to the host's body. Like a mosquito, the leech sucks blood. Turtles sometimes have leeches stuck between their legs and on their chests. Leeches sometimes will attach themselves between a swimmer's toes or around the waistband of a bathing suit.

1. How is a parasite different from a predator?

_____

_____

_____

_____

2. What do we call the plant or animal that a parasite lives on? _____

3. Why do female mosquitoes need blood?

_____

_____ **W   D**

4. How do forest animals sometimes escape from fleas and ticks?

_____

_____

_____ **W   D**

5. Name two plant parasites that live on other plants.

_____

_____

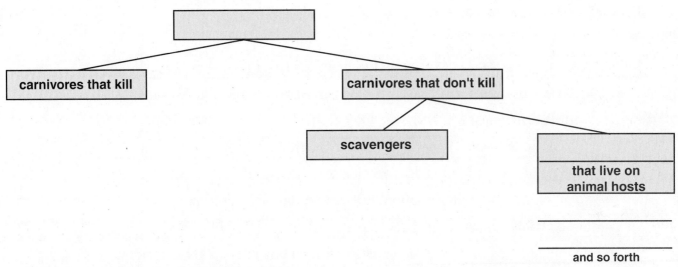

6. Fill in the two empty boxes in the chart below. Then list two types of animals that live on animal hosts.

_____

_____

and so forth

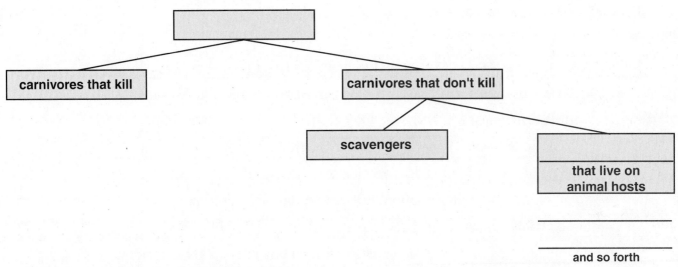

D For each item, write a sentence that means the same thing by changing the underlined word or words.

1. A strange <u>event</u> caused the <u>fear</u> that she <u>showed.</u>

_____

_____

2. Tom <u>showed</u> <u>fear</u> at the sight of a snake.

_____

_____

3. The erupting volcano caused an unusual <u>event.</u>

_____

_____

_____

4. The horses showed their fear by rearing.

_____

_____

_____

E You will be tested on some facts presented in this lesson. These facts are:

1. **Mistletoe and dodder are parasites that live on plants.**
2. **Fleas, ticks, mosquitoes, and leeches are parasites that live on animals.**

Study these facts. Repeat them to yourself. Writing these facts may help you remember them.

F Read this: A title is a piece of paper that tells who owns something. When you buy a car, for example, you take title to the car. When you apply for license plates, you must show that you have title to the car. You must also show that you have title to the car when you sell it.
Use the facts to fill out the form.

Facts: Your name is Adrian Garner and you are applying for a new driver's license. You were born March 1, 1980, in Sarasota, Florida. You live with your parents, Mr. and Mrs. Guy Garner. Your address is 1440 Temple in Sarasota. You passed both the written and the driving test. Your total score on the road-signs test was 18 out of 20 correct. Your score on the driver-information test was 15 out of 20 correct. You drive a 1987 Ramrod. The license plate number is HL 6747. Plates and title to the car are in your name. The title number is #6009-87-567. The serial number of the car is C320-4687-49. You have good eyesight without glasses. You are 5 feet 8 inches tall, you weigh about 145 pounds, your hair is brown, and your eyes are blue. Your Social Security number is 435-77-3008. Your insurance company is Western Insurance. The insurance policy number is 477-09-89.

State of Florida—Driver's License Application

Name _____ Age _____

Date of birth _____ Place of birth _____

Present address _____

Social Security number _____

Is this an application for a new license or a renewal of an old one? old _____ new _____

Height _____ Weight _____

Hair color _____ Eye color _____

Eyesight without glasses: good _____ poor _____ Eyesight with glasses: good _____ poor _____

Name of insurance company that insures car _____

Insurance policy number _____

G Each argument below breaks one of these rules:

Rule 1. Just because two things happen around the same time doesn't mean one thing causes the other thing.

Rule 2. Just because you know about a part doesn't mean you know about the whole thing.

Rule 3. Just because you know about a part doesn't mean you know about another part.

Rule 4. Just because you know about the whole thing doesn't mean you know about every part.

Rule 5. Just because words are the same doesn't mean they have the same meaning.

Rule 6. Just because the writer presents some choices doesn't mean there aren't other choices.

After each argument below, write the number of the rule the argument breaks.

1. The introduction of front-wheel drive has caused cars to become smaller. In the 1960s, cars were large and only a few had front-wheel drive. The number of front-wheel drive cars went up and up in the 1970s, and the average car got smaller and smaller.

_____

2. You asked me whether the voters in the west suburb will vote Democratic or Republican. I'll tell you this. The voters in the downtown district voted Democratic. So did the voters in the east suburb. There's no doubt that the voters in the west suburb will vote Democratic.

_____

3. That football team has lost nine games in a row. Their quarterback must be a terrible

player. _____

4. Every time it rains at night, the crickets stop chirping just before the storm. I have observed this trend for twelve years. My chart shows that every time it has rained, the crickets stopped chirping. I know that it will rain tonight because the crickets had been chirping, but they stopped about five minutes

ago. _____

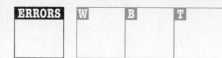

LESSON 87

ERRORS	W	B	T

★ **A** For each item, write a sentence that means the same thing by changing the underlined word or words.

1. A strange <u>event</u> caused the <u>fear</u> that she <u>showed</u>.

_____

_____

_____

2. An unusual weather <u>event</u> damaged the crop.

_____

_____

_____

3. The brave woman <u>showed</u> no <u>fear</u>.

_____

_____

4. They <u>showed</u> photos of the eclipse, a rare <u>event</u>.

_____

_____

_____

B Look at diagram 1.

Diagram 1

You can't see the dots, but **all the dots are in the circle.**

1. Complete the deduction.

   All the dots are in the circle.
   Part of the circle is in the square.

So, _____

_____

• Look at diagram 2.

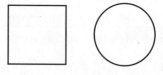

Diagram 2

You can't see the dots, but **all the dots are in the circle.**

2. Complete the deduction.

   All the dots are in the circle.
   None of the circle is in the square.

So, _____

_____

3. Draw the dots in diagram 2.

Each argument below breaks one of these rules:

Rule 1. Just because two things happen around the same time doesn't mean one thing causes the other thing.

Rule 2. Just because you know about a part doesn't mean you know about the whole thing.

Rule 3. Just because you know about a part doesn't mean you know about another part.

Rule 4. Just because you know about the whole thing doesn't mean you know about every part.

Rule 5. Just because words are the same doesn't mean they have the same meaning.

Rule 6. Just because the writer presents some choices doesn't mean there aren't other choices.

After each argument, write the number of the rule the argument breaks.

1. An officer stopped a man on the freeway for speeding. The man had been traveling at about 85 miles per hour and had been weaving in and out of traffic.

   When the officer began writing the first of three tickets, the man said: "But, officer, you don't understand. I must get home. I left home about an hour ago, and I forgot that I had left my welding torch on in the basement. If somebody doesn't turn it off very soon, it will burn up the house. My wife is in the house. If I don't get home right now, I'm going to lose my home and my

   wife." _____

2. Bob said that he'd give me a ring Thursday, and all he did was call me on the phone. I wonder if I should even see him again.

   _____

3. I'm sure that she has pretty feet. Her legs

   and arms are very attractive. _____

4. Not everybody's going to agree with me, but I don't think Mary Cass is right for the job of union official. I know what others have said. Even the president of the union called Mary a stout supporter of the union. But that's the problem. We don't need a stout supporter. We need somebody who is slim, somebody who can get out there and fight.

   _____

LESSON 87

 D Here's what we know:

> **Many people think the words in his songs are redundant.**

For each item, combine one of the sentences below with the sentence in the box.

- **Some people refuse to buy any more of his CDs.**
- **His last three albums were best-sellers.**

1. Make a combined sentence with **however**.

_____

_____

_____

_____

_____

2. Make a combined sentence with **therefore**.

_____

_____

_____

_____

_____

★ **A** Each argument that follows is faulty.

• Our sun is not even two million kilometers across, and Red Giant stars are more than ten million kilometers across. Therefore, Red Giant stars must be brighter than our sun.

1. What does the writer want us to conclude?

_____

_____

_____

2. How could you show that the argument is faulty?

_____

_____

_____

_____

• I support the mayor for reelection. He has the experience and knowledge necessary to run our city. Our city government works very well. The mayor is part of the city government, so it follows that he must be doing good work, too.

3. What does the writer want us to conclude?

_____

_____

_____

4. How could you show that the argument is faulty?

_____

_____

_____

_____

• When the cost of raw materials goes up, we have no choice but to raise the price of our cars. Either you let us price our cars however we please, or you destroy the very foundation of our economy. The choice is up to you.

5. What does the writer want us to conclude?

_____

_____

_____

_____

6. How could you show that the argument is faulty?

_____

_____

_____

_____

ERRORS	W	B	T

B Underline the redundant part in each sentence below. Then explain why the underlined part is redundant by filling in the blanks.

1. **"Yes," she said, agreeing.**

   If _____

   _____,

   then _____

   _____.

2. **To change some of her money, she converted it.**

   If _____

   _____,

   then _____

   _____.

3. **"Ouch, that thing hurts," he screamed in pain.**

   If _____

   _____,

   then _____

   _____.

C For each item, write a sentence that means the same thing by changing the underlined word or words.

1. A strange event caused the fear that she showed.

   _____

   _____

   _____

2. An earthquake is a geological event that creates fear.

   _____

   _____

   _____

3. Sam showed no fear when he jumped from the airplane.

   _____

   _____

   _____

4. A hurricane can be a destructive event.

   _____

   _____

D Select the right word for combining each pair of sentences below. Then write the combined sentence. Remember to punctuate each sentence correctly.

1. Police officers need to learn new laws. They go to police school.

   therefore   **but**

   _____

   _____

   _____

2. The bank's computer broke down. The bank clerk couldn't tell me the exact amount in my savings account.

   so   **however**

   _____

   _____

   _____

   _____

   _____

3. The newspaper photographer ran out of film. She was unable to take a picture when the building collapsed.

   therefore   **however**

   _____

   _____

   _____

   _____

   _____

4. Don had to return some books. They were overdue.

   who   **which**

   _____

   _____

   _____

5. Many people enjoy seeing dolphins perform at water shows. Dolphins seem to enjoy performing tricks for crowds.

   and   **but**

   _____

   _____

   _____

   _____

   _____

   _____

6. Cats love Susan. Susan is our animal doctor.

   who   **which**

   _____

   _____

ERRORS	W	B	T

★ **A** For each item, write a sentence that means the same thing by changing the underlined words.

1. They <u>made up</u> a <u>fitting plan</u>.

_____

_____

2. She had a <u>chance</u> to present the facts about the frightening <u>event</u>.

_____

_____

3. Bev experienced <u>fear</u> before she found her missing <u>money</u>.

_____

_____

4. The <u>rule</u> was very <u>unclear</u>.

_____

_____

B Read each item. Cross out the irrelevant words in the second piece of evidence, and write the conclusion for each item.

1. **Mailing packages costs more than mailing letters.**

   Our books are mailed in brown paper packages.

   _____

   _____

2. **Some periodicals contain advertising.**

   Newsmagazines are informative periodicals.

   _____

   _____

3. **Cold temperatures preserve food.**

   Household freezers have unwavering cold temperatures.

   _____

   _____

Ⓒ Each argument that follows is faulty.

• Three years ago, I had a bad cough. Dr. Samuel made me take some medicine. It tasted awful, but my cough went away in one day. Later, I had the flu. I had to take a different kind of medicine. It tasted bad too, but the next day I felt fine. My dad has some medicine that is supposed to make hair grow. If this medicine tastes bad, I know it will work and I will have lots of hair tomorrow.

1. What does the writer want us to conclude?

   _____

   _____

   _____

2. How could you show that the argument is faulty?

   _____

   _____

   _____

   _____

   _____

• Would you rather pay $20,000 for this automobile and have something that you will love and all your friends will admire? Or would you prefer to drive that junk you've got now and have everybody think you're a slob?

3. What does the writer want us to conclude?

   _____

   _____

   _____

4. How could you show that the argument is faulty?

   _____

   _____

   _____

   _____

• Sue must not have any friends, because she always goes to the movies by herself.

5. What does the writer want us to conclude?

   _____

   _____

6. How could you show that the argument is faulty?

   _____

   _____

   _____

   _____

   _____

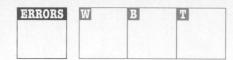
★ **A** Each argument that follows breaks one of these rules:

Rule 1. Just because two things happen around the same time doesn't mean one thing causes the other thing.

Rule 2. Just because you know about a part doesn't mean you know about the whole thing.

Rule 3. Just because you know about a part doesn't mean you know about another part.

Rule 4. Just because you know about the whole thing doesn't mean you know about every part.

Rule 5. Just because words are the same doesn't mean they have the same meaning.

Rule 6. Just because the writer presents some choices doesn't mean there aren't other choices.

After each argument that follows, write the number of the rule the argument breaks.

1. Poor Morey. His mother said he seemed to have lost his senses since the accident. Can you imagine not being able to hear, smell, or see? I hope it's not permanent. _____

2. What kind of a suggestion is that? How could we possibly drop our athletic program? Do you realize that you're talking about St. Francis University, which has a tradition of sports excellence that dates back to Knute Dropley, the first football coach to have a national champion at St. Francis? Do I have to remind you that the very fiber of this university is woven from the principles that are formed on the athletic field and in athletic competition? Athletes are real men and women, strong and knowledgeable about how to share and how to be a member of a working group. If we do away with our athletic program, we will turn out people who are weak and know nothing of what it is like to compete for excellence. _____

3. The army is not efficient, so we cannot expect Major Schlock to do an efficient job.

_____

4. The Johnsons had a serious fight. Mr. Johnson left this morning with a suitcase, and that's just what happens after married people have a big fight. _____

B Use the rule in the box and the evidence to answer the questions.

All fires need air.

• **Sam lit a candle.**

1. What's the conclusion?

_____

_____

• **There was a fire in the fireplace.**

2. What's the conclusion?

_____

_____

• **There is no air on the moon.**

3. What's the conclusion?

_____

_____

C Underline the redundant part in each sentence below. Then explain why the underlined part is redundant by filling in the blanks.

1. He halted by coming to a complete stop.

If _____

_____,

then _____

_____.

2. She was the kind of employee who worked for somebody.

If _____

_____,

then _____

_____.

3. That car didn't move as long as it was standing still.

If _____

_____,

then _____

_____.

D For each item, write a sentence that means the same thing by changing the underlined words.

1. A strange <u>event</u> caused the <u>fear</u> that she <u>showed</u>.

_____

_____

_____

2. The crooks had a <u>plan</u> for making <u>money</u>.

_____

_____

3. He <u>showed</u> his <u>fear</u> when he <u>paused</u>.

_____

_____

_____

4. His paper was <u>filled</u> with <u>irrelevant</u> facts.

_____

_____

E Each argument that follows is faulty.

- I think my Aunt Alice is very strange. She's always been a little bit odd. As long as I've known her, she's had a tendency to put things in strange places. She once put a statue of a giant swan on her roof. Another time, she put a little folding table in the back seat of the car. She even put a little tiny television set inside her doghouse.

  When I got the last letter from Aunt Alice, I knew that she had gone too far putting things in strange places. She wrote that she was going to the dentist's office to have a bridge put in her mouth. I don't know if it's a railroad bridge or a bridge for cars, but I do know that poor Aunt Alice has lost her mind.

1. What does the writer want us to conclude?

   _____

   _____

   _____

2. How could you show that the argument is faulty?

   _____

   _____

   _____

- Primp circuit boards are recognized as the finest in the world. You know that any company that produces such a circuit board must be the world leader in electronic components.

3. What does the writer want us to conclude?

   _____

   _____

   _____

4. How could you show that the argument is faulty?

   _____

   _____

   _____

- J. Paul Getty was an American, and he had more than a billion dollars. John Jackson is an American, so he must be rich too.

5. What does the writer want us to conclude?

   _____

   _____

6. How could you show that the argument is faulty?

   _____

   _____

   _____

★ **A** In the passage below, the verbs **has** and **have** and the verbs **is** and **are** are used incorrectly six times. Cross out each incorrect word. Write the correct word above it.

Everybody in my class are very excited when we have a substitute teacher. Some students in the class has many ways to upset a substitute teacher. But usually, if the substitute are prepared for class, everybody have a good day. Some classes are rowdy and has a bad reputation with substitutes. But our regular teacher always leaves lots of work for us to do. Our class are always too busy to fool around.

B Underline the redundant part in each sentence below. Then explain why the underlined part is redundant by filling in the blanks.

1. **As a boss, she managed other people.**

If _____

_____,

then _____

_____.

2. **I got sick last winter and wasn't healthy.**

If _____

_____,

then _____

_____.

3. **The clarity of his argument made it clear.**

If _____

_____,

then _____

_____

_____.

ERRORS | W | B | T

★ **A** Read the passage. Find a statement that contradicts an earlier statement.

- Underline the statement you assume to be true.
- Circle the contradiction.
- Make up an if-then statement that explains the contradiction.

Mr. Flimp was in favor of using the death penalty for a wide range of crimes. "Times are not what they used to be, because the cities are different and the problems in the cities are different from the problems experienced in the past." He continued, "The best way to hold crime down is to let criminals know that if they get caught, they will receive the death penalty." Mr. Flimp concluded his argument by saying, "As Andrew Jackson said in 1814, 'They won't steal if they know they will die for their crime.' The words of Andrew Jackson are as true today as they were in 1814."

B Underline the redundant part in each sentence below. Then explain why the underlined part is redundant by filling in the blanks.

1. **We had to row the boat to shore, dipping our paddles into the water.**

   If _____

   _____,

   then _____

   _____.

2. **She exhibited her art by showing it at the museum.**

   If _____

   _____,

   then _____

   _____.

3. **She was a cautious buyer who was careful about what she bought.**

   If _____

   _____,

   then _____

   _____.

★ **A** Write the verb **has** or **have** in each blank.

1. Nobody with brains _____ any reason to worry.

2. Some players on the team _____ gotten their tickets already.

3. You _____ a good opportunity to be first in line.

4. The rain in those four counties _____ ruined all the crops.

5. Wrestlers on the squad _____ to do a lot of push-ups.

6. One of the vacationers _____ more than one boat.

B Underline the redundant part in each sentence below. Then explain why the underlined part is redundant by filling in the blanks.

1. **The music created a sad mood, filling us with a feeling of sorrow.**

   If _____

   _____,

   then _____

   _____

   _____.

2. **He was no longer afraid when he lost his fear.**

   If _____

   _____,

   then _____

   _____.

3. **They devised a new sales strategy by making up a new sales plan.**

   If _____

   _____

   _____,

   then _____

   _____

   _____.

C Noreen sometimes has trouble using the words **who** and **which.** Below is a report she wrote. Cross out the words **who** and **which** if they are used incorrectly. Write the correct word above every crossed-out word.

People which climb mountains are often very interesting. Some of the most interesting mountain climbers are people which climb for a living. These people are called Sherpas, and they live near very high mountains, who are both dangerous and beautiful. These mountains, which are called the Himalayas, have many peaks over 25,000 feet high. The Sherpas guide visitors who come to climb the Himalayas. They often accompany the climbers which hire them to tops of mountains. Mount Everest, who is the highest mountain in the world, was first climbed by a person who was a Sherpa.

D Rewrite each sentence below, using the word **usually, occasionally,** or **rarely.**

1. The girl (almost never) went to football games.

   _____

   _____

2. (Once in a while) Tom likes to study.

   _____

   _____

3. It (almost never) rains in the desert.

   _____

   _____

★ **A** Rewrite each sentence below, using the word **usually, occasionally,** or **rarely.**

1. Our baseball team (almost never) wins.

_____

_____

2. (Once in a while) Sarah likes to sing.

_____

_____

3. Tom is (most of the time) a good student.

_____

_____

B Underline the redundant part in each sentence that follows. Then explain why the underlined part is redundant.

1. I found his repetitive statements redundant.

_____

_____

_____

2. I know that we've made progress because we have moved forward.

_____

_____

_____

3. He had the kind of bird that has wings, feathers, and two legs.

_____

_____

_____

C Each argument that follows is faulty.

• We know that our mayor belongs to the Zeep Club, a club which does not allow black people or women to be members. We can hardly expect the mayor to give all people equal consideration in the course of his duties. We should elect someone new to run our city.

1. What does the author want us to conclude?

_____

_____

2. How could you show that the argument is faulty?

_____

_____

_____

• I can prove beyond any doubt that Abraham Lincoln was never president of the United States. In the mid-1800s, when he was supposed to be president, there were over thirty million people in the United States. There was only one president. The chance of any one person being president was 1 in 30 million. When the odds get this small, we can say there is just about no chance of any one person being president. Therefore, Lincoln could not have been president.

3. What does the author want us to conclude?

_____

_____

_____

• Good steaks are rare these days. You shouldn't order yours well done.

4. What does the author want us to conclude?

_____

_____

_____

_____

5. How could you show that the argument is faulty?

_____

_____

_____

A The passage below contains a word you may not know. Read the passage and answer the questions.

The owner of the house felt that windows are very important, so you can understand why the house was so well fenestrated. The fenestration, which had been laid out by an architect who loved stained glass, allowed much light and air into all the rooms. When the sunlight came through the stained glass, the rooms shone with the glory of colored light.

1. Circle the answer.

Fenestration probably means:

ceiling   light   the arrangement of windows

2. Write any sentence from the passage that contradicts the idea that **fenestration** means **light.**

_____

_____

_____

_____

B Underline the redundant part in each sentence that follows. Then explain why the underlined part is redundant.

1. He bought the kind of automobile that is designed to take people from one place to another.

_____

_____

_____

2. My apartment had been robbed, and some of my things had been stolen.

_____

_____

_____

_____

3. He was a salesperson who sold things.

_____

_____

_____

_____

C Rewrite each sentence below, using the word **usually, occasionally,** or **rarely.**

1. Ron (once in a while) likes to watch television.

_____

_____

2. He (almost never) brushes his teeth.

_____

_____

3. Oranges are (most of the time) sweet and juicy.

_____

_____

ERRORS	W	B	T

★ **A** Rewrite each sentence below, using the word **usually, occasionally,** or **rarely.**

1. John (almost never) exercises.

   _____

   _____

2. (Once in a while) she says something silly.

   _____

   _____

3. The sun (most of the time) shines in the summer.

   _____

   _____

4. People (almost never) insult her mother.

   _____

   _____

5. (Most of the time) she goes to bed early.

   _____

   _____

B In the passage below, the verbs **has** and **have** are used incorrectly five times. Cross out each incorrect word. Write the correct word above it.
There are also three redundant parts in the passage below. Cross out each redundant part.

On January 1, the first day of the new year, many of us has New Year's resolutions. Nobody have as many resolutions as I do, since I always have more than anyone. All of these resolutions has been on my list for a long time. My brother has forgotten most of his already, and he doesn't remember what they were. Anybody who have any kind of sense can remember their resolutions all year. I has remembered the same resolutions for three years now. My only problem is that I can't keep them!

C Read the passage below and answer the questions. Circle **W** if the question is answered by words in the passage. Circle **D** if the question is answered by a deduction. If you circle **W** for an item, underline the words in the passage that give the answer.

Any living thing is called an organism. Some organisms, such as a monkey or an oak tree, are very complicated. Other organisms are very small and simple. Some are so small that we cannot see them without using a strong magnifying glass. Millions of these small organisms live in our bodies. The picture shows what you might see if you looked at a speck of saliva through a microscope. Some of the organisms you see have hairs and move like worms. Others are shaped like spirals. Still others look like little disks.

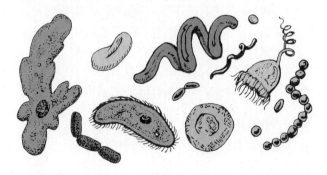

Different types of organisms live in different parts of our body. They perform different jobs. If we didn't have some types of organisms in our blood, our body couldn't fight diseases. When unwanted organisms get in the blood, the organisms that protect the body fight them and try to get rid of them. Other organisms help us digest different kinds of food.

These tiny organisms are also found outside the body. A drop of water from a lake is loaded with such organisms. If the water is clean, there are fewer organisms than there are in polluted or dirty water.

Polluted water makes people sick, because it contains organisms that can overpower the organisms in the body. When these outside organisms win, the person gets sick. Often, the person will develop a fever. Drugs, such as penicillin, contain very strong organisms that can usually overpower the outside organisms.

1. What do we call any living thing?

_____ **W** **D**

2. Which has more organisms in it, tap water or sewer water?

_____ **W** **D**

3. Why is polluted water dangerous to people?

_____

_____

_____

_____

4. How does penicillin work?

_____

_____

_____

_____

_____

5. Fill in the empty box below.

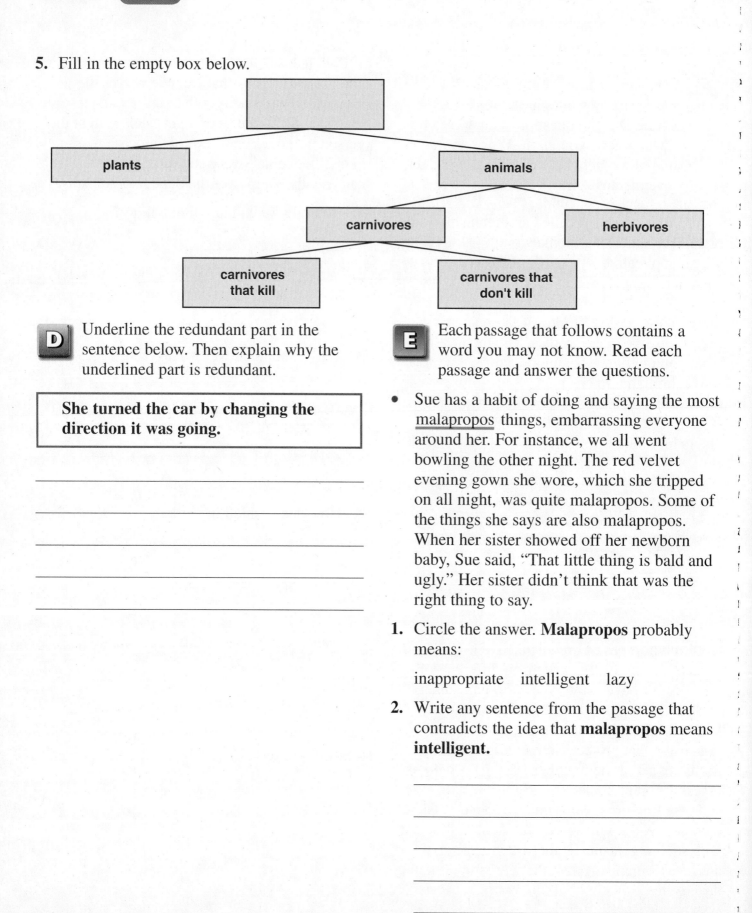

D Underline the redundant part in the sentence below. Then explain why the underlined part is redundant.

> **She turned the car by changing the direction it was going.**

_____

_____

_____

_____

_____

E Each passage that follows contains a word you may not know. Read each passage and answer the questions.

• Sue has a habit of doing and saying the most malapropos things, embarrassing everyone around her. For instance, we all went bowling the other night. The red velvet evening gown she wore, which she tripped on all night, was quite malapropos. Some of the things she says are also malapropos. When her sister showed off her newborn baby, Sue said, "That little thing is bald and ugly." Her sister didn't think that was the right thing to say.

1. Circle the answer. **Malapropos** probably means:

inappropriate   intelligent   lazy

2. Write any sentence from the passage that contradicts the idea that **malapropos** means **intelligent.**

_____

_____

_____

_____

_____

• The handsome musketeer had such <u>panache</u> that all the ladies loved him. The way he swept off his hat and kissed their hands, the dashing way he had of leaping onto his horse and galloping off—these things thrilled the ladies at court. He always had a witty remark and was never afraid. Other young soldiers tried to copy his panache.

3. Circle the answer. **Panache** probably means:

   pancake   greediness   a dashing charm

4. Write any sentence from the passage that contradicts the idea that **panache** means **pancake.**

   _____

   _____

   _____

   _____

   _____

   _____

 You will be tested on a fact presented in this lesson. This fact is:

Any living thing is an organism.

Study this fact. Repeat it to yourself. Writing this fact may help you remember it.

LESSON 97

6. Write any sentence from the passage that contradicts the idea that **malign** means **cheer someone up.**

_____

_____

_____

_____

E Rewrite each sentence that follows, using the word **usually, occasionally,** or **rarely.**

1. My brother (almost never) goes to bed early.

_____

_____

2. (Once in a while) Fred goes to the movies.

_____

_____

3. We (most of the time) eat our biggest meal in the evening.

_____

_____

_____

4. The woman (almost never) ate a large dinner.

_____

_____

5. (Most of the time) our football team wins.

_____

_____

F You will be tested on a fact presented in this lesson. This fact is:

Plants are different from animals in several ways: (a) plants "breathe in" carbon dioxide; (b) plants "exhale" oxygen; and (c) plants make their own food.

Study the fact. Repeat it to yourself. Writing this fact may help you remember it.

A Rewrite each sentence below, using the word **usually, occasionally,** or **rarely.**

1. Our basketball team (almost never) loses a game.

_____

_____

2. I (most of the time) go to the movies on a Saturday.

_____

_____

3. She likes to stay at home (once in a while).

_____

_____

4. Most people (almost never) go ice-skating in the summer.

_____

_____

5. (Most of the time) Jane goes to the grocery store after work.

_____

_____

B In the passage below, the verbs **was** and **were** are used incorrectly six times. Cross out each incorrect word. Write the correct word above it.

There are also three redundant parts in the passage below. Cross out each redundant part.

Last summer I were camping up at Gold Lake with my best friend, who I like better than any other pal. I had never been camping before, so she were showing me how to do everything, since it was a new experience for me. We pitched the tent and gathered firewood. She were up there to go fishing, so we went down to the river, which were near our campsite. While we was down there, she taught me how to cast a line out into the water. We caught trout for dinner and cooked them up for our evening meal. It were tons of fun.

 C Each passage contains a word you may not know. Read each passage and answer the questions.

• They took the prisoner in for <u>interrogation</u>. He was taken to the interrogation room, where three officers began to question him. The interrogation consisted of thousands of questions asked over and over by the officers.

1. Circle the answer.

   Interrogation probably means:

   sleeping   eating   questioning

2. Write any sentence from the passage that contradicts the idea that **interrogation** means **sleeping.**

_____

_____

_____

_____

• She <u>tenaciously</u> held onto her position in the argument. Everybody tried to attack what she said, but she would not give an inch. She fought back. She was so tenacious that the people who tried to attack her argument finally got tired and gave up. She won the argument because she was so tenacious.

3. Circle the answer.

Tenacious probably means:

tenderness   timid   stubborn

4. Write any sentence from the passage that contradicts the idea that **tenacious** means **to be timid.**

_____

_____

_____

_____

• His problem was that he was too <u>loquacious</u>. In fact, he never shut up. He talked all the time, day and night. He was so loquacious that people would avoid him. They couldn't stand to hear him talk, talk, talk, talk, talk.

5. Loquacious probably means:

talkative   lazy   shy   skinny

6. Write any sentence from the passage that contradicts the idea that **loquacious** means **shy.**

_____

_____

_____

_____

D Underline the redundant part in the sentence below. Then explain why the underlined part is redundant.

The little girl raced down the street on a tricycle with three wheels.

_____

_____

_____

_____

E Write whether each statement below is a **statement of ought** or a **statement of fact.**

1. The death penalty is being used again in several states.

_____

2. We should outlaw the death penalty.

_____

3. Canada depends heavily on oil imports.

_____

4. Mike likes to go to the game.

_____

★ **A** Read the passage below.

> Ancient Egyptian legend tells of a time when the world was all water. The water receded, leaving a tall hill of sand. A magic bird rose up from the center of the hill, soared into the sky, and became the sun.
>
> Ancient Egyptian kings believed that when they died, they would join the sun and rise and set with it forever. They had huge pyramids built over their graves so that after they died, the trip to the sun would be easier. To an ancient Egyptian, the pyramid was a symbol of the creation of the world as well as a stairway to the sun.

• Here's a conclusion:

   The ancient Egyptians believed in an afterlife.

1. Does the passage contain evidence to support this conclusion or evidence to contradict this conclusion?

   _____

   _____

2. Which sentence contains the evidence?

   _____

   _____

   _____

   _____

• Here's another conclusion:

   The Egyptians did not believe in magic.

3. Does the passage contain evidence to support this conclusion or evidence to contradict this conclusion?

   _____

   _____

4. Which sentence contains the evidence?

   _____

   _____

   _____

• Here's another conclusion:

   A pyramid had no special meaning to the ancient Egyptians.

5. Does the passage contain evidence to support this conclusion or evidence to contradict this conclusion?

   _____

   _____

6. Which sentence contains the evidence?

   _____

   _____

   _____

   _____

- Here's another conclusion:

  Pyramids served as tombs.

7. Does the passage contain evidence to support this conclusion or evidence to contradict this conclusion?

   _____

   _____

8. Which sentence contains the evidence?

   _____

   _____

   _____

   _____

B Underline the redundant part in the sentence below. Then explain why the underlined part is redundant.

Matt hated his job and didn't like his occupation.

_____

_____

_____

_____

C Each passage contains a word you may not know. Read each passage and answer the questions.

- I liked that suntan lotion except that it was very <u>unctuous</u>. In fact, when I put it on, I felt like a greased pig. The lotion was so unctuous that sand stuck to me and I had trouble getting it off. I think I prefer a lotion that is less unctuous.

1. Circle the answer.

   Unctuous probably means:

   oily   pleasant   yellow   warm

2. Write any sentence from the passage that contradicts the idea that **unctuous** means **yellow**.

   _____

   _____

   _____

   _____

- When the sun is beating down in the desert, you might see something that looks like a lake off in the distance. This is an <u>illusion</u>, because the lake isn't really there. An illusion of a lake is caused by heat waves. Many thirsty people in the desert have wandered after illusions of cool water only to find hills of dry sand.

3. Circle the answer.

   Illusion probably means:

   laughter

   solid substance

   gold or silver

   something that doesn't exist

4. Write any sentence from the passage that contradicts the idea that **illusion** means **solid substance.**

_____

_____

_____

_____

• It is useless to discuss anything with him because all of his arguments are obviously fallacious. The conclusions he comes up with are always wrong. For instance, he said his neighbors were criminals, just because he saw a cop car outside their home. Actually, his neighbors had called the police themselves, because they had been robbed. I have no patience with his fallacious reasoning.

5. Circle the answer.

Fallacious probably means:

full of error   full of fear   frisky   serious

6. Write any sentence from the passage that contradicts the idea that **fallacious** means **serious.**

_____

_____

_____

_____

D Rewrite each sentence below, using the word **usually, occasionally,** or **rarely.**

1. Ann likes to take a long walk (once in a while).

_____

_____

2. Our radio (almost never) works.

_____

_____

3. (Most of the time) he drinks milk with his breakfast.

_____

_____

4. (Once in a while) my car runs smoothly.

_____

_____

5. The school is (most of the time) closed on Saturday.

_____

_____

LESSON 99

Tomorrow you will be tested on facts you have learned. The test will include the fact presented in Lesson 97 and some of the facts from earlier lessons. These facts are:

1. In 1969, the first person walked on the moon.

2. In 1869, the first coast-to-coast railroad in the United States was completed.

3. The teeth and the eyes of herbivorous mammals are well designed for grazing.

4. The eyes of herbivorous mammals allow them to eat and to watch out for enemies at the same time.

5. The right and the left eye of many herbivorous mammals see different things.

6. The teeth and the eyes of carnivorous mammals are well designed for hunting.

7. The right and the left eye of many carnivorous mammals see nearly the same thing.

8. The teeth of a herbivorous mammal are flat, and the teeth of a carnivorous mammal are pointed.

9. Plants are different from animals in several ways: (a) plants "breathe in" carbon dioxide; (b) plants "exhale" oxygen; and (c) plants make their own food.

10. Study the chart below. Make sure that you can fill in this chart.

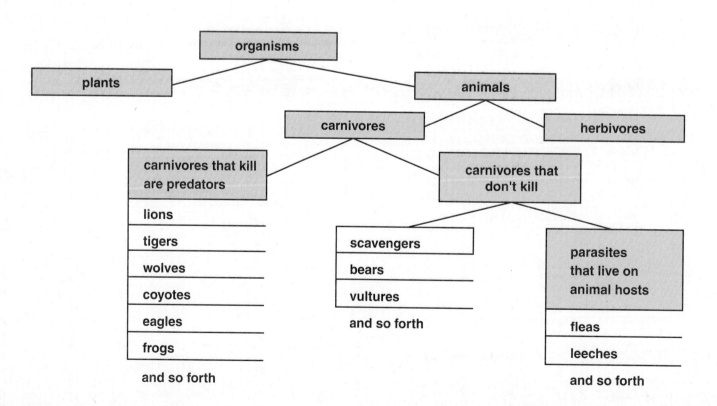

A **INFORMATION TEST.** Answer each item. You have fourteen minutes.

1. Name three ways that plants are different from animals.

_____

_____

_____

_____

2. Name the two parts of a herbivorous mammal that are well designed for grazing.

_____

3. Name the two parts of a carnivorous mammal that are well designed for hunting.

_____

4. Do both eyes of a herbivorous mammal see almost the same thing? _____

5. Do both eyes of a carnivorous mammal see almost the same thing? _____

6. When did the first person walk on the moon? _____

7. When was the first coast-to-coast railroad in the United States completed? _____

8. Why do herbivorous mammals need the kind of eyes they have?

_____

_____

_____

9. How are the teeth of a herbivorous mammal different from the teeth of a carnivorous mammal?

_____

_____

_____

_____

10. Fill in the chart below.

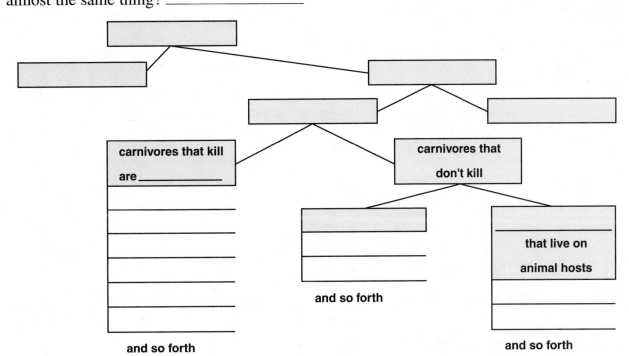

carnivores that kill

are _____

and so forth

carnivores that
don't kill

and so forth

that live on
animal hosts

and so forth

LESSON 100

★ **B** Read the facts and the items. If an item is relevant to fact A, write **relevant to fact A.** If an item is relevant to fact B, write **relevant to fact B.** If an item is irrelevant to both facts, write **irrelevant.**

Fact A. **Kim works as a teacher's aide.**

Fact B. **Kim is taking flying lessons.**

1. Kim was disappointed when fog closed the airport.

_____

2. Kim doesn't make much money.

_____

3. Kim has always wanted to be an airline pilot.

_____

4. Both of Kim's sisters work as nurses.

_____

C Write whether each statement below is a **statement of ought** or a **statement of fact.**

1. Mara should go to college.

_____

2. Mara is planning to go to college.

_____

3. Henry doesn't want to take a typing class.

_____

4. I ought to help my mother after school.

_____

D Rewrite each sentence below, using the word **usually, occasionally,** or **rarely.**

1. The man (almost never) raised his voice.

_____

_____

2. She (most of the time) takes a bath in the morning.

_____

_____

3. I (almost never) eat my entire dinner.

_____

_____

4. Alice rides her bike to school (once in a while).

_____

_____

5. (Most of the time) we take a vacation in September.

_____

_____

A In the passage below, the verbs **has** and **have** are used incorrectly six times. Cross out each incorrect word. Write the correct word above it.
There are three redundant parts in the passage below. Cross out each redundant part.

This city have the best bus system in Canada, better than any you will find for miles around. All you has to know is the bus number, where you are going, and when the bus arrives. (Each bus route have its own printed schedule that shows when the buses arrive and depart.) Everybody have to has correct change because the driver doesn't make change on the bus. Children and those over fifty-five years old has special fares, and they pay a different fare from that paid by other people.

B Read the evidence and write the conclusion for each item.

1. Here's the evidence:

   Each part of the nervous system responds to electric current.
   A lightbulb responds to electric current.

   What's the conclusion?

   _____

   _____

2. Here's the evidence:

   Things that spill oil are fire hazards.
   Beached tankers spill oil.

   What's the conclusion?

   _____

   _____

3. Here's the evidence:

   All dogs are canines.
   An albatross is not a canine.

   What's the conclusion?

   _____

   _____

C For each item, write a sentence that means the same thing by changing the underlined words.

1. The major <u>argued</u> that he had <u>sound</u> <u>reasons</u> for <u>hiding</u> the <u>facts</u>.

_____

_____

_____

2. Tim's <u>reasons</u> for stealing tires were not <u>sound</u>.

_____

_____

3. The police were <u>hiding</u> the <u>facts</u> regarding the crime.

_____

_____

_____

4. Were they trying to <u>hide</u> their real <u>reasons</u> for raising prices?

_____

_____

_____

5. The lawyer will <u>argue</u> that his client's <u>reasons</u> are <u>sound</u>.

_____

_____

_____

A Underline the redundant part in each sentence below. Then explain why the underlined part is redundant.

1. Feeling sleepy, the children were somnolent after lunch.

_____

_____

_____

2. The elephant was a rogue that traveled alone.

_____

_____

_____

B For each item, write a sentence that means the same thing by changing the underlined words.

1. The major argued that he had sound reasons for hiding the facts.

_____

_____

_____

2. What reasons does Helen have for hiding her love from Tom?

_____

_____

_____

3. The manager argued that his facts proved that the Devils had won the game.

_____

_____

_____

_____

4. The spy was hiding the secret facts in a brown bag.

_____

_____

_____

_____

C In the passage below, the verbs **is** and **are** are used incorrectly five times. Cross out each incorrect word. Write the correct word above it.

There are **two** redundant parts in the passage below. Cross out each redundant part.

Almost every country are famous for a particular dish. Italy are famous for its spaghetti, and Germany is famous for its sausages. The United States has become well known for several dishes. For instance, hamburgers originated in the United States, where they were made for the first time. Hamburgers is popular all over the world, and people in many places like to eat them. Hush puppies, which is balls of fried cornmeal, is popular in the southern states.

ERRORS | W | B | T |

A
For each item, write a sentence that means the same thing by changing the underlined words.

1. The major argued that he had sound reasons for hiding the facts.

_____

_____

_____

2. The salesman argued that his reasons for raising his prices were sound.

_____

_____

_____

3. Sound newspaper reporting is based on facts.

_____

_____

4. She must have had a reason for hiding her money in a pillow.

_____

_____

_____

5. Was the report based on sound facts?

_____

_____

B
Write the instructions for this diagram.

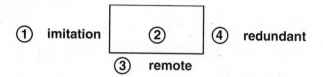

1. (what) _____

_____

2. (what and where) _____

_____

_____

3. (what and where) _____

_____

_____

4. (what and where) _____

_____

_____

C In the passage below, the verbs **was** and **were** are used incorrectly five times. Cross out each incorrect word. Write the correct word above it.
There are **two** redundant parts in the passage below. Cross out each redundant part.

In the 1960s, it were very common to see hitchhikers along the road. They was usually kids who wanted to travel, but they was too poor to pay for plane fare or bus tickets. Hitchhiking were dangerous, and it was also unsafe. Often the kids were hurt by people who picked them up. However, some kids was lucky. They saw a lot of their own country on very little money, and they didn't spend much. Some of them got to meet lots of interesting people.

D Write whether each statement below is a **statement of ought** or a **statement of fact.**

1. It is against the law to kill other people.

   _____

2. You should not kill other people.

   _____

3. We ought to plan a vacation for September.

   _____

4. She shouldn't be out after 11 P.M.

   _____

★ A For each item, write a sentence that means the same thing by changing the underlined word or words.

1. The major <u>argued</u> that he had <u>sound</u> reasons for <u>hiding</u> the <u>facts</u>.

_____

_____

_____

2. Did Art have a <u>sound</u> excuse for <u>hiding</u> his laundry?

_____

_____

_____

3. How can you <u>argue</u> that you won when you're <u>hiding</u> the truth?

_____

_____

_____

4. His report was filled with useless <u>facts</u>.

_____

_____

B Each sentence below has two possible meanings. Read each sentence and answer the questions.

• **She told the tailor to mind his business.**

1. What's the intended meaning of the sentence?

_____

_____

2. What's the unintended meaning?

_____

_____

3. Which word is involved in the two meanings?

_____

• **She said, "Your brother is on the phone. Make him get off it."**

4. What's the intended meaning of the sentence?

_____

_____

5. What's the unintended meaning?

_____

_____

6. Which words are involved in the two meanings?

_____

Read this:

A lease is an agreement to pay for the use of an apartment or house or car for a set length of time.

Use the facts to fill out the form.

Facts: Your name is Sarah Templeton and you are applying to rent a new apartment. You currently live with your parents at 1617 Augusta in Oak Park, Illinois. Your social security number is 443-76-9008. Your present phone number is 383-0907. You work as a cashier in Kenwood's Drug Store at 123 Oak Park Mall. Your pay is $7 an hour and you make $1100 a month. Your expenses are $500 a month. Your father is a painter for New Era Construction Company in Oak Park, and your mother is a salesperson in a small novelty shop in the mall. Your parents live together, and their combined earnings are $38,000 a year. The person who knows you best is Mr. Jim Rowe, who is your supervisor at Kenwood's. His phone number is 434-6758. The bank where you cash your paycheck is Oak Park Trust, 1345 Ridgeland Avenue, in Oak Park. You wish to sign a one-year lease. You have no pets, and you don't own a waterbed.

<u>Application for Apartment Rental</u>

Name _____ Phone number _____

Address _____
                                                  City   State

Employment _____ Reference _____
                 Company name

_____ Phone _____
                     Address

Hourly rate of pay _____ Earnings per month _____

Parents' address _____
                                                  City   State

Occupation of father _____ Occupation of mother _____

Current monthly expenses _____ Bank where you do business _____

Lease desired: 1 year   2 years   3 years   (Circle one)

Do you wish to keep pets in the apartment? Yes _____ No _____

Do you own a waterbed? Yes _____ No _____

★ Look at this diagram:

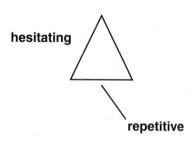

hesitating

repetitive

The diagram contradicts part of these instructions:

1. Draw a triangle.

2. Write the word **hesitating** to the left of the triangle.

3. Under the triangle, make a line that slants up to the right.

4. At the bottom of the slanted line, write the word **repetitive.**

Circle the instruction that the diagram contradicts.
Draw a new diagram that follows the instructions.

B Each sentence that follows has two possible meanings. Read each sentence and answer the questions.

● **He looked for Jane's residence in the telephone book.**

1. What's the intended meaning of the sentence?

_____

_____

2. What's the unintended meaning?

_____

_____

3. Which word is involved in the two meanings?

_____

● **The headline read, "New business folds."**

4. What's the intended meaning of the sentence?

_____

_____

5. What's the unintended meaning?

_____

_____

6. Which word is involved in the two meanings?

_____

C Write whether each statement below is a **statement of ought** or a **statement of fact.**

1. Most people ought to buy our brand of toothpaste.

   _____

2. Most people bought our brand of toothpaste.

   _____

3. Many of the customers wanted spaghetti for dinner.

   _____

4. Eighty percent of the people in this town use our garbage service.

   _____

D For each item, write a sentence that means the same thing by changing the underlined words.

1. He showed new facts that supported his argument.

   _____

   _____

2. Mayor Bill's answer was very unclear.

   _____

   _____

3. The crook was hiding the money in a paper bag.

   _____

   _____

LESSON 106

ERRORS W B T

★ **A** For each item, write a sentence that means the same thing by changing the underlined words.

1. The major argued that he had sound reasons for hiding the facts.

_____

_____

_____

2. The student's answer was quite fitting, and she was filled with pride.

_____

_____

_____

3. His report was repetitive and showed no understanding of the topic.

_____

_____

_____

4. The prisoner didn't have the chance to break any rules.

_____

_____

_____

B Each sentence that follows has two possible meanings. Read each sentence and answer the questions.

• **The chairperson said, "We stand for everything worthwhile."**

1. What's the intended meaning of the sentence?

_____

_____

2. What's the unintended meaning?

_____

_____

3. Which words are involved in the two meanings?

_____

• **The city manager said, "We will support the new building."**

4. What's the intended meaning of the sentence?

_____

_____

5. What's the unintended meaning?

_____

_____

6. Which word is involved in the two meanings?

_____

- **An army colonel said, "I will stand behind my troops."**

7. What's the intended meaning of the sentence?

_____

_____

8. What's the unintended meaning?

_____

_____

9. Which words are involved in the two meanings?

_____

 You will be tested on a fact presented in this lesson. This fact is:

> **When an animal hibernates, it curls up in a safe place and sleeps for a long period of time.**

Study this fact. Repeat it to yourself. Writing this fact may help you remember it.

★ **A** Each sentence that follows has two possible meanings. Read each sentence and answer the questions.

• **That solution seems very simple to me.**

1. What's the intended meaning of the sentence?

   _____

   _____

2. What's the unintended meaning?

   _____

   _____

3. Which word is involved in the two meanings?

   _____

• **They found the used-car salesman to be very slippery.**

4. What's the intended meaning of the sentence?

   _____

   _____

5. What's the unintended meaning?

   _____

   _____

6. Which word is involved in the two meanings?

   _____

• **In the end, he received a series of rabies shots.**

7. What's the intended meaning of the sentence?

   _____

   _____

8. What's the unintended meaning?

   _____

   _____

9. Which words are involved in the two meanings?

   _____

B Underline the redundant part in each sentence below. Then explain why the underlined part is redundant.

1. He sanctioned her action, approving of what she did.

_____

_____

_____

_____

_____

2. She was scrupulous about her work, attending carefully to every detail.

_____

_____

_____

_____

_____

_____

3. The project was completely finished.

_____

_____

_____

_____

C You will be tested on a fact presented in this lesson. This fact is:

Inflation means that prices keep going up.

Study this fact. Repeat it to yourself. Writing this fact may help you remember it.

ERRORS	W	B	T

★ **A** In the passage below, the verbs **has** and **have** are used incorrectly five times. Cross out each incorrect word. Write the correct word above it.

There are three redundant parts in the passage below. Cross out each redundant part.

This year our soccer team have won every game so far, beating every team we've played. The coaches has helped a lot with our offense. Most of the players has done a good job on defense, especially me. Some members of the team has been playing soccer for only a couple of years, but they do all right considering that they haven't played the game for more than two years. Our best player is from England. He have been scoring about two goals a game. Nobody's legs are more powerful than his, which are more powerful than anyone else's.

B In each deduction below, the rule is missing. Read each deduction and then answer the questions.

• **If you stay slim, you'll live longer. Therefore, you should stay slim.**

1. What kind of statement is the conclusion?

_____

2. So, what do you know about the missing rule?

_____

_____

3. Write the missing rule.

_____

_____

• **If you work hard at your studies, you'll get smart. Therefore, you should work hard at your studies.**

4. What kind of statement is the conclusion?

_____

5. So, what do you know about the missing rule?

_____

_____

6. Write the missing rule.

_____

_____

C Each sentence that follows has two possible meanings. Read each sentence and answer the questions.

- **The ghost felt he needed somebody to lift his spirits.**

1. What's the intended meaning of the sentence?

_____

_____

_____

2. What's the unintended meaning?

_____

_____

_____

3. Which word is involved in the two meanings?

_____

- **For three years, quarterback Bosse carried the entire team.**

4. What's the intended meaning of the sentence?

_____

_____

_____

_____

5. What's the unintended meaning?

_____

_____

_____

6. Which word is involved in the two meanings?

_____

- **He decided to run for the office of mayor.**

7. What's the intended meaning of the sentence?

_____

_____

8. What's the unintended meaning?

_____

_____

9. Which words are involved in the two meanings?

_____

★ **A** Read each deduction and write the answers to the questions.

- **We shouldn't damage our ears.**
  Listening to extremely loud music damages our ears.
  Therefore, we shouldn't listen to extremely loud music.

1. What kind of statement does the deduction begin with?

_____

2. Is the deduction valid?

_____

3. Explain.

_____

_____

_____

- **Coyotes kill chickens and sheep.**
  We like chickens and sheep.
  Therefore, we should kill coyotes.

4. What kind of statement does the deduction begin with?

_____

5. Is the deduction valid?

_____

6. Explain.

_____

_____

_____

_____

B Read the passage and answer the questions. Circle **W** if the question is answered by words in the passage. Circle **D** if the question is answered by a deduction. If you circle **W** for an item, underline the words in the passage that give the answer.

Some things will rot if they are left in the air. Another word for **rot** is **decompose.** Things that decompose start out as one material and turn into another material. Rocks do not decompose, nor does water. Leaves decompose and turn into a soggy mass that no longer looks like leaves. When animals decompose, their flesh becomes rotten. If they decompose long enough, they will become shriveled.

Tiny organisms are responsible for much of the change that occurs when matter decomposes. These organisms are called **decomposers.** They are very small plants that have no chlorophyll; therefore, they cannot convert sunlight into food. They get their food by eating the flesh or waste material of other organisms.

When you read about decomposers, you may think they are nothing but filthy little organisms, but think of what the world would be like if there were no decomposers. Leaves from hundreds of years ago would be piled on the ground along with remains of other plants. The bodies of dead animals and their waste material would be piled hundreds of kilometers high.

The decomposers do more than rid the world of this dead matter. As they eat the remains of the animals, they give off waste matter that is high in nitrogen. Nitrogen helps plants grow, so the decomposers actually help many things live.

1. Why can't decomposers convert sunlight into food?

_____

_____ **W   D**

2. How do decomposers get their food?

_____

_____

_____ **W   D**

3. Are decomposers plants, or are they animals?

_____ **W   D**

4. How do decomposers help plants?

_____

_____

_____

_____

5. What would the world look like if there were no decomposers?

_____

_____

_____

_____

6. What's another word for **rot?**

_____

7. Why is nitrogen important to a tree?

_____

_____ **W   D**

8. Fill in the chart below. List three types of plants that have chlorophyll. Fill in the name for the plants that do not have chlorophyll.

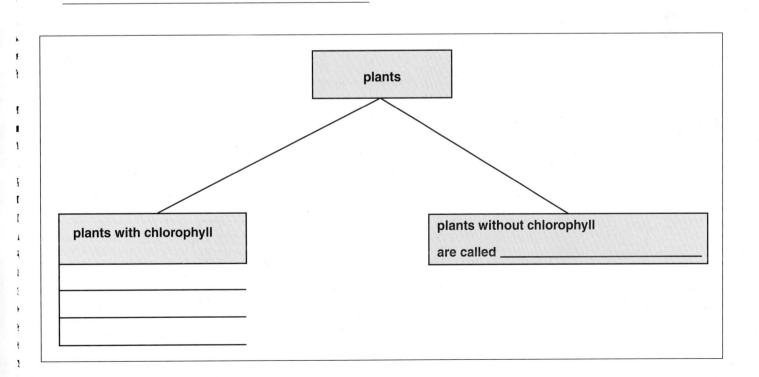

plants

plants with chlorophyll

_____

_____

_____

plants without chlorophyll

are called _____

C Each passage that follows contains a word you may not know. Read each passage and answer the questions.

- The soil here is so <u>fecund</u> that plants grow ten feet tall. You can scatter corn seeds on top of the ground, and two months later you'll have cornstalks taller than you are. The fecundity of this soil is amazing. This ground grows everything from watermelons to strawberries as big as your fist.

1. Circle the answer.

   Fecund probably means:

   painful   fierce   fertile   barren

2. Write any sentence from the passage that contradicts the idea that **fecund** means **barren.**

   _____

   _____

   _____

- She always spoke deprecatingly about her former husband. She pointed out his faults and weaknesses, and she had no kind words for him. Her friends learned to stop asking her about him, because she never missed a chance to <u>deprecate</u> him in public. There was no doubt that she despised him and blamed him for all her troubles.

3. Circle the answer.

   Deprecate probably means:

   nervous   to express approval of
   to express disapproval of   sweetly

4. Write any sentence from the passage that contradicts the idea that **deprecate** means **sweetly.**

   _____

   _____

   _____

   _____

- He <u>extolled</u> her beauty in poems and songs. He extolled her to his friends by speaking of her grace and her kindness, her wisdom and her generosity. He seemed unable to say anything but good about her. According to him, she was the best at everything.

5. Circle the answer.

   Extol probably means:

   eat   speak evil of   listen   praise

6. Write any sentence from the passage that contradicts the idea that **extol** means **speak evil of.**

   _____

   _____

   _____

   _____

D You will be tested on a fact presented in this lesson. This fact is:

> **Plants that do not have chlorophyll are decomposers.**

Study this fact. Repeat it to yourself. Writing this fact may help you remember it.

E Tomorrow you will be tested on facts you have learned. The test will include all of the facts presented in Lessons 97–107, and some of the facts from earlier lessons. These facts are:

1. The word **ecology** comes from a Greek word that means **house.**

2. A hundred years ago, people were not concerned with ecology because they believed there was no end to different types of wildlife.

3. Living things are designed to keep living.

4. Leonardo da Vinci was an inventor, a painter, a musician, and a scientist.

5. A cold war happens when two countries are close to being in a shooting war with each other.

6. Plants are different from animals in several ways: (a) plants "breathe in" carbon dioxide; (b) plants "exhale" oxygen; and (c) plants make their own food.

7. When an animal hibernates, it curls up in a safe place and sleeps for a long time.

8. Inflation means that prices keep going up.

9. Carnivorous animals eat other animals.

10. Study the chart below. Make sure that you can fill in this chart.

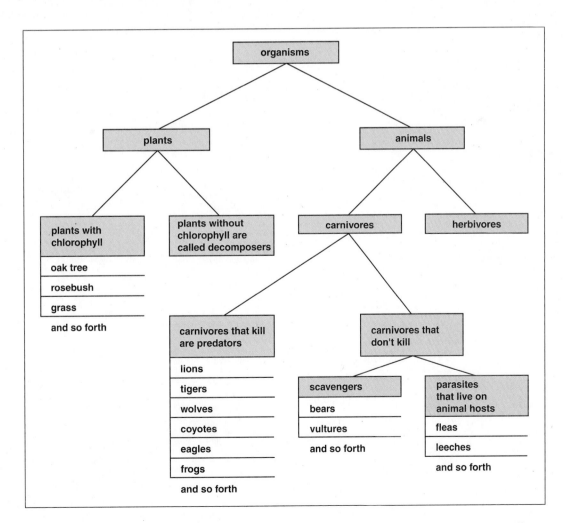

ERRORS | W | B | T

A **INFORMATION TEST.** Answer each item. You have fourteen minutes.

1. What do we mean when we say that an animal hibernates?

_____

_____

_____

2. Name three ways that plants are different from animals.

_____

_____

_____

_____

3. What does inflation mean?

_____

_____

4. What is a cold war?

_____

_____

_____

5. Name three different things that Leonardo da Vinci did.

_____

_____

6. The word **ecology** comes from a Greek word that means

_____

7. Why weren't people concerned with ecology a hundred years ago?

_____

_____

_____

8. What is a basic goal of all living things?

_____

9. What do we mean when we say that an animal is carnivorous?

_____

_____

10. Fill in the boxes in the chart on the next page.

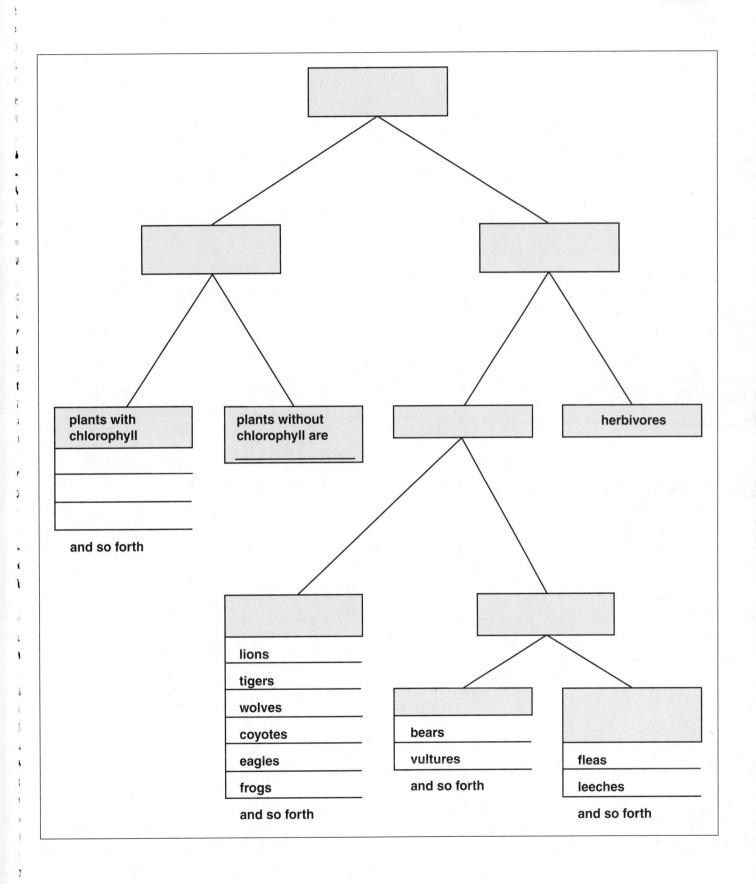

B Read each deduction and write the answers to the questions.

- **High-rise buildings are very impressive. More people than ever before are living in high-rise buildings. Therefore, we ought to build more high-rise buildings.**

1. What kind of statement does the deduction begin with?

   _____

2. Is the deduction valid? _____

3. Explain.

   _____

   _____

   _____

   _____

- **The United States uses more oil than any other country. Huge oil tankers bring the oil to the United States from other countries. Therefore, we should build more huge oil tankers.**

4. What kind of statement does the deduction begin with?

   _____

5. Is the deduction valid? _____

6. Explain.

   _____

   _____

   _____

   _____

C Jim sometimes has trouble using the words **who** and **which.** Below is a letter that he wrote to his friend Ted. Cross out the words **who** and **which** if they are used incorrectly. Write the correct word above every crossed-out word.

Dear Ted,

I have a friend who would like to meet you. He knows which you are because my sister told him that you run for the Rockets Track Club. He lives in Alton, who is near Parkvale. His favorite sport, which is track, is very popular in Alton. He knows which lane each runner must run in at the local track meets. He has several friends who used to run for your track team. The team they run for, which is called the Flying Pizzas, has some world-class runners. The people who sponsor the Flying Pizzas give a free pizza to any athlete who comes in first. Who knows, maybe you will win a pepperoni pizza, which is the grand prize. Let me know where you plan to stay when you run in Alton, and I'll tell my friend to look for you. His name is Randy, which is a nice name.

Jim

D Each sentence that follows has two possible meanings. Read each sentence and answer the questions.

• **When Jack went out dancing, he was dressed to kill.**

1. What's the intended meaning of the sentence?

_____

_____

_____

2. What's the unintended meaning?

_____

_____

3. Which words are involved in the two meanings?

_____

• **It was now Rick's turn to step into his dad's shoes.**

4. What's the intended meaning of the sentence?

_____

_____

5. What's the unintended meaning?

_____

_____

6. Which words are involved in the two meanings?

_____

• **She was the brightest student in the class.**

7. What's the intended meaning of the sentence?

_____

_____

8. What's the unintended meaning?

_____

_____

9. Which word is involved in the two meanings?

_____

★ **A** Read each deduction and write the answers to the questions.

- **We should try to lower the crime rate.**
  Good police enforcement lowers the crime rate.
  Therefore, we should insist on good police enforcement.

1. What kind of statement does the deduction begin with?

   _____

2. Is the deduction valid? _____

3. Explain. _____

   _____

   _____

- **Digger High has the best basketball team in the state.**
  Digger High spends more money on basketball than our high school does.
  Therefore, our high school should spend more money on basketball.

4. What kind of statement does the deduction begin with?

   _____

5. Is the deduction valid? _____

6. Explain. _____

   _____

   _____

   _____

B Write each sentence below with the word **especially.**

1. She was really happy on her birthday.

   _____

   _____

   _____

2. The lake is very full in the spring.

   _____

   _____

   _____

3. The ground was very soggy after the storm.

   _____

   _____

   _____

   _____

C

Underline the redundant part in each sentence below. Then explain why the underlined part is redundant.

1. She nibbled at the cheese, taking small bites.

_____

_____

_____

_____

2. For a lazy person, he was very indolent.

_____

_____

_____

_____

3. The fire was burning.

_____

_____

_____

_____

★ **A** After each statement, write a statement that is more general by using the name of a larger class for each underlined part.

1. Lobster, clams, and sea bass are served at Barney's Diner.

_____

_____

2. Sparrows and pigeons often perch on that tall, gray skyscraper.

_____

_____

B Write each sentence below with the word **especially.**

1. The dog was very glad to come into the house.

_____

_____

2. The dog was really wet and muddy.

_____

_____

3. Victoria Island is a very popular tourist spot.

_____

_____

C Read each deduction and write the answers to the questions.

• **We should fail all students who do not perform well.**
Students who do not perform well score less than 95 percent on tests.
Therefore, we should fail all students who score less than 95 percent on all tests.

1. What kind of statement does the deduction begin with?

_____

2. Is the deduction valid? _____

3. Explain. _____

_____

_____

• **Beethoven's Ninth Symphony may be the most famous symphony ever written.**
Many people have not heard Beethoven's Ninth Symphony.
Therefore, these people should listen to Beethoven's Ninth Symphony.

4. What kind of statement does the deduction begin with?

_____

5. Is the deduction valid? _____

6. Explain. _____

_____

_____

D Read the rule and each piece of evidence. Write a conclusion after each piece of evidence.

> Rule. **Parasites grow, feed, and live on other animals.**

Evidence   Conclusion

1. An ant does not grow, feed, or live on

   other animals.   _____

2. A tick is a parasite.   _____

                                         _____

3. A tapeworm is a parasite.   _____

                                         _____

4. The dwarf pygmy goby does not grow, feed, or   _____

   live on other animals.   _____

E Underline the redundant part in the sentence below. Then explain why the underlined part is redundant.

   The necessary ingredients in the recipe were vital.

   _____

   _____

   _____

   _____

ERRORS | W | B | T

A In the item below, the underlined sentence has two possible meanings. The sentence that follows the underlined sentence makes it clear which meaning is intended. Read the item and answer the questions.

• The boy ate the cake on the table.
When his mother saw him there, she told him to get down.

1. What are the two possible meanings of the underlined sentence?

_____

_____

_____

_____

2. What is the intended meaning?

_____

_____

_____

B After each statement, write a statement that is more general by using the name of a larger class for each underlined part.

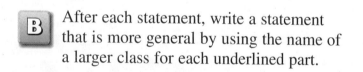

1. A tall, muscular soldier was carrying a rifle, a pistol, and hand grenades.

_____

_____

2. That hardworking janitor scrubbed the walls, polished the floor, and wiped the windows.

_____

_____

C Write each sentence below with the word **especially.**

1. These books are really hard to read.

_____

_____

2. Joanne is a very good auto mechanic.

_____

_____

3. On spring days, I'm really glad when school is over.

_____

_____

_____

D Write the verb **was** or the verb **were** in each blank.

1. I met some people who _____ strangers to me.

2. You and I _____ the only ones who got the right answer.

3. Gravel _____ a lot cheaper a few years ago.

4. Most of the students _____ going to class.

5. Every one of the flowers _____ wilting.

6. Each of these records _____ a big hit.

A In each item that follows, the underlined sentence has two possible meanings. The sentence that follows the underlined sentence makes it clear which meaning is intended. Read the items and answer the questions.

- He set a ladder against the wall and broke it. He had to buy a new ladder.

1. What are the two possible meanings of the underlined sentence?

_____

_____

_____

_____

2. What is the intended meaning?

_____

_____

_____

- When she added ice cubes to the glasses of hot tea, they broke. The tea ran all over the counter.

3. What are the two possible meanings of the underlined sentence?

_____

_____

_____

_____

_____

4. What is the intended meaning?

_____

_____

_____

_____

- Let Mr. Fixit repair your house and save money. He charges less than anybody else in town.

5. What are the two possible meanings of the underlined sentence?

_____

_____

_____

_____

_____

6. What is the intended meaning?

_____

_____

_____

_____

B After each statement, write a statement that is more general by using the name of a larger class for each underlined part.

1. Sweet, juicy grapefruits and oranges are grown in California, Texas, and Florida.

   _____

   _____

   _____

2. The short, red-haired typist likes chocolate, jelly beans, and red licorice.

   _____

   _____

   _____

3. That collie eats orange peels, coffee grounds, and old food that's been thrown away.

   _____

   _____

C You will be tested on a fact presented in this lesson. This fact is:

> **The roots of plants help prevent the formation of a desert by holding down the soil.**

Study this fact. Repeat it to yourself. Writing this fact may help you to remember it.

A In each deduction below, the rule is missing. Read each deduction and then answer the questions.

- **Smoking is bad for you.**
  Therefore, you shouldn't smoke.

1. What kind of statement is the conclusion?

_____

2. So, what do you know about the missing rule?

_____

_____

3. Write the missing rule.

_____

_____

_____

- **If you exercise, you'll stay in good health.**
  Therefore, you ought to exercise.

4. What kind of statement is the conclusion?

_____

5. So, what do you know about the missing rule?

_____

_____

6. Write the missing rule.

_____

_____

_____

B After each statement, write a statement that is more general by using the name of a larger class for each underlined part.

1. Lions, wolves, dogs, and eagles eat mice, rabbits, and gophers.

_____

_____

_____

2. Young boys, older boys, and grown men usually like football, baseball, soccer, swimming, bowling, golf, and all kinds of racing.

_____

_____

_____

3. That strange-looking gentleman in the black suit and tie eats nothing but potato chips, corn chips, soft drinks, and ice-cream cones.

_____

_____

_____

LESSON 116

A Select the right word for combining each pair of sentences. Then write the combined sentence. Remember to punctuate each sentence correctly.

1. The mechanic worked all morning on your car. Your car still will not start.   **so   but**

_____

_____

_____

2. The cement truck backed over the fire hydrant. Water was spraying all over the street.   **and   however**

_____

_____

_____

_____

3. We tease Mrs. Tremain. She is the school librarian.   **who   which**

_____

_____

_____

4. The nurse told Kathleen that the shot wouldn't hurt. Kathleen's arm hurt all the next day.   **therefore   however**

_____

_____

_____

_____

5. Phyllis doesn't like to watch daytime television shows. She did enjoy that game show.   **and   but**

_____

_____

_____

6. Mark got a haircut this afternoon. His father still thought that Mark's hair was too long.   **so   however**

_____

_____

_____

_____

B In each item that follows, the underlined sentence has two possible meanings. The sentence that follows the underlined sentence makes it clear which meaning is intended. Read the items and answer the questions.

• <u>She was looking for her glasses on her knees</u>. She finally found them under the bed.

1. What are the two possible meanings of the underlined sentence?

_____

_____

_____

_____

2. What is the intended meaning?

_____

_____

_____

- <u>My neighbor beat his dog</u>. They often have races.

3. What are the two possible meanings of the underlined sentence?

_____

_____

_____

4. What is the intended meaning?

_____

_____

_____

- <u>She hung a picture on the wall and it fell down</u>. She called a carpenter to put the wall back up.

5. What are the two possible meanings of the underlined sentence?

_____

_____

_____

_____

6. What is the intended meaning?

_____

_____

_____

C Write each sentence below with the word **particularly.**

1. It was a very cold day.

_____

_____

2. His feet look big, especially when he wears sandals.

_____

_____

_____

3. It rains a lot in Seattle, especially in the winter.

_____

_____

_____

4. She was a very good student in high school.

_____

_____

_____

LESSON 116

D In each deduction, the rule is missing. Read each deduction and then answer the questions.

- **Photography interests you.**
  Therefore, you should learn more about photography.

1. What kind of statement is the conclusion?

   _____

2. So, what do you know about the missing rule?

   _____

   _____

3. Write the missing rule.

   _____

   _____

- **If you eat the right kinds of foods, you'll be healthier.**
  Therefore, you should eat the right kinds of foods.

4. What kind of statement is the conclusion?

   _____

5. So, what do you know about the missing rule?

   _____

   _____

6. Write the missing rule.

   _____

   _____

★ **A** Write each sentence that follows with the word **particularly.**

1. Fran's hair is curly, especially after she washes it.

_____

_____

_____

2. He is a very good writer.

_____

_____

3. She likes to watch football games, especially on Saturday afternoon.

_____

_____

_____

_____

4. Sam has a really well-trained dog.

_____

_____

★ **A** In each item that follows, the underlined sentence has two possible meanings. The sentence that follows the underlined sentence makes it clear which meaning is intended. Read the items and answer the questions.

• Don laid the book on the table just as someone spilled coffee on it. He wiped off the book before the coffee stained it.

1. What are the two possible meanings of the underlined sentence?

_____

_____

_____

_____

2. What is the intended meaning?

_____

_____

_____

_____

• Her dress was not fitting. Everyone else at the party was wearing blue jeans.

3. What are the two possible meanings of the underlined sentence?

_____

_____

_____

4. What is the intended meaning?

_____

_____

• The woman took out a cigarette, lit a match, and began to smoke. The waiter poured some water on her to put out the fire.

5. What are the two possible meanings of the underlined sentence?

_____

_____

_____

_____

6. What is the intended meaning?

_____

_____

_____

B Underline the redundant part in each sentence that follows. Then explain why the underlined part is redundant.

1. A car is a lethal object, capable of killing living things.

_____

_____

_____

_____

340 *LESSON 118*

2. The preceding event occurred earlier.

_____

_____

_____

_____

3. The bolts were made of metallic steel.

_____

_____

_____

_____

C Read the passage and answer the questions. Circle **W** if the question is answered by words in the passage. Circle **D** if the question is answered by a deduction. If you circle **W** for an item, underline the words in the passage that give the answer.

Even though a cow does not eat animals the way a carnivore does, it receives much of its nourishment from very small animals that live in one of its stomachs. That's right, a cow has more than one stomach. Here's how a cow "eats animals."

The cow eats grass. Grass is mostly cellulose, a kind of woody material. If a carnivore ate only grass, the carnivore would not get much nourishment from the meal because the carnivore has no way to break the cellulose down into materials the body can use to build muscle or to provide energy.

Cows and some other grazing animals are different. They have a way of converting grass into a meal that is rich in protein. A cow eats grass, and the grass goes into the cow's first stomach. Inside this stomach are animals that can digest cellulose. These tiny organisms eat the grass.

While billions of these organisms are eating the grass, the organisms and the grass move to the next stomach. This stomach digests protein. The organisms that eat cellulose are rich in protein, so the stomach digests them. Although the cow is eating only grass, the cow is also digesting protein. This process continues as long as the cow lives. In the cow's first stomach, organisms digest the cellulose contained in plants. In the cow's second stomach, the organisms are digested. Without these organisms that eat cellulose, the cow would not receive the nourishment that it needs, and it would soon die.

1. What is grass mainly composed of?

_____ **W** **D**

2. Why can't a lion get nourishment from eating only grass?

_____

_____

_____ **W** **D**

3. Explain what happens in the first stomach of a cow.

_____

_____

_____

_____

4. Explain what happens in the second stomach of a cow.

_____

_____

_____

_____

5. What would happen to a cow if it had no organisms that eat cellulose in its stomach?

_____

_____

_____

_____ **W   D**

D Each sentence that follows has two possible meanings. Read each sentence and answer the questions.

• **The Tigers slaughtered the Buckeyes in tonight's game.**

1. What's the intended meaning of the sentence?

_____

_____

2. What's the unintended meaning?

_____

_____

3. Which word is involved in the two meanings?

_____

• **The headline read, "Stock market crashes."**

4. What's the intended meaning of the sentence?

_____

_____

_____

5. What's the unintended meaning?

_____

_____

6. Which word is involved in the two meanings?

_____

• **They had a heated argument.**

7. What's the intended meaning of the sentence?

_____

_____

8. What's the unintended meaning?

_____

_____

9. Which word is involved in the two meanings?

_____

E Copy each sentence that follows, using the word **especially** or **particularly** to fill in the blank. Use **especially** in two sentences and **particularly** in two sentences.

1. The sun is _____ hot today.

_____

_____

2. She likes to fix cars, _____ old convertibles.

_____

_____

3. He reads a lot, _____ mystery novels.

_____

_____

4. They are building that house _____ fast.

_____

_____

F You will be tested on some facts presented in this lesson. These facts are:

> **1. In a cow's first stomach, organisms digest the cellulose contained in plants.**
> **2. In a cow's second stomach, the organisms are digested.**

Study these facts. Repeat them to yourself. Writing the facts may help you to remember them.

A The arguments below have an ought statement for a conclusion. Complete the deductions after each argument by writing the missing rule and the conclusion. The evidence that the author uses in the argument is already written for you.

1. The judge leaned closer to the defendant. "You shouldn't steal, because stealing is against the law," the judge said. "Next time it happens, I'll see that you go to jail."

   ▌ *Rule:* _____

   _____

   _____

   ▌ *Evidence:* Stealing is against the law.

   ▌ *Conclusion:* _____

   _____

   _____

2. You're old enough to know better. Smoking is very bad for you, so you shouldn't smoke. That's the last time I'm going to tell you. From now on, it's up to you.

   ▌ *Rule:* _____

   _____

   _____

   ▌ *Evidence:* Smoking is very bad for you.

   ▌ *Conclusion:* _____

   _____

   _____

★ **B** After each statement, write a statement that is more general by using the name of a larger class for each underlined part.

1. The little dark-eyed girl who served customers in the resturant carried a tray full of hamburgers, milkshakes, fries, hotdogs, and soft drinks.

   _____

   _____

   _____

   _____

2. That half-grown colt rubbed against a thick-trunked black oak.

   _____

   _____

   _____

3. Spoons, forks, and knives were rattling around inside a dishwasher.

   _____

   _____

   _____

   _____

C Read the passage and answer the questions. Circle **W** if the question is answered by words in the passage. Circle **D** if the question is answered by a deduction. If you circle **W** for an item, underline the words in the passage that give the answer.

In Africa, there is a special partnership between tickbirds and large land animals such as the rhinoceros. Both the rhino and the tickbird benefit from this partnership.

The tickbird is a medium-sized bird that gets food from the rhino's hide. The bird spends most of its life riding on the rhino's back, pecking away at the ticks that get into folds of the skin and ears. (Ticks are small parasites that dig into the skin and drink the host's blood.) The tickbird is well equipped for eating these ticks. It has special claws that enable it to walk upside down on the rhino's belly and pick lice and ticks from places that are hard to reach. One of the few times the tickbird leaves the rhino is when the rhino wallows and rolls in a muddy marsh.

The tickbird benefits from the partnership because the rhino provides its food. The tickbird also gets free transportation. The rhino benefits because the tickbird gets rid of bothersome parasites. The rhino receives another benefit—a pair of sharp eyes. The rhinoceros cannot see very far, but the tickbird has keen eyes. When an animal (or hunter) approaches, the tickbird lets out a distinctive cry, a warning to the nearsighted rhino. If the rhino is sleeping or does not pay attention to the tickbird's

warning, the tickbird will hop onto the rhino's head and give it a few brisk pecks on the top of the skull. The rhino usually responds to this second warning.

1. Name two benefits the host receives from the partnership explained in the story.

_____

_____

_____ **W**   **D**

2. Name two benefits the tickbird receives from the partnership.

_____

_____ **W**   **D**

3. How does the tickbird first signal danger?

_____

_____

4. What do the bird's special claws enable it to do?

_____

_____

5. What part of the host would not receive attention if the tickbird did not have these claws?

_____ **W**   **D**

_____

6. Why does the tickbird sometimes peck the host on the head?

_____

_____

_____

7. Why would rhinos feel a lot worse if there were no tickbirds?

_____

_____

_____ **W   D**

D Each argument below is faulty. Read the argument and answer the questions.

• Animals used to live much longer than they live today. I read that the brontosaurus lived for over five million years.

1. What does the writer want us to conclude?

_____

_____

_____

2. How could you show that the argument is faulty?

_____

_____

_____

_____

• Last winter, the city of Dayton used more electricity than the city of Memphis. It is quite apparent that every person in Dayton uses more electricity than every person in Memphis.

3. What does the writer want us to conclude?

_____

_____

_____

4. How could you show that the argument is faulty?

_____

_____

_____

• Don't be ridiculous. I have statistics to show that this prison is the most escape-proof prison in the country. On the average, it has less than one escape every five years. Compare this to Drearing State Penitentiary, which averages over eleven escapes every five years. The statistics show that the chances of escape are very low, so you're being ridiculous when you tell me that there has been a breakout in cell block 13.

5. What does the author want us to conclude?

_____

_____

_____

6. How could you show that the argument is faulty?

_____

_____

_____

E Copy each sentence below, using the word **especially** or **particularly** to fill in the blank. Use **especially** in two sentences and **particularly** in two sentences.

1. She gets along well with her family,

_____ with her brother.

_____

_____

_____

2. He had a _____ good opportunity to get a job.

_____

_____

_____

3. Lynn goes to bed early, _____ on Sunday nights.

_____

_____

_____

4. These new regulations are _____ strict.

_____

_____

_____

F You will be tested on some facts presented in this lesson. These facts are:

1. **A rhinoceros provides food and transportation for a tickbird.**
2. **A tickbird removes parasites from a rhinoceros and signals danger.**

Study these facts. Repeat them to yourself. Writing these facts may help you to remember them.

G Tomorrow you will be tested on facts you have learned. The test will include all of the facts presented in Lessons 106–119, and some of the facts from earlier lessons. These facts are:

1. When an animal hibernates, it curls up in a safe place and sleeps for a long period of time.
2. Inflation means that prices keep going up.
3. The roots of plants help prevent the formation of a desert by holding down the soil.
4. In a cow's first stomach, organisms digest the cellulose contained in plants.
5. In a cow's second stomach, the organisms are digested.
6. A rhinoceros provides food and transportation for a tickbird.

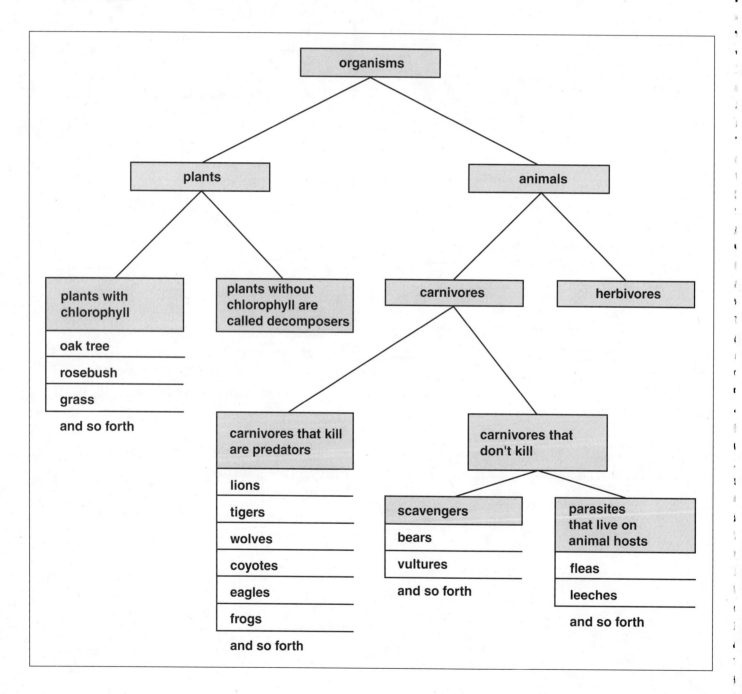

LESSON 119

7. A tickbird removes parasites from a rhinoceros and signals danger.
8. The study of ecology is the study of living things in the world and how they affect each other.

9. An endangered species is one that is nearly extinct.
10. Study the chart below. Make sure that you can fill in this chart.

A **INFORMATION TEST.** Answer each item. You have twelve minutes.

1. Why are plants important in preventing the formation of a desert?

   _____

   _____

2. Name two benefits a rhinoceros receives from its partnership with a tickbird.

   _____

   _____

   _____

3. Name two benefits a tickbird receives from its partnership with a rhinoceros.

   _____

   _____

   _____

4. Explain what happens in the first stomach of a cow.

   _____

   _____

   _____

5. Explain what happens in the second stomach of a cow.

   _____

   _____

6. What do we mean when we say that an animal hibernates?

   _____

   _____

   _____

7. What does inflation mean?

   _____

   _____

8. When you study ecology, what do you study?

   _____

   _____

   _____

9. What is an endangered species?

   _____

   _____

10. Fill in the chart on page 350.

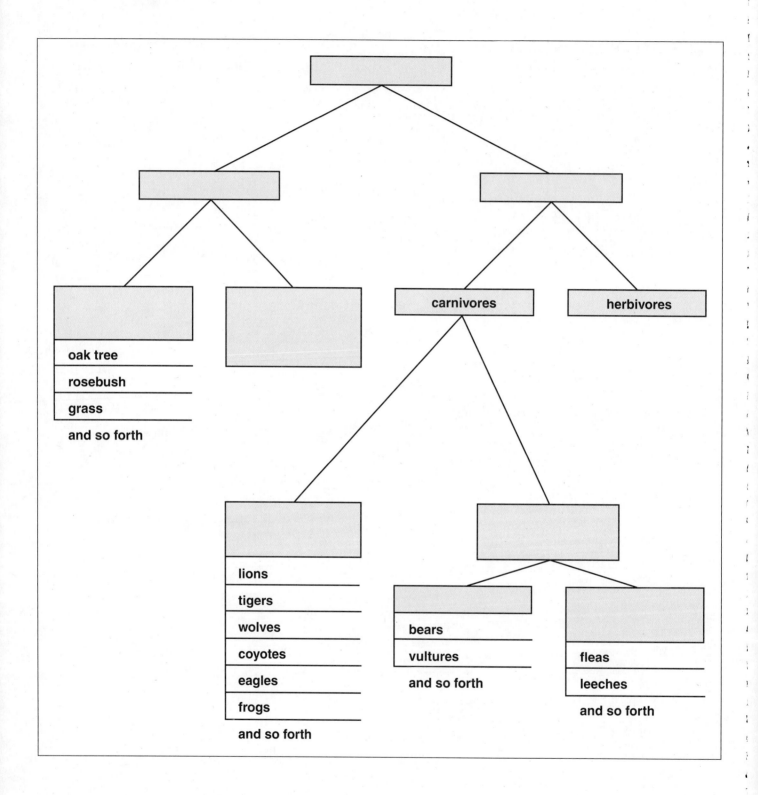

★ **B** The arguments below have an ought statement for a conclusion. Complete the deduction after each argument by writing the missing rule and the conclusion. The evidence that the author uses in the argument is already written for you.

1. The Carlsons were trying to decide where to spend their next vacation. "Let's go someplace in the desert," Kathy said.

"We've been there," her brother said. "Let's go camping in the woods instead."

"We were there last year," their mother said. "How about Lake Gitchie Goomie?"

"Yeah," said Kathy's brother. "We've never been to Lake Gitchie Goomie, so we should go there."

■ *Rule:* _____

_____

_____

■ *Evidence:* The Carlsons have never been to Lake Gitchie Goomie.

■ *Conclusion:* _____

_____

_____

2. Sharon sat next to Nancy in the cafeteria. "Sometimes the food in this place is just terrible," Sharon said. "Look here—canned peas again. Most kids hate canned peas. We shouldn't have to eat them."

■ *Rule:* _____

_____

_____

■ *Evidence:* Most kids hate canned peas.

■ *Conclusion:* _____

_____

_____

LESSON 120

C In each item that follows, the underlined sentence has two possible meanings. The sentence that follows the underlined sentence makes it clear which meaning is intended. Read each item and answer the questions.

- The football star made a play for the cheerleader. She turned him down.

1. What are the two possible meanings of the underlined sentence?

_____

_____

_____

_____

_____

2. What is the intended meaning?

_____

_____

_____

- She put tuna on the lettuce before she noticed it was moldy. She threw out the tuna.

3. What are the two possible meanings of the underlined sentence?

_____

_____

_____

_____

_____

4. What is the intended meaning?

_____

_____

_____

- They stopped the train near the truck so they could load it more easily. When they were done loading the truck, the train went on to the station.

5. What are the two possible meanings of the underlined sentence?

_____

_____

_____

_____

_____

_____

_____

6. What is the intended meaning?

_____

_____

_____

_____

A Write whether each statement below is a **statement of ought** or a **statement of fact.**

1. He plans to go home after work.

_____

2. He ought to go home after work.

_____

3. We will elect a new governor next fall.

_____

4. Minimum attendance at school should be required for graduation.

_____

B The argument below has an ought statement for a conclusion. Complete the deduction after the argument by writing the missing rule and the conclusion. The evidence that the author uses in the argument is already written for you.

First, there was ordinary cleanser. Then there was extra strength cleanser. Then there was Crud-Zip, and people all over the country thought that the perfect cleanser had finally arrived. But now there is something better. Scientists at the Crud-Zip laboratories have come up with a new, super strength formula. That's right. Crud-Zip is new and improved. You should buy yourself a can today.

Rule: _____

_____

Evidence: Crud-Zip is new and improved.

Conclusion: _____

_____

★ **A** The argument below has an ought statement for a conclusion. Complete the deduction after the argument by writing the missing rule and the conclusion. The evidence that the author uses in the argument is already written for you.

In 1996, we began a careful study of different food products, concentrating on what is referred to as "junk food." The tests we did were designed to indicate how much nutritional value each product has. Among the products that we tested was a popular brand of cold cereal called Sugar Crunchos. Our studies showed that Sugar Crunchos have fewer important vitamins and minerals than any other cereal. Since Sugar Crunchos are worthless as a food, the public should stop buying them.

Rule: _____

_____

_____

Evidence: Sugar Crunchos are worthless as a food.

Conclusion: _____

_____

_____

A Underline the redundant part in each sentence below. Then explain why the underlined part is redundant.

1. The organization hired a typist to type things.

_____

_____

_____

_____

2. I noted that all the events that followed were subsequent.

_____

_____

_____

_____

3. Her brother, who had a sister, was the tallest person in the family.

_____

_____

_____

_____

B Each passage that follows contains a word you may not know. Read each passage and answer the questions.

• He was exonerated from the charge of speeding through the city. His lawyer pointed out that he was the only doctor who could help a patient at the County Hospital and that the patient would have died if he had not been operated on within an hour. When the judge exonerated the doctor from the charge of speeding, the judge told the police officer to tear up the speeding ticket.

1. Circle the answer.

   Exonerated probably means:

   painted green   accused   religious
   freed from blame

2. Write any sentence from the passage that contradicts the idea that **exonerated** means **accused.**

_____

_____

_____

_____

• The captain made an <u>innuendo</u> at dinner. He hinted that he might quit his job. What he actually said was, "I won't be here much longer." He said it in a meaningful way. I'm fairly sure that his innuendo meant that he was quitting his job.

3. Circle the answer.

Innuendo probably means:

a story   something said as a hint

something that is said very clearly

4. Write any sentence from the passage that contradicts the idea that **innuendo** means **something that is said very clearly.**

_____

_____

_____

 Read the passage and answer the questions. Circle **W** if the question is answered by words in the passage. Circle **D** if the question is answered by a deduction. If you circle **W** for an item, underline the words in the passage that give the answer.

There are over forty types of cleaner fish. These fish provide a special service to the larger ocean animals, and these animals often travel long distances to receive the cleaner fish's attention. The name "cleaner fish" describes this service. They clean other fish. Sharks covered with lice are often found near a cleaner fish station. Sometimes fish may actually wait in line while the cleaner fish works on other fish!

The cleaner fish goes over the body of the shark or other fish like a vacuum cleaner, removing lice and other parasites. The cleaner fish removes rotten flesh from any injured areas. If a shark has mouth parasites, it will open its mouth and allow the cleaner fish to swim in and eat the parasites. When the parasites are removed from the shark's mouth, the cleaner fish swims out. No other fish could swim into the mouth of a shark and survive.

Many large fish depend on the services of the cleaner fish. Sometimes cleaner fish follow whales and other extremely large ocean animals. A dozen whales can keep many cleaner fish busy.

1. What kind of water do cleaner fish live in?

_____ **W** **D**

2. Would whales be followed by cleaner fish if the whales moved into deep water?

_____

3. How many types of cleaner fish are there?

_____

4. What do they eat?

_____

_____

5. What would happen to the population of cleaner fish if no other fish visited their station?

_____

_____

_____

6. Do parasites attack sea animals other than sharks?

_____ **W D**

7. What does a shark do when a cleaner fish goes into its mouth?

_____

_____

_____

 D You will be tested on some facts presented in this lesson. These facts are:

> 1. **Cleaner fish eat parasites from larger ocean animals.**
> 2. **Sharks allow cleaner fish to eat things inside their mouths.**

Study these facts. Repeat them to yourself. Writing these facts may help you to remember them.

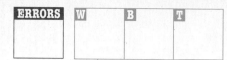
★ **A** Read the argument below and answer the questions.

> We really can't accept you for this job, Ms. Jones. While reading over your job application, I noticed that you held your last job for only six months. I'm afraid we are looking for someone who will stay at this job for a much longer period of time.

1. What does the writer want us to conclude?

_____

_____

_____

2. What evidence does the writer use to support this conclusion?

_____

_____

_____

3. What rule does the writer's argument break?

_____

_____

_____

_____

4. How could you show that the conclusion may not be valid?

_____

_____

_____

_____

B Ed sometimes has trouble using the words **who** and **which.** Following is a letter that he wrote to the Foodville Market. Cross out the words **who** and **which** if they are used incorrectly. Write the correct word above every crossed-out word.

Dear Foodville Market,

Chocolate-covered ants, which are the only things that I can eat, are out of stock at your store. I recently spoke with your manager, who promised me that she would order more ants right away. That was over three weeks ago, and now any girl which looks at me thinks I'm sick because I'm so skinny. The doctor which examined me told me that I must get some ants to eat soon or I will become even skinnier. Which brings me to the point of this letter. Do you realize that there are many other people which need to eat chocolate-covered ants? I have several other friends who have decided to shop at another market because they can't purchase ants at your store. I would like to know who hired your manager. Perhaps I could speak directly with this person, and he or she could order these ants, who

I need to keep up my strength. Please reply soon because I'm getting weaker every day.

Sincerely yours,

Edward Entomol

C Read the passage and answer the questions. Circle **W** if the question is answered by words in the passage. Circle **D** if the question is answered by a deduction. If you circle **W** for an item, underline the words in the passage that give the answer.

Below is a picture of a crab. Crabs live in water and on beaches. The crab's hard shell is solid except for one small tender spot on the underside of its body.

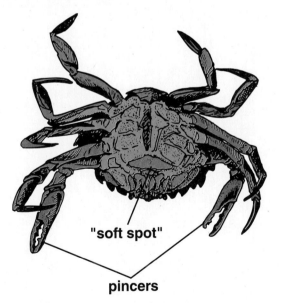

"soft spot"

pincers

Most smaller predators could not kill a crab by attacking its back or its front. Attacking a crab from the front is not a good idea, because the crab's pincers are so strong that they could snip off the end of a stick (or the end of your finger). But if a predator could reach the soft spot on the crab's underside, the predator could easily kill the crab.

Reaching that tender spot may seem like an easy thing to do. However, in addition to using their pincers, crabs have developed other methods of protection that make the predator's job very difficult.

The hermit crab hides itself whenever it can. It will hide in nearly anything that offers protection for its midsection—shells of other animals, tin cans, or anything else that can serve as a hard overcoat. While wearing this borrowed covering, the hermit crab can move. It scoots along the sandy bottom of the ocean, looking like some sort of shellfish with crab legs sticking out of the bottom. This sight is not funny for the predators, however, because as long as the hermit crab stays inside the covering, the predators won't be able to eat it.

Some crabs get additional protection from small stinging animals called sea anemones. The crab pulls the sea anemones from a rock and places them on its shell. The stinging tentacles of sea anemones discourage predators from trying to dig into the shell. One type of crab carries a sea anemone in each claw. Whenever a predator approaches, the crab holds the anemones up, and the predator leaves.

Some crabs disguise themselves by attaching plants or other animals to their shells. Doing this makes the shells blend in with the surroundings. The spider crab attaches seaweed or other small animals to its shell. Other crabs protect the tender part of their shells by attaching a piece of sponge directly over the tender spot. Predators rarely eat sponges and, therefore, the sponge disguises the crab's tender spot. Another type of crab disguises itself to look like coral.

1. What part of their body do crabs have to protect?

   _____ **W   D**

2. Does the sting of the sea anemone bother a crab?

   _____ **W   D**

3. How does the hermit crab protect its tender part?

   _____

   _____

   _____

4. Name a sea animal with a hard shell.

   _____

5. Why do some crabs place a piece of sponge on the underside of their bodies?

   _____

   _____

6. How do some crabs disguise themselves?

   _____

   _____

   _____

7. Fill in the chart on the next page so that it tells four ways that crabs protect themselves.

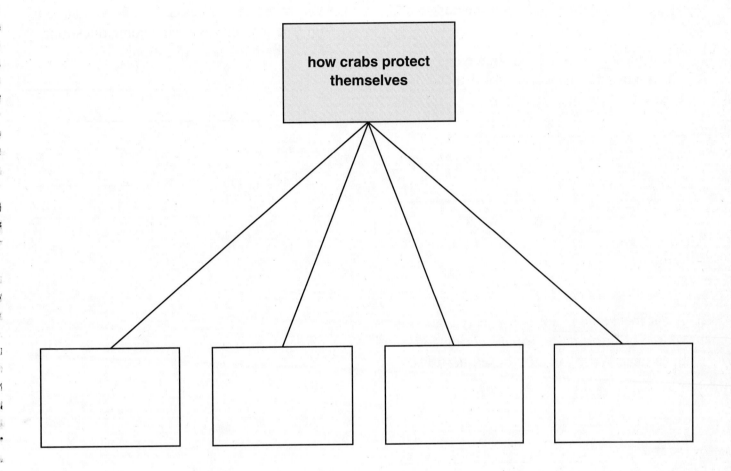

how crabs protect themselves

LESSON 124

Read each item and write the answers.

1. A car mechanic is a good source of information for answering some questions. Write three of those questions.

_____

_____

_____

_____

_____

2. A car mechanic is not necessarily a good source of information for answering some questions. Write three of those questions.

_____

_____

_____

_____

_____

3. A farmer is a good source of information for answering some questions. Write three of those questions.

_____

_____

_____

_____

_____

4. A farmer is not necessarily a good source of information for answering some questions. Write three of those questions.

_____

_____

_____

_____

_____

E In the passage below, the verbs **is** and **are** are used incorrectly five times. Cross out each incorrect word. Write the correct word above it.
There are two redundant parts in the passage below. Cross out each redundant part.

One of the best things you can do for yourself is learn a sport. Some of the more popular sports is fishing, jogging, tennis, and swimming. Each of these sports are guaranteed to keep you in shape both mentally and physically, in your mind and in your body. Jogging, swimming, and tennis is good for your circulatory system and your muscles. Fishing, since it often involves hiking or canoeing, are also good exercise. Fishing are a fine way to spend time outdoors, out of the house. If you get a chance, buy yourself a fishing rod or a tennis racket and learn to use it.

F You will be tested on some facts presented in this lesson. These facts are:

Crabs have different ways to protect themselves from predators:

1. **Crabs have strong pincers.**
2. **Hermit crabs live inside hard objects.**
3. **Some crabs carry sea anemones.**
4. **Some crabs disguise themselves with plants and other animals.**

Study these facts. Repeat them to yourself. Writing these facts may help you to remember them.

★ **A** Underline the redundant part in each sentence below. Then explain why the underlined part is redundant.

1. He was a very intelligent genius.

   _____

   _____

   _____

   _____

2. The giraffe she saw was tall and had four legs.

   _____

   _____

   _____

   _____

3. That winter, which followed autumn, set five records for low temperatures.

   _____

   _____

   _____

   _____

B The argument below has an ought statement for a conclusion. Complete the deduction after the argument by writing the missing rule and the conclusion. The evidence that the author uses in the argument is already written for you.

> "Look, Ralph, there's one of those Multipurpose Kitchen Wizards with fourteen interchangeable attachments. Give me the checkbook, will you, dear?"
>
> "Oh, Martha, you shouldn't buy that thing."
>
> "Why not?"
>
> "Because we don't need it, that's why not."

Rule: _____

_____

Evidence: Martha and Ralph don't need the Multipurpose Kitchen Wizard.

Conclusion: _____

_____

C Read each argument below and answer the questions.

- **I doubt if we will be able to accept your application to this university, Joe. Your record from Smith State is very poor. You skipped classes and almost flunked out your first term. We don't want students like that here.**

1. What does the writer want us to conclude?

_____

_____

_____

2. What evidence does the writer use to support this conclusion?

_____

_____

_____

3. What rule does the writer's argument break?

_____

_____

_____

4. How could you show that the conclusion may not be valid?

_____

_____

_____

- **This guy is very qualified for the job. Unfortunately, he has a prison record. Once a crook, always a crook. He'll just have to find another sucker to hire him.**

5. What does the writer want us to conclude?

_____

_____

_____

6. What evidence does the writer use to support this conclusion?

_____

_____

7. What rule does the writer's argument break?

_____

_____

_____

8. How could you show that the conclusion may not be valid?

_____

_____

_____

D In each item that follows, the underlined sentence has two possible meanings. The sentence that follows the underlined sentence makes it clear which meaning is intended. Read each item and answer the questions.

• I leaned against the building to light my cigar just before it blew up. Bricks and boards flew all over the place.

1. What are the two possible meanings of the underlined sentence?

_____

_____

_____

_____

_____

2. What is the intended meaning?

_____

_____

_____

• My neighbors make good hamburgers, but they're too cheesy. Last time I ate a burger at their house, all they did was talk about cheap schemes for making money.

3. What are the two possible meanings of the underlined sentence?

_____

_____

_____

_____

_____

4. What is the intended meaning?

_____

_____

_____

• She tied the hat to her doll's head so it wouldn't blow away. The wind was too strong and blew the hat off anyway.

5. What are the two possible meanings of the underlined sentence?

_____

_____

_____

_____

_____

6. What is the intended meaning?

_____

_____

_____

E Read each item and write the answers.

1. A truck driver is a good source of information for answering some questions. Write three of those questions.

_____

_____

_____

_____

2. A truck driver is not necessarily a good source of information for answering some questions. Write three of those questions.

_____

_____

_____

_____

3. A telephone operator is a good source of information for answering some questions. Write three of those questions.

_____

_____

_____

_____

4. A telephone operator is not necessarily a good source of information for answering some questions. Write three of those questions.

_____

_____

_____

_____

5. A librarian is a good source of information for answering some questions. Write three of those questions.

_____

_____

_____

_____

6. A librarian is not necessarily a good source of information for answering some questions. Write three of those questions.

_____

_____

_____

_____

★ **A** The argument below has an ought statement for a conclusion. Complete the deduction after the argument by writing the missing rule and the conclusion. The evidence that the author uses in the argument is already written for you.

> "Let's go to the store and get some Smackin' Goo. I heard it's the best bubble gum ever made."
>
> "Who told you that?"
>
> "That guy who dresses up like a clown on television."
>
> "That doesn't mean that it's really any good."
>
> "Why?"
>
> "The guy on television is just trying to sell you something. You shouldn't believe what he says."

Rule: _____

_____

_____

Evidence: The guy on television is trying to sell you something.

Conclusion: _____

_____

_____

B Read each item and write the answers.

1. A doctor is a good source of information for answering some questions. Write three of those questions.

_____

_____

_____

_____

_____

2. A doctor is not necessarily a good source of information for answering some questions. Write three of those questions.

_____

_____

_____

_____

_____

3. A football star is a good source of information for answering some questions. Write three of those questions.

_____

_____

_____

_____

_____

4. A football star is not necessarily a good source of information for answering some questions. Write three of those questions.

_____

_____

_____

_____

_____

5. A plumber is a good source of information for answering some questions. Write three of those questions.

_____

_____

_____

_____

_____

6. A plumber is not necessarily a good source of information for answering some questions. Write three of those questions.

_____

_____

_____

_____

_____

ERRORS | W | B | T

A The argument below has an ought statement for a conclusion. Complete the deduction after the argument by writing the missing rule and the conclusion. The evidence that the author uses in the argument is already written for you.

> Last weekend, I was out rafting on the river and I was shocked to see how much pollution was in the water. I passed one huge factory on the river, the Acme Company's textile mill. I could actually see the goop they were dumping in the river. The textile mill should be closed.

Rule: _____

_____

_____

Evidence: The textile mill is polluting the river.

Conclusion: _____

_____

_____

B Underline the redundant part in each sentence below. Then explain why the underlined part is redundant.

1. That act was followed by a subsequent one.

_____

_____

_____

_____

2. He was a stingy miser.

_____

_____

_____

3. Her dog, a canine named Judy, was always barking.

_____

_____

_____

C Each argument that follows is faulty. Read each argument and answer the questions.

● Look at his entire record. He has entered that little number 35 racer in over 100 races, and he has the longest record of wins in the NASCAR. He's the biggest money winner in the history of stock-car racing. I haven't heard the results of last Saturday's race, but I don't have to hear. I know what must have happened—he won again.

1. What does the writer want us to conclude?

_____

_____

2. How could you show that the argument is faulty?

_____

_____

_____

● The increase in average wealth per person is causing the national debt to rise. The average wealth per person in the United States is now more than four times what it was in 1950. Since 1950, the national debt has also greatly increased. There is no doubt that the richer our people get, the more they put our country in debt. If we want to get rid of our national debt, we should all become poor.

3. What does the writer want us to conclude?

_____

_____

_____

4. How could you show that the argument is faulty?

_____

_____

_____

_____

● The locks on the doors of Mazzo cars are the finest in the industry. They've outperformed the locks of all other cars. They're safer and more reliable. With the finest-engineered door locks in the world, you know that Mazzo cars must be the safest, best-engineered cars in the world.

5. What does the writer want us to conclude?

_____

_____

_____

6. How could you show that the argument is faulty?

_____

_____

_____

_____

D Read the passage and answer the questions. Circle **W** if the question is answered by words in the passage. Circle **D** if the question is answered by a deduction. If you circle **W** for an item, underline the words in the passage that give the answer.

Some trees do not need much sunlight to survive. These trees are called **tolerant.** A tolerant tree is tolerant of shade, which means it can get along in shade. Trees that are not tolerant can't survive in shade. They are called intolerant. The top of an intolerant tree must be in full sunlight. Some trees are fairly tolerant when they are young, but become very intolerant as they mature. Other trees are intolerant from the time they are tiny seedlings.

You can tell whether a tree is tolerant by its shape and by the pattern of leaves on the tree. Stand under a tree and look up. Can you see the sunlight or the sky? If not, the tree is probably intolerant. Intolerant trees usually try to shade everything beneath them. To do this, they put out lots of leaves on top—so many leaves that no sunlight can reach the ground beneath the tree. If there is no sunlight beneath the tree, no competing vegetation can spring up next to the tree to take water or to block the sunlight.

Find a tree whose lower branches are always shaded by its upper ones. If the lower branches are bare and the upper leaves are dense, the tree is probably an intolerant one. On an intolerant tree, leaves that are always shaded die.

Intolerant trees are usually fast growers. They have to grow fast to survive. If seeds from different trees fall on the bank of a river, the fastest-growing trees are going to get the sunlight. The slower-growing trees will be shaded by the faster-growing trees. If the intolerant trees were slow growers, they would be shaded and then die. Just as intolerant trees are usually fast growers, tolerant trees are usually slow growers. They can survive in the shade; therefore, they don't have to grow fast and be the first to reach for the sunlight.

1. A Douglas fir is a very intolerant tree. Is it probably a fast-growing tree or a slow-growing one?

   _____ **W D**

2. In which of these places would you probably find a healthy, young Douglas fir growing—an open field, a forest, or a deep canyon?

   _____

3. A Douglas fir is shaped like an upside-down ice-cream cone. Why would this shape help the bottom branches of the tree?

   _____

   _____

4. What would happen to the bottom branches of a Douglas fir if the tree were shaped like a globe?

   _____

   _____ **W D**

5. What are trees called that can't survive in shade?

   _____ **W D**

6. What are trees called that can survive in shade?

_____

7. You can find young white oak trees growing beneath Douglas fir trees. What do you know about those white oaks?

_____

_____

8. The picture below shows eight trees that are the same age.

- Put an **F** on each fast-growing tree.
- Put an **S** on each slow-growing tree.
- Put a **T** on each tolerant tree.
- Put an **I** on each intolerant tree.

LESSON 127

E Use the rule in the box and the evidence to answer the questions.

> **Every insect has six legs.**

Tom has two insects in his pocket.

1. What's the conclusion?

   _____

   _____

2. How do you know?

   _____

   _____

Rita's pet animal does not have six legs.

3. What's the conclusion?

   _____

   _____

4. How do you know?

   _____

   _____

There are forty-two insect legs in hill 1 and sixty insect legs in hill 2.

5. What's the conclusion?

   _____

   _____

6. How do you know?

   _____

   _____

F You will be tested on some facts presented in this lesson. These facts are:

> 1. **Tolerant trees do not need much sunlight to survive.**
> 2. **Intolerant trees cannot survive in the shade.**

Study these facts. Repeat them to yourself. Writing these facts may help you to remember them.

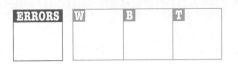

★ **A** Read the rule and each piece of evidence. Write a conclusion after each piece of evidence.

> Rule. **Omnivorous animals eat plants and other animals.**

Evidence	**Conclusion**

1. Armadillos are omnivorous animals. _____

_____

2. Pandas do not eat plants and other animals. _____

_____

3. Pangolins do not eat plants and other animals. _____

_____

4. Rats are omnivorous animals. _____

_____

B Here's what we know:

> **The regulation requires firefighters to wear uniforms.**

For each item, combine one of the sentences with the sentence in the box.

- **Every firefighter owns at least two uniforms.**
- **They don't have to wear their jackets in the summer.**

1. Make a combined sentence with **but.**

_____

_____

_____

_____

2. Make a combined sentence with **and.**

_____

_____

_____

_____

C The arguments below have an ought statement for a conclusion. Complete the deduction after each argument by writing the rule, the evidence, and the conclusion.

1. Over 85 percent of the citizens of Ultuga believe that it is all right to eat another human being if the moon is full. Since most of the people believe that you may eat a person if the moon is full, we should let Ultugans eat people when the moon is full.

   Complete the deduction:

   ▌ *Rule:* _____

   _____

   _____

   ▌ *Evidence:* _____

   _____

   _____

   ▌ *Conclusion:* _____

   _____

2. One man said, "I think that fool we call a president is doing everything completely wrong!"

   "Listen, buddy," the other man said, "around here, we don't like to hear people talk like that. We ought to lock you up for what you said."

   ▌ *Rule:* _____

   _____

   _____

   ▌ *Evidence:* _____

   _____

   _____

   ▌ *Conclusion:* _____

   _____

   _____

Each passage that follows contains a word you may not know. Read each passage and answer the questions.

- When the president was proven to be a cheater and a thief, the country was shocked at such <u>ignominious</u> behavior. Members of the president's staff were later suspected of behaving just as ignominiously and were brought to trial. Many of them went to jail.

1. Circle the answer.

   Ignominious probably means:

   disgraceful   bouncy

   trusting   praiseworthy

2. Write any sentence from the passage that contradicts the idea that **ignominious** means **trusting.**

   _____

   _____

   _____

- The pain was so <u>excruciating</u> that he fainted. When he came to in the hospital, the pain was still excruciating, so he was given a shot to knock him out. The next morning, he could stand the pain. Later that day, the pain became excruciating again, and again he was given a drug to ease the pain.

3. Circle the answer.

   Excruciating probably means:

   unbearable   a tingling feeling
   praise   pleasant

4. Write any sentence from the passage that contradicts the idea that **excruciating** means **pleasant.**

   _____

   _____

   _____

   _____

- The soldiers were camped in ice and snow for weeks at a time without food or warm clothes. They exhibited a great deal of <u>fortitude</u>. Although they were hungry and cold, no one complained. Some of them even joked about the weather. The commander was very proud of his people. He admired them for their great fortitude during these terrible times.

5. Circle the answer.

   Fortitude probably means:

   sorrow   fat   courage   hunger

6. Write any sentence from the passage that contradicts the idea that **fortitude** means **sorrow.**

   _____

   _____

   _____

ERRORS | W | B | T

★ **A** The argument below has an ought statement for a conclusion. Complete the deduction after the argument by writing the rule, the evidence, and the conclusion.

> Lots of people feel that they just don't have enough time to do everything that they want to. Their problem is that they don't know how to do things efficiently. For example, some people walk or ride their bikes to work. Driving cars everywhere saves time. People should drive their cars everywhere.

■ *Rule:* _____

_____

■ *Evidence:* _____

_____

■ *Conclusion:* _____

_____

B Read the passage. Find a statement that contradicts an earlier statement.

● Underline the statement you assume to be true.
● Circle the contradiction.
● Make up an if-then statement that explains the contradiction.

> We had suffered a drought of more than two years. Our land was dry and dusty, and we couldn't grow anything on it. For the first year, we lived by selling our cattle and chickens. We didn't have water for them either. One evening at dinnertime, my husband said, "I think we should sell the farm and move to the city."
>
> "Let's enjoy our dinner and talk about it later," I said, trying to cheer him up. "Everything in the salad is fresh from the garden."
>
> Well, as it turned out, we didn't have to talk about it. By the time we were eating dessert, it had started to rain.

_____

_____

_____

_____

C In each item that follows, the underlined sentence has two possible meanings. The sentence that follows the underlined sentence makes it clear which meaning is intended.

● <u>She put rings in her doll's ears, but they fell off</u>. So, she pasted the ears back on with glue.

1. What are the two possible meanings of the underlined sentence?

_____

_____

_____

_____

2. What is the intended meaning?

_____

_____

_____

- The car was on the bridge when it blew up. Fortunately, the only damage was to one end of the bridge.

3. What are the two possible meanings of the underlined sentence?

_____

_____

_____

4. What is the intended meaning?

_____

_____

- She put a spoon in the soup and it turned green. Nobody wanted green soup, so she threw it out.

5. What are the two possible meanings of the underlined sentence?

_____

_____

_____

6. What is the intended meaning?

_____

_____

D Each argument that follows breaks one of these rules:

Rule 1. Just because two things happen around the same time doesn't mean one thing causes the other thing.

Rule 2. Just because you know about a part doesn't mean you know about the whole thing.

Rule 3. Just because you know about a part doesn't mean you know about another part.

Rule 4. Just because you know about a whole thing doesn't mean you know about every part.

Rule 5. Just because words are the same doesn't mean they have the same meaning.

Rule 6. Just because the writer presents some choices doesn't mean there aren't other choices.

Rule 7. Just because events have happened in the past doesn't mean they'll always happen.

After each argument below, write the number of the rule the argument breaks.

1. When I asked if I should turn left at the stoplight, the man replied, "Right," so I went right. I went three miles out of my way just because that man gave me the wrong directions.

_____

2. We took dirt samples from the east side of the slope and from the south side. Both samples contained far too much ash. I think that it's safe to say that the north side of the slope has soil with too much ash.

_____

3. Sarah had a weakness for gambling. She bet on everything. She tried every game of chance. For a while, she made money gambling, but then her luck turned bad and she lost everything she and her husband owned: the house, the car, and the furniture.

Although her husband, Bill, loved her, he finally decided to leave her. He felt that she had too much desire for taking a chance—a chance on which card would turn up or on which horse would win.

As he left, he turned to Sarah and said, "You've always been a gambler and you'll never change."

_____

4. The principal of a large, city high school said this to a committee: "We have made a decision to permit students to attend only those classes that they wish to attend. We will not give students grades, and we will not require them to come to class every day. Of course, we will try to encourage them to come to class; however, attendance is not required. Our decision to change our school policies in this way is based on the fact that there has been a steady drop in enrollment. Students are not attending classes. They are doing things that are more interesting. So, it was a choice of making the classes easier for the students, or serving fewer and fewer students."

_____

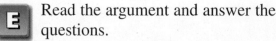 **E** Read the argument and answer the questions.

My name is Giovanni Berlucci. You may not recognize me, because I am an Italian film actor. I've made thirty movies since I was twelve years old, some of which were released here in Canada. This is my first trip to your country, and while I'm here I'd like to tell you about a fine new car, the Distaray. It is tastefully designed to look expensive even though it really isn't. It has a smooth ride, even over bumpy roads. For a mid-sized car, the mileage is great. Just between you and me, let me tell you: The Distaray is the best designed and most expertly built car sold in Canada.

1. The argument uses Giovanni Berlucci as a source for what kind of information?

_____

_____

2. Is Giovanni Berlucci a good source for this information?

_____

3. For what kind of information would Giovanni Berlucci be a good source?

_____

_____

_____

_____

F Underline the redundant part in each sentence below. Then explain why the underlined part is redundant.

1. Every time he purchased something, he spent money.

   _____

   _____

   _____

2. She was an outgoing extrovert.

   _____

   _____

   _____

3. All at once, there was a sudden burst of fire.

   _____

   _____

   _____

G Tomorrow you will be tested on facts you have learned. The test will include facts presented in Lessons 114–127 and some of the facts from earlier lessons. These facts are:

1. In a cow's first stomach, organisms digest the cellulose contained in plants.

2. In a cow's second stomach, the organisms are digested.

3. The roots of plants help prevent the formation of a desert by holding down the soil.

4. A rhinoceros provides food and transportation for a tickbird.

5. A tickbird removes parasites from a rhinoceros and signals danger.

6. Cleaner fish eat parasites from larger ocean animals.

7. Sharks allow cleaner fish to eat things inside their mouths.

8. Tolerant trees do not need much sunlight to survive.

9. Intolerant trees cannot survive in the shade.

10. Study the first chart on page 382. Make sure that you can fill in this chart.

11. Study the second chart on page 382. Make sure that you can fill in this chart.

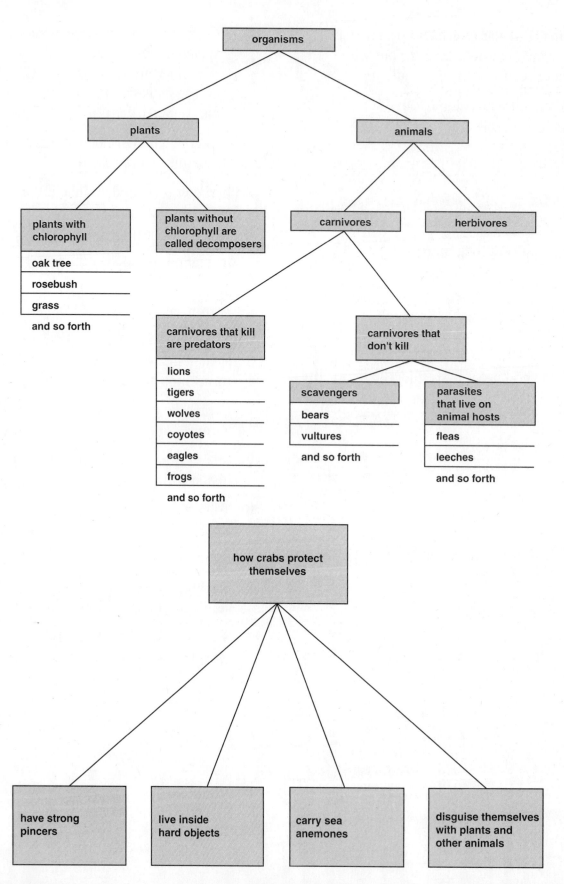

INFORMATION TEST. Answer each item. You have sixteen minutes.

1. What do cleaner fish eat?

_____

_____

2. What do we call trees that do not need much sunlight?

_____

3. What does a shark do when a cleaner fish goes into its mouth?

_____

_____

4. What do we call trees that cannot survive in the shade?

_____

5. Explain what happens in the first stomach of a cow.

_____

_____

_____

6. Explain what happens in the second stomach of a cow.

_____

_____

7. Name two benefits a tickbird receives from its partnership with a rhinoceros.

_____

_____

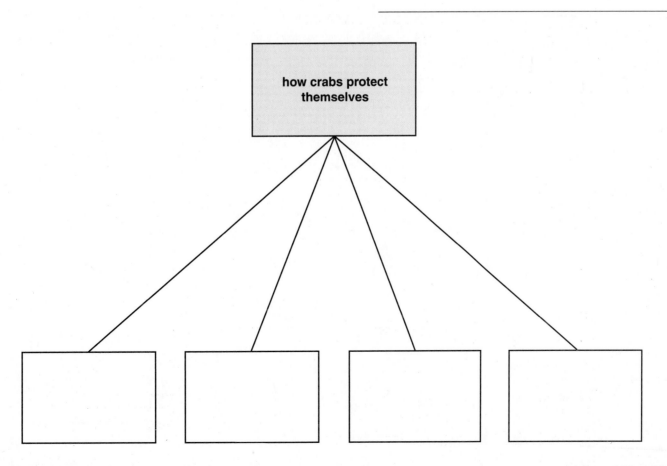

how crabs protect themselves

8. Why are plants important in preventing the formation of deserts?

_____

_____

9. Name two benefits a rhinoceros receives from its partnership with a tickbird.

_____

_____

10. Fill in the chart on page 383.

11. Fill in the chart below.

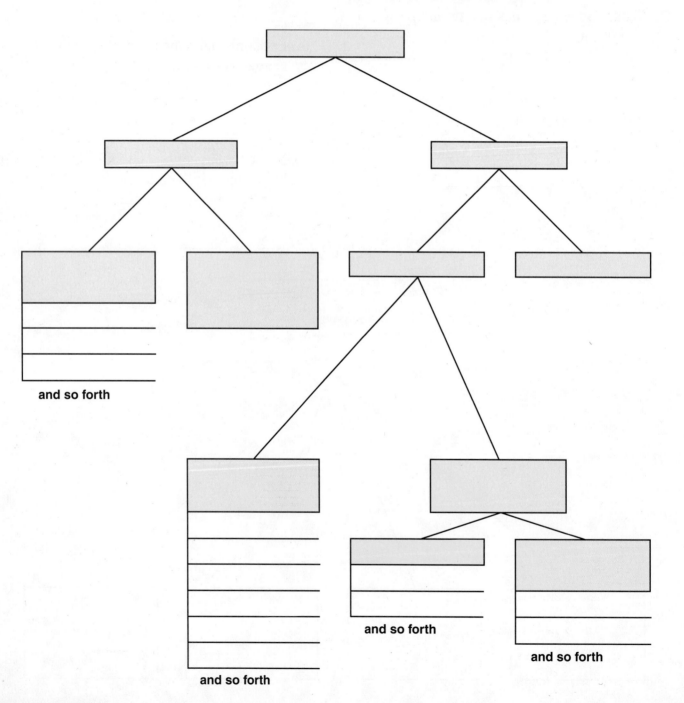

and so forth

and so forth

and so forth

and so forth

★ **B** Read the ads and answer the questions.

● The combined experience of the ten salespeople at Frank's Car Lot is over 100 years. That means that the average salesperson at Frank's Car Lot has over ten years of experience. That's a lot of experience. Come down to Frank's and talk to one of our friendly and knowledgeable salespeople.

1. Does the ad actually say that each salesperson has over ten years of experience?

_____

2. Write a sentence that would be in the ad if the ad said that each of the salespeople had over ten years of experience.

_____

_____

_____

● Five people tried Slimmmm diet pills. Every single one of the people who tried Slimmmm lost over five pounds in one week. What about you? Wouldn't you like to lose some of that unattractive fat around your middle?

3. Does the ad actually say that Slimmmm will help **you** lose weight?

_____

4. Write a sentence that would be in the ad if the ad said that Slimmmm would help you lose weight.

_____

_____

C Read the evidence and write the conclusion for each item.

1. Here's the evidence:

> **High mountain peaks have cold weather.**
> **Alaska has cold weather.**

What's the conclusion?

_____

_____

2. Here's the evidence:

> **Good insulation retains heat.**
> **Glass does not retain heat.**

What's the conclusion?

_____

_____

3. Here's the evidence:

> **A good soccer team must have a strategy that works.**
> **This school has a good soccer team.**

What's the conclusion?

_____

_____

LESSON 130

D The argument below has an ought statement for a conclusion. Complete the deduction after the argument by writing the rule, the evidence, and the conclusion.

"Turn that stereo down this minute. If I've told you once, I've told you a thousand times: You shouldn't listen to such loud music because you'll damage your ears."

Rule: _____

_____

_____

Evidence: _____

_____

_____

Conclusion: _____

_____

E Read the argument and answer the questions.

Ms. Smith has been counseling married couples for over twenty years. She is considered to be among the best five marriage counselors in Canada.

"Many people come to me because they are worried about their marriages," says Ms. Smith. "They are bored and blame their boredom on their partner. They think that the only way to overcome this boredom is to get a divorce. I tell them to take up a new hobby together. Any husband and wife who start climbing mountains or parachuting from a plane will not stay bored for long."

Ms. Smith has been married for thirty years and has three children and twelve grandchildren. If you are having problems with your marriage, I would recommend a visit to Ms. Smith.

1. The argument uses Ms. Smith as a source for what kind of information?

_____

_____

2. Is Ms. Smith a good source for this information?

_____

3. For what kind of information would Ms. Smith be a good source?

_____

_____

★ **A** Read the ads and answer the questions.

• Professional tennis players are very critical about the equipment they use. Among the fussiest of all is Gron Grog, the current Wibley champion. Shortly before the Wibley tournament, Grog switched to the Neilson tennis racket, with the patented vulcanized handle. Here's what Grog said about this racket.

"My game improved perhaps 25 percent with the Neilson racket. It's amazing. In the finals, I beat Trebling, a player I have never defeated before."

Wouldn't you like to play 25 percent better? Try the Neilson racket.

1. Does the ad actually say that the Neilson racket will improve your game?

_____

2. Write a sentence that would be in the ad if the ad said that the Neilson racket would improve your game.

_____

_____

_____

• The Highlander is the toughest jeep on the road. This jeep has been tested for traction over muddy mountain roads, sand dunes, and rocky trails. It has been driven over the roughest terrain we could find, and it keeps its traction better than any other leading jeep. Since the Highlander can perform in rough country, think of what an easy time it will have doing everyday driving chores, such as taking you to the grocery store.

3. Does the ad actually say that the Highlander is the best jeep for **you?**

_____

4. Write a sentence that would be in the ad if the ad said that the Highlander is the best jeep for you.

_____

_____

_____

_____

LESSON 131

B   For each item, write a sentence that means the same thing by changing the underlined words.

1. The <u>rule</u> <u>limited</u> their parking.

_____

_____

2. She had an excellent <u>chance</u> to <u>show</u> her paintings.

_____

_____

_____

3. He <u>hid</u> his true feelings by presenting <u>irrelevant</u> <u>facts</u>.

_____

_____

_____

4. The frightening <u>event</u> <u>changed</u> their excitement into <u>fear</u>.

_____

_____

_____

C   Write the instructions for this diagram.

③ **ambiguous**

② (triangle)   ① (circle)

④ **strategy**

1. (what) _____

_____

2. (what and where) _____

_____

_____

3. (what and where) _____

_____

4. (what and where) _____

_____

D Read the arguments and answer the questions.

• Professor Johnson has been with the University of Idaho for twelve years and is chairperson of the history department. He has received awards for his outstanding research in the field of nineteenth-century bonnets and hats. All those who have worked with him have the highest respect for his keen, inquiring mind. Now Professor Johnson is urging that the city close four junior high schools. Surely it is foolish to ignore the wisdom this most worthy man is offering us.

1. The argument uses Professor Johnson as a source for what kind of information?

_____

_____

_____

2. Is Professor Johnson a good source for this information?

_____

3. For what kind of information would Professor Johnson be a good source?

_____

_____

_____

• Don is an auto mechanic. Don never watched television until about a year ago, when someone gave him an old Stella television set. It must be five years old, but he's never had a problem with it. If you are thinking of buying a television set, Don definitely recommends a Stella. He says it will last forever.

4. The argument uses Don as a source for what kind of information?

_____

_____

5. Is Don a good source for this information?

_____

6. For what kind of information would Don be a good source?

_____

_____

_____

A Read the rule and each piece of evidence. Write a conclusion after each piece of evidence.

> Rule. **One-celled animals can live in one drop of water.**

Evidence	**Conclusion**
1. A paramecium is a one-celled animal.	_____
	_____
2. A sand dollar cannot live in one drop of water.	_____
	_____
3. An amoeba is a one-celled animal.	_____
	_____
4. A sea perch cannot live in one drop of water.	_____
	_____

B Write the verb **is** or the verb **are** in each blank.

1. Several stockbrokers in that firm _____ predicting a poor year for the stock market.

2. You _____ in a better position to decide the answer.

3. Black sand _____ made from volcanic rock.

4. Tables _____ frequently made with wood-veneer tops.

5. Canoes at the lake _____ all rented for the afternoon.

6. Most fresh vegetables _____ very inexpensive at this time of year.

Use the facts to fill out the form.

Facts: Your name is Sarah Liebmann and you are applying for a National Direct Student Loan with the Financial Aid Office of the University of New Orleans. You are a second-year student. Your major subject is biology. Your social security number is 556-56-7090. Your campus address is 1416 Pontchartrain Drive, and your campus phone number is 868-6364. Your parents now reside in Baton Rouge, Louisiana. Your father is a building contractor in Baton Rouge, and your mother is an interior designer. Their combined income for the year is $85,000. They live at 4350 Highland Road in Baton Rouge. You are single and were born June 5, 1978. The loan amount you want is $3000 to cover your expenses for a year. Mr. Nick Boudreaux is the person who knows you best. His address is 1418 Perkins Road in Baton Rouge, Louisiana, and his phone number is 322-4567. The bank in your hometown—where you have both a checking and a savings account—is the Baton Rouge Federal Bank, 123 Government Ave., in Baton Rouge, Louisiana.

Office of Student Financial Aid
University of New Orleans, New Orleans, Louisiana

Student's name ——————————————————————————————————————
　　　　　　　　　　　　Last　　　　　　　　　　　　　　　　First

Telephone number (campus) —————————————　Social Security number —————————

Home address ——————————————————————————————————————

Campus address —————————————————————————————————————

Father's occupation —————————————————————————————————

Mother's occupation ————————————————————————————————

Parents' combined income for the year ——————————————————————

Your year in school:　1　2　3　4　(Circle one)　Major subject ———————————

Amount of the loan you are requesting ——————————————————————
List the name and address of a reference:

Name ——————————————————————　Address ———————————————

Name of the bank in your home city ——————————————————————

Address of bank ——————————————————
Type of account:　Savings　　yes　　no
　　　　　　　　　　Checking　yes　　no

D Read the ads and answer the questions.

- All Miter toys are totally nontoxic. That means that we use paint and other materials that are nonpoisonous. Children playing with Miter toys are totally safe from any possible poisoning caused by paint or glue. If we go to the trouble of making sure that there is no possible way that our toys can poison your children, you can imagine the care we take with every other detail of our toys.

1. Write a sentence that would be in the ad if the ad said that the toys were completely safe.

_____

_____

_____

_____

- Here's some good news for those who suffer from bad breath. Pure and Fresh mouthwash has been designed to fight the germs that cause mouth odor. Pure and Fresh is made from the purest spring waters, and it contains active chemical ingredients that fight ugly bad breath. Available now at your local drugstore.

2. Write a sentence that would be in the ad if the ad said that Pure and Fresh mouthwash gets rid of bad breath.

_____

_____

_____

_____

E Read the passage below.

In early civilizations, people used to celebrate when the shortest day of the year passed and the days started getting longer again. In the Northern Hemisphere, the shortest day comes late in December, which is when the celebration would occur. Many people believe that the Christian celebration of Christmas at this same time of year is really a holdover from the earlier custom of celebrating the return of the sun. Actually, many people believe that Christ was probably born sometime in June or July.

- Here's a conclusion:

> **People in early times were indifferent to the changing seasons.**

1. Does the passage contain evidence to support this conclusion or evidence to contradict this conclusion?

_____

_____

2. Which sentence contains the evidence?

_____

_____

_____

_____

_____

- Here's another conclusion:

  Christmas should probably be a summer holiday.

3. Does the passage contain evidence to support this conclusion or evidence to refute this conclusion?

   _____

   _____

4. Which sentence contains the evidence?

   _____

   _____

   _____

   _____

ERRORS | W | B | T

★ **A** Underline the redundant part in each sentence below. Then explain why the underlined part is redundant.

1. His extraneous remarks were irrelevant to the discussion.

   _____

   _____

   _____

2. She was an average person, like most other people.

   _____

   _____

   _____

3. She permitted the children to work alone by allowing independent activities.

   _____

   _____

   _____

   _____

B In each item below, the underlined sentence has two possible meanings. The sentence that follows the underlined sentence makes it clear which meaning is intended. Read the items and answer the questions.

● My friends told me to eat eggs, but I can't stand them. Eggs always make me sick.

1. What are the two possible meanings of the underlined sentence?

   _____

   _____

   _____

   _____

2. What is the intended meaning?

   _____

   _____

   _____

● The goat took a pear out of the basket and then ate it. It got straw all over its whiskers.

3. What are the two possible meanings of the underlined sentence?

   _____

   _____

   _____

   _____

   _____

4. What is the intended meaning?

   _____

   _____

   _____

- She took the cake from the oven and it collapsed. She fed the cake to the dog and made another one.

5. What are the two possible meanings of the underlined sentence?

_____

_____

_____

_____

6. What is the intended meaning?

_____

_____

_____

 Look at this diagram:

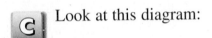

The diagram contradicts part of these instructions:

1. Draw a circle.

2. Write the word **chance** inside the circle.

3. Draw a rectangle under the circle.

4. Write the word **opportunity** under the rectangle.

Circle the instruction that the diagram contradicts.

Draw a new diagram that follows the instructions.

D Read the facts and the items. If an item is relevant to fact A, write **relevant to fact A.** If an item is relevant to fact B, write **relevant to fact B.** If an item is irrelevant to both facts, write **irrelevant.**

Fact A. **Allen hates to travel in airplanes.**

Fact B. **Allen doesn't know how to drive a car.**

1. Allen hesitated when he was asked to fly to the meeting in Los Angeles.

_____

2. Allen rides a ten-speed bicycle to work.

_____

3. Allen doesn't have a driver's license.

_____

4. Allen refused to fly to Hawaii for a vacation that he won.

_____

E Select the right word for combining each pair of sentences that follow. Then write the combined sentence. Remember to punctuate each sentence correctly.

1. Five boys ran after the robber. The robber had stolen fifty-five glazed donuts.
who   which

_____

_____

2. The bus ran through a red light. The police officer gave the bus driver a traffic ticket.
   therefore   but

   _____

   _____

   _____

3. George ate a candy bar. The candy bar was on the shelf.   **who   which**

   _____

   _____

4. Aaron was supposed to go to bed early. He stayed up late listening to the radio.
   and   however

   _____

   _____

   _____

5. Marlene is working her way through college. She works as a waitress three nights a week.
   so   but

   _____

   _____

   _____

6. It rained for five days in a row. The stream did not overflow its banks.
   therefore   however

   _____

   _____

   _____

F Read the passage below. Find a statement that contradicts an earlier statement.

- Underline the statement you assume to be true.
- Circle the contradiction.
- Make up an if-then statement that explains the contradiction.

> It was one of those rare winter days high in the mountains of Colorado. As sometimes happens, a hot wind called the chinook began to blow down the valley. Within three hours, the temperature had risen more than thirty degrees Celsius. Snow that had accumulated on the ridges was melting, as were the icicles hanging from bare tree limbs.
>
> It was so warm outside that Jan and Eddie went into their backyard and sat on a blanket under the maple. Hearing the warm chinook rustling the oak leaves above her head, Jan said, "This feels just like summer."

_____

_____

_____

_____

★ **A** Read the argument and answer the questions.

> We interviewed three chefs concerning our new product, Hamburger-Delight. These people are featured at some of the finest hotels in Europe. We just mixed a little Hamburger-Delight with tomatoes, onions, and hamburger (so easy even **you** can do it) and asked these fine chefs to taste the results. "Remarkable," said the first chef. "Amazing," said the second chef. "Fantastic," said the third chef.
>
> If it pleases these experts, it's bound to please you. Run down to your local grocery and buy some today—but don't be surprised if you can't find it! Hamburger-Delight is selling too fast for grocers to keep it in stock!

1. The argument uses three chefs as a source for what kind of information?

_____

_____

2. Are these chefs a good source for this information?

_____

3. For what kind of information would the chefs be a good source?

_____

_____

B Read the paragraph below.

> Sue worked in a restaurant and rented a room in a nearby boardinghouse. Sue got a new job installing telephones. She moved to a house on Llewellyn Avenue.

1. The paragraph gives a clue about what caused Sue to move to a house on Llewellyn Avenue. What caused her to move?

_____

_____

2. Name two ways that your answer to question 1 could cause Sue to move.

_____

_____

_____

C Read the passage and answer the questions. Circle **W** if the question is answered by words in the passage. Circle **D** if the question is answered by a deduction. If you circle **W** for an item, underline the words in the passage that give the answer.

Graph A shows how a population cycle works. The broken line shows the food supply for an area. The solid line shows the number of animals that live in the area. When the food supply goes up, the number of animals goes up. When the food supply goes down, the number of animals goes down.

Number
of living
things

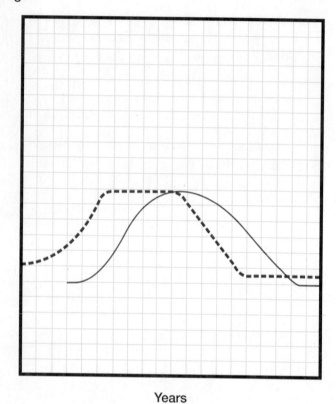

Years

Graph A

Here's an example of how the population cycle works. Let's say that the number of prairie rats increases. These rats are food for other animals. When the number of rats increases, the food supply for other animals, such as coyotes and owls, increases. As their food supply increases, so does the number of coyotes and owls—until there are too many predators for the food supply. When this happens, too many rats get eaten and the number of rats goes down. This means that the food supply for the predators goes down, and many of them starve. When there are fewer predators to eat the rats, more and more rats survive. This increase in the rat population means an increase in the food supply for certain predators, and so the number of those predators also increases.

You won't become confused about population cycles if you remember that the population of animals depends on the food supply. When the supply goes up, more animals can eat and live. If too many of them eat, they will reduce the food supply. When the food supply goes down, the population of the animals will go down also.

1. When the food supply goes up in an area, what happens to the number of animals in that area?

   _____ **W   D**

2. Let's say that the number of predators that eat squirrels increased. What would happen to the squirrel population?

   _____ **W   D**

3. Let's say that the number of insects that woodpeckers eat decreased. What would happen to the woodpecker population?

   _____ **W   D**

4. Write what would happen next in the population cycle for sparrows and their predators:

   The number of predators that eat sparrows decreases.

   The population of sparrows increases.

   The number of predators that eat sparrows increases.

   Then what happens?

   _____

   _____

5. Look at graph B. The dotted line shows how much grass there is in an area. The solid line shows how many herbivores are in that area. If the solid line is below the dotted line, there is more than enough grass for the herbivores. But if the solid line goes above the dotted line, there is not enough grass for the herbivores.

- Complete the dotted line using these facts:
  In 1995, the amount of grass drops to 30.
  In 1996, the amount of grass stays at 30.
  In 1997, the amount of grass rises to 50.

- Answer these questions:
  In 1993, is there enough grass for the herbivores?

  _____

  In 1995, is there enough grass for the herbivores?

  _____

  In 1996, is there enough grass for the herbivores?

  _____

  What happens to the number of herbivores in 1997?

  _____

  Why? _____

  _____

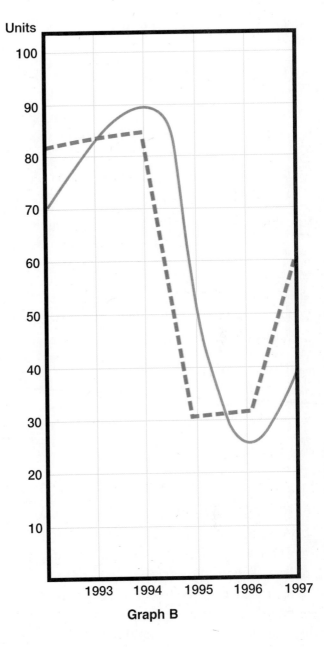

Graph B

D Each argument that follows is faulty.

- The senator said, "Mr. Jenkins says that my bill is absurd. Is this the same Mr. Jenkins who made a $30,000 mistake in the 1992 audit? Is this the same Mr. Jenkins who made a false statement before a committee in 1995? Need I say more about Mr. Jenkins?"

1. What does the writer want us to conclude?

_____

_____

2. How could you show that the argument is faulty?

_____

_____

_____

_____

- I don't know why my dad got so mad at me. Before I left on the date, he said, "You must be home by a quarter of twelve."

  I told him I would, and I went out on the date. When I got home, you should have heard him. He yelled and screamed about how late I got in. I don't know what he was so excited about. He said to get home by a quarter of twelve, and I did. Three is a quarter of twelve, and I got home at 3 A.M.

3. What does the writer want us to conclude?

_____

_____

_____

4. How could you show that the argument is faulty?

_____

_____

_____

_____

- Don't tell me about that mountain. I've flown over it a hundred times. I know just how it's shaped. I know where the glacier on it is, and how it runs. You tell me there's a big cave in that mountain, and I say you're wrong. I've observed that mountain quite carefully.

5. What does the writer want us to conclude?

_____

_____

_____

6. How could you show that the argument is faulty?

_____

_____

_____

E Each sentence that follows has two possible meanings. Read each sentence and answer the questions.

- **Our team quickly jumped ahead of the other team.**

1. What's the intended meaning of the sentence?

_____

_____

_____

2. What's the unintended meaning?

_____

_____

_____

3. Which words are involved in the two meanings?

_____

- **Buffy is a spoiled child.**

4. What's the intended meaning of the sentence?

_____

_____

5. What's the unintended meaning?

_____

_____

6. Which word is involved in the two meanings?

_____

- **When their eyes met, sparks flew.**

7. What's the intended meaning of the sentence?

_____

_____

8. What's the unintended meaning?

_____

_____

9. Which words are involved in the two meanings?

_____

ERRORS | W | B | T

★ **A** Read the argument and answer the questions.

> I'm Alvin Cleats, first baseman for the Tule Lake Tubes. Maybe you remember that great play I made in the World Series. Yes, baseball has been a great life for me. I've had as many thrills as you have had watching me. If you want to keep watching me, let me recommend this PDZ-440 color television. It's made by the folks at Power Drain Enterprises. And I can tell you, they know how to make them so that they last and last. Get the PDZ-440, and I'll see you in next year's World Series. PDZ-440: It's the best, like me!

1. The argument uses Alvin Cleats as a source for what kind of information?

_____

_____

2. Is Mr. Cleats a good source for this information?

_____

3. For what kind of information would Mr. Cleats be a good source?

_____

_____

B Write whether each statement below is a **statement of ought** or a **statement of fact.**

1. A regulation should be made to restrict smoking to certain areas of this restaurant.

_____

2. A regulation restricts smoking to certain areas in this restaurant.

_____

3. Those schools shouldn't be so competitive.

_____

4. Most people should drive their cars less.

_____

C Read the paragraph below.

> Old Mr. Jones could always be seen on summer days kneeling on his lawn, digging out dandelions. Ever since that day a long, black car was parked in front of his house, we haven't seen Mr. Jones.

1. The paragraph gives a clue about why Mr. Jones has not been seen. What is the clue?

_____

_____

2. Name two reasons for Mr. Jones not being seen.

_____

_____

_____

D Read each deduction and write the answers to the questions.

- **We should do what is necessary to have a good school program.**
  In a good school program, students attend classes all day.
  Therefore, we should make sure that students attend classes all day.

1. What kind of statement does the deduction begin with?

_____

2. Is the deduction valid? _____

3. Explain. _____

_____

_____

- **This machine will keep very old people alive for ten years or more.**
  There are thousands of old people who would like to live longer.
  Therefore, we should use this machine to keep these old people alive.

4. What kind of statement does the deduction begin with?

_____

5. Is the deduction valid? _____

6. Explain. _____

_____

_____

E Here's what we know:

> **The police officer's directions were ambiguous.**

For each item, combine one of the sentences below with the sentence in the box.

- **We found the correct street without too much trouble.**
- **We got lost on our way to the meeting hall.**

1. Make a combined sentence with **but.**

_____

_____

_____

_____

2. Make a combined sentence with **so.**

_____

_____

_____

_____

LESSON 136

A Underline the redundant part in each sentence below. Then explain why the underlined part is redundant.

1. He was sad, and he wasn't very happy.

_____

_____

_____

2. The cabin was in proximity to the riverbank, near the water's edge.

_____

_____

_____

_____

_____

3. Their infant, not yet an adult, had black hair and brown eyes.

_____

_____

_____

_____

B Read the ads and answer the questions.

• If you have ever suffered from dandruff, you know how embarrassing it can be. It messes your clothing, and it itches. Well, here's some good news. Feel Free dandruff shampoo is now available in all drugstores. Feel Free is a shampoo that contains powerful chemicals that will help control those ugly white flakes. Mary Morse, star of *Starship*, says: "This is the shampoo that makes my hair shine."
   Why not try some today?

1. Write a sentence that would be in the ad if the ad said that Feel Free gets rid of dandruff.

_____

_____

_____

• Five people have driven the Hodo moped around New York City for a week. Their average gas mileage was 132.8 miles per gallon. In this day of rising gas prices, shouldn't you consider a Hodo moped?

2. Write a sentence that would be in the ad if the ad said that you would get 132.8 miles per gallon on the Hodo moped.

_____

_____

_____

C In the passage below, the verbs **was** and **were** are used incorrectly five times. Cross out each incorrect word. Write the correct word above it.

There are three redundant parts in the passage below. Cross out each redundant part.

> In the 1930s and 1940s, it were common to see hitchhikers hitching rides on the road. However, these people was not kids traveling for fun. These hitchhikers was adults who were heading west. They had hopes of getting jobs in California and finding work. The homes they was coming from had been destroyed by great dust storms. They was poor and homeless, without money or a home.

D Read the paragraph below and answer the questions.

Anne went outside dressed in her shorts and carrying a picnic basket. She stood in front of her house and looked around. "Darn it," she said, and went back inside.

1. The paragraph gives a clue about what caused Anne to go back inside the house. What caused her to go back?

_____

_____

2. Name two causes for Anne going back inside the house.

_____

_____

_____

E Read each item. Cross out the irrelevant words in the second piece of evidence, and write the conclusion for each item.

1. All ships have drag.
A submarine is a submersible ship.

_____

_____

2. Some fruit seeds contain poisonous chemicals.
Apples contain dark, bitter seeds.

_____

_____

★ **A** Ray sometimes has trouble using the words **who** and **which**. Below is a letter that he wrote to his friend Slim. Cross out the words **who** and **which** if they are used incorrectly. Write the correct word above every crossed-out word.

Dear Slim,

I used our money to buy a company, who has invented some interesting products. Our company, who is named Knot-So-Brite, is sure to be a success. The people which work for us are very smart. They have invented a machine that uses milk instead of oil for fuel. Some of our employees, which are famous scientists, are working on a machine that will convert mud into chocolate pudding. Guess which works in our art department? The same men who painted our house! You'll be pleased to know that the men who sold us this company are the same men which sold us the swampland in Florida.

Your pal,

Ray

B Read the ads and answer the questions.

• We have put this engine through a torture test. First, we filled the crankcase with Nu-Lube oil, with the patented graphite base. This is the famous black oil that has been revolutionizing motoring. Then, while the engine ran, we drained out the oil. But did the engine freeze up? No. Did the metal parts begin to grind each other into piles of metal filings? No. Has there been any sign of wear on this engine in the hour that it has run without oil? No. Imagine how Nu-Lube will save the life of your engine. Buy it now at leading gas stations.

1. Write a sentence that would be in the ad if the ad said that Nu-Lube is the best oil for your car.

_____

_____

_____

• Come Hither is a new perfume from the makers of the world-famous Aroma No. 9. Some of the richest and most beautiful women in the world wear Come Hither. This perfume costs a little more—but then, it's only for special people. Would you like to be like those women who wear Come Hither? Remember to buy some soon.

2. Write a sentence that would be in the ad if the ad said that Come Hither will make you a special person.

_____

_____

_____

Each argument that follows breaks one of these rules:

Rule 1. Just because two things happen around the same time doesn't mean one thing causes the other thing.

Rule 2. Just because you know about a part doesn't mean you know about the whole thing.

Rule 3. Just because you know about a part doesn't mean you know about another part.

Rule 4. Just because you know about a whole thing doesn't mean you know about every part.

Rule 5. Just because words are the same doesn't mean they have the same meaning.

Rule 6. Just because the writer presents some choices doesn't mean there aren't other choices.

Rule 7. Just because events have happened in the past doesn't mean they'll always happen.

After each argument that follows, write the number of the rule the argument breaks.

1. If the National Food Corporation is earning a huge profit, you can bet that every employee of that company is rich.

_____

2. Sharon is on the witness stand.

   District Attorney: "Isn't it true that you were a car thief when you were a teenager?"

   Sharon: "Yes, it's true."

   District Attorney: "Why shouldn't we believe that you still commit crimes?"

   _____

3. A survey of families who started out poor and became rich has been completed. This survey shows that the number of telephones in a house is related to the achievement of the children living in the house. When the families had no phones, the achievement of the children was very low. When the families had an average of one phone, the achievement level of the children went up greatly. When these families had an average of 2.3 phones, the achievement level of the children was the highest. This survey shows that we can improve the achievement of children by putting more phones in the house.

   _____

4. Cars, trucks, and buses make noise, pollute the atmosphere, use up gasoline or diesel fuel, and cause many accidents. Cars and trucks and buses are vehicles. The bicycle is also a vehicle. So, the bicycle must have the same faults as cars and trucks and buses. We should outlaw all these vehicles.

   _____

D Read the passage below. Find a statement that contradicts an earlier statement.

- Underline the statement you assume to be true.
- Circle the contradiction.
- Make up an if-then statement that explains the contradiction.

Garlic is a wonderful herb. Perhaps because of its powerful smell (and the telltale breath it leaves), people used to think it could ward off vampires and give soldiers courage. In truth, garlic will take the sting out of insect bites if you crush a clove and apply it to your skin. Planted near certain crops, it will keep insects away. Garlic provides protection against certain germs. The next time you feel a cold coming on, try chewing a few cloves of garlic—they may help your cold. Garlic is also a good breath freshener because of its mild odor. It can be used in almost any dish—casseroles, vegetables, even meat. Powdered garlic can be used, but fresh cloves are much better.

_____

_____

E Write the instructions for this diagram.

② currency ① ③

④ _____

1. (what) _____

_____

2. (what and where) _____

_____

3. (what and where) _____

_____

4. (what and where) _____

_____

F Each passage below contains a word you may not know. Read each passage and answer the questions.

• Her mind had <u>obliterated</u> all memory of that terrible night. She no longer remembered the flames and the smoke. Unfortunately, the memory of her childhood also was obliterated. She couldn't even recognize her mother and father.

1. Circle the answer.

   Obliterated probably means:

   recognized   increased   destroyed   saved

2. Write any sentence from the passage that contradicts the idea that **obliterated** means **saved.**

   _____

   _____

   _____

• She is very <u>diligent</u>. She carefully attends to details and checks everything twice to make sure it is correct. This diligence may slow her down a little, but she keeps plugging away and never makes a mistake. Sometimes she spends an hour or two double-checking her figures and outlining her next job.

3. Circle the answer.

   Diligent probably means:

   careful   dopey   quick   careless

4. Write any sentence from the passage that contradicts the idea that **diligent** means **quick.**

   _____

   _____

   _____

   _____

• I've never met a person with a better <u>aesthetic</u> sense than Mildred. Have you seen what she's done to her house? It's magnificent inside. The colors, the arrangement of pictures, and the choice of plants are all very tasteful. Also, the lighting is very impressive. Mildred's aesthetic abilities simply amaze me.

5. Circle the answer.

   Aesthetic probably means:

   vulgar   sleepy   artistic   writing

6. Write any sentence from the passage that contradicts the idea that **aesthetic** means **vulgar.**

   _____

   _____

   _____

   _____

ERRORS | W | B | T

★ **A** Read the evidence and write the conclusion for each item.

1. Here's the evidence:

   All immersible appliances are waterproof.
   Toasters are not waterproof.

   What's the conclusion?

   _____

   _____

2. Here's the evidence:

   Broccoli is a plant with chlorophyll.
   Chlorophyll makes plants green.

   What's the conclusion?

   _____

   _____

3. Here's the evidence:

   Some banks exchange currency.
   The American is a bank.

   What's the conclusion?

   _____

   _____

B Read the argument and answer the questions.

Joe Block led the New York Bullets basketball team to a victory over the Minnesota Pugs last season. The Bullets were predicted to lose by at least twenty points, but the Bullets won. So, when Joe says, "Light and Fluffy popcorn is the best popcorn on the market," you can bet that he is right again! Put a little Light and Fluffy in your life—tonight!

1. The argument uses Joe Block as a source for what kind of information?

   _____

   _____

2. Is Joe Block a good source for this information?

   _____

   _____

3. For what kind of information would Joe Block be a good source?

   _____

   _____

Read the passage and answer the questions. Circle **W** if the question is answered by words in the passage. Circle **D** if the question is answered by a deduction. If you circle **W** for an item, underline the words in the passage that give the answer.

The population cycle depends on the food supply. When the food supply is large in an area, the area can support many animals. When the number of animals becomes so great that they eat most of the food supply, animals starve. Now there aren't as many animals to eat the food, so the food supply grows again. Soon the supply is large, so the area can once more support a large number of animals.

Predators control the population of many animals. Predators keep the number of these animals from becoming too great. However, some animals have no natural enemies, so predators do not hold down their population growth. The Norwegian lemming is one of these animals. The lemming is a furry cousin of the rat that is about five inches long. Normally, lemmings live in the mountains. About every five years, the lemming population increases greatly. The number of lemmings is greater than the food supply. But the lemmings do something about this problem. They begin to march from the mountains into the lowlands, where many predators live. Hundreds of thousands of lemmings join the march, moving steadily in the same direction. Nothing seems to stop them. If a lake is in their way, they try to swim across, and many drown. With each mile, hundreds of lemmings die. Sometimes the march continues all the way to the ocean. The lemmings continue

their journey into the sea, where most of them drown. A few lemmings survive, and these lemmings return to the mountains. Now there is ample food for the lemmings, and the population begins to grow and grow. Five years later, the lemming population will again be very large, and the lemmings will start another march into the lowlands.

1. What does the population cycle of animals depend on?

_____ **W** **D**

2. Write what would happen next in the population cycle for rabbits and predators that eat rabbits:

The number of predators that eat rabbits decreases.

The population of rabbits increases.

The number of predators that eat rabbits increases.

Then what happens?

_____

_____

3. Where do lemmings normally live?

_____ **W** **D**

4. Why does the lemming population sometimes get too big?

_____

_____ **W** **D**

5. How do lemmings reduce their population?

_____

_____

D Read the ads and answer the questions.

- The Lakeview lawn mower has an adjustable blade that lets you cut your grass with a minimum of effort. In the spring, your grass is long and hard to cut. With the Lakeview, you simply adjust the blade to a higher position, which makes the grass much easier to mow. In the summer, adjust the blade to a lower position. Your lawn will be as smooth as any lawn in your neighborhood. This adjustable blade is only one of the many features on the Lakeview mower. Don't you think that we take as much care with all of these features as we do with the adjustable blade? Lakeview, the premium lawn mower!

1. Write a sentence that would be in the ad if the ad said that all the features were as carefully designed as the special blade.

   _____

   _____

   _____

- The Hammon Moto 600 is the fastest motorcycle on the road today. It can accelerate up to 100 miles per hour in ten seconds. The Hammon Moto gets about 50 miles per gallon of gasoline—almost twice as much mileage as you get from an old-fashioned car. When you consider speed performance and mileage, it's no wonder that over 10,000 people switched from old-fashioned cars to the Hammon Moto 600. These people are convinced that the Hammon is the best vehicle on the road today.

2. Write a sentence that would be in the ad if the ad said that the Hammon Moto 600 is the best vehicle on the road today.

   _____

   _____

   _____

   _____

E Read the facts and the items. If an item is relevant to fact A, write **relevant to fact A.** If an item is relevant to fact B, write **relevant to fact B.** If an item is irrelevant to both facts, write **irrelevant.**

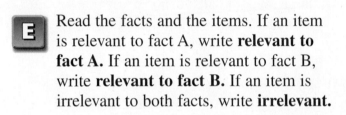

Fact A. **Susan and Michael are excellent cooks.**

Fact B. **Susan is trying to quit smoking.**

1. Because they both studied oriental art, Susan and Michael enjoyed their visit to the Art Institute of Chicago.

   _____

2. Susan knows that smoking cigarettes can be harmful to her health.

   _____

3. All of their friends enjoy the dinner parties Susan and Michael give.

   _____

4. Neither Michael nor Susan can decide whose omelettes are better.

   _____

You will be tested on some facts presented in this lesson. These facts are:

> 1. **Lemmings normally live in the mountains.**
> 2. **The lemming population sometimes gets too big because there are not many predators in the mountains.**
> 3. **Lemmings reduce their population by marching to the sea.**

Study these facts. Repeat them to yourself. Writing these facts may help you to remember them.

★ **A** Underline the redundant part in each sentence below. Then explain why the underlined part is redundant.

1. "That's it!" he exclaimed emphatically.

_____

_____

_____

_____

2. She drew a four-cornered rectangle.

_____

_____

_____

3. By the time a year was over, twelve months had passed.

_____

_____

_____

B Look at diagram 1.

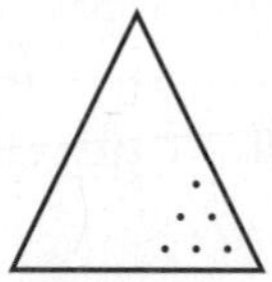

Diagram 1

You can see the dots and the triangle, but you can't see the circle.

1. Complete the deduction:

All the dots are in the triangle.
Part of the triangle is in the circle.

So, _____

_____

2. Draw a circle in diagram 1.

• Look at diagram 2.

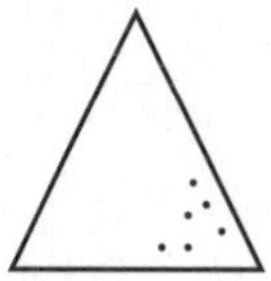

Diagram 2

You can see the dots and the triangle, but you can't see the circle.

3. Complete the deduction:

All the dots are in the triangle.
None of the triangle is in the circle.

So, _____

_____

4. Draw a circle in diagram 2.

Read the paragraph below.

> I was watching a biography of Edna St. Vincent Millay on television when a big thunderstorm started. I missed the end of the show.

1. The paragraph gives a clue about what caused the writer to miss the end of the show. What caused the writer to miss it?

_____

_____

2. Name two ways that your answer to question 1 could cause the writer to miss the end of the show.

_____

_____

_____

_____

_____

_____

 Read the arguments and answer the questions.

• Mike Hanney has worked as an engineer for twenty years. He has completed skyscrapers in New York and built many bridges in Peru and Central America. He says we should build a floating bridge between the mainland and Strawberry Island. If he says the bridge should be a floating bridge, I think we should seriously consider building that type of bridge.

1. The argument uses Mike Hanney as a source for what kind of information?

_____

_____

2. Is Mike Hanney a good source for this

information? _____

3. For what kind of information would Mike Hanney be a good source?

_____

_____

• The University of Washington spends more money on its science departments than on any other department. The oceanography and fisheries departments are excellent. Teachers and students take boats out on the ocean to study sea life. These boats are equipped with the most modern devices for studying life under the sea. The University of Washington receives millions of dollars from the government for research. Its professors and students are carefully selected. This group of people agrees that the salmon season should be cut short this year. I think we should follow their advice.

1. The argument uses the University of Washington as a source for what kind of information?

_____

_____

2. Is the University of Washington a good

source for this information? _____

3. For what kind of information would the University of Washington be a good source?

_____

E Read the passage below.

For generations, people all over the world have watched horse races and horse shows. Many others have enjoyed riding or hunting or the game of polo. Horses are also a popular theme in pictures, beginning centuries ago with paintings and continuing through modern times with photographic stories.

It wasn't until the camera was invented that a startling discrepancy was discovered. Popular paintings up to the nineteenth century showed horses flying over the ground with all four legs outstretched. When the camera was perfected in the 1870s, snapshots showed that horses never run that way. As a horse's front legs leave the ground, its back legs come down for the next stride. No horse could extend all four of its legs without falling on its stomach!

When painters applied this new knowledge to their work and began painting horses as they actually run, everyone complained that their pictures looked wrong.

- Here's a conclusion:

   Some paintings of horses are more than 100 years old.

1. Does the passage contain evidence to support this conclusion or evidence to refute this conclusion?

   _____

   _____

2. Which sentence contains the evidence?

   _____

   _____

   _____

   _____

   _____

- Here's another conclusion:

   People don't like art unless it is realistic.

3. Does the passage contain evidence to support this conclusion or evidence to refute this conclusion?

   _____

   _____

4. Which sentence contains the evidence?

   _____

   _____

   _____

   _____

   _____

   _____

- Here's another conclusion:

  Horseback riding and hunting are unpopular.

5. Does the passage contain evidence to support this conclusion or evidence to refute this conclusion?

_____

_____

6. Which sentence contains the evidence?

_____

_____

_____

_____

- Here's another conclusion:

  There are horses in many countries.

7. Does the passage contain evidence to support this conclusion or evidence to refute this conclusion?

_____

_____

8. Which sentence contains the evidence?

_____

_____

_____

_____

LESSON 139

F Read this: A title is a piece of paper that tells who owns something. When you buy a car, for example, you take title to the car. When you apply for license plates, you must show that you have title to the car. You must also show that you have title to the car when you sell it. Use the facts to fill out the form.

Facts: Your name is Rebecca Lynn. You are applying for a new driver's license in Vancouver, British Columbia. You are eighteen years old and were born April 22, 1980, in Butte, Montana. You are 5 feet 4 inches tall, you weigh about 115 pounds, your hair is black, and your eyes are brown. You live with your parents, John and Mary Lynn, at 1230 Stapleton in Vancouver. You passed both the written and driving tests given by the province. Your score on the road-signs test was 85 percent correct, and your score on the driver-information test was 98 percent correct. You drive a 1990 Ford. The license plate number is BC 2356. The car's title is in your name. The title number is 3945-84-87. The car's serial number is A543-4HL2-450. You must use your glasses to drive because, without them, your eyesight is poor. The car is insured by Safeink Insurance Company.

Province of British Columbia

Driver's License Application Form

Name _____

Date of birth _____ Place of birth _____

City

Present address _____

Street   City   State/Province

Is this application for a new license or for a renewal of an old one?   new_____   old _____

Eyesight without glasses   good _____   poor _____

Eyesight with glasses   good _____   poor _____

Height _____ Weight _____

Hair color _____ Eye color _____

Percent correct on driver-information test _____ Percent correct on road-signs test _____

What is the license plate number of the vehicle you own? _____

What is the title number of the vehicle? _____

Whose name is on the title? _____

What is the serial number of the vehicle? _____

Name of your insurance company _____

G Tomorrow you will be tested on facts you have learned. The test will include all of the facts presented in Lessons 123–138, and some of the facts from earlier lessons. These facts are:

1. Lemmings normally live in the mountains.

2. The lemming population sometimes gets too big because there are not many predators in the mountains.

3. Lemmings reduce their population by marching to the sea.

4. Tolerant trees do not need much sunlight to survive.

5. Intolerant trees cannot survive in the shade.

6. Cleaner fish eat parasites from larger ocean animals.

7. Sharks allow cleaner fish to eat things inside their mouths.

8. When an animal hibernates, it curls up in a safe place and sleeps for a long period of time.

9. Inflation means that prices keep going up.

10. Study the chart below. Make sure that you can fill in this chart.

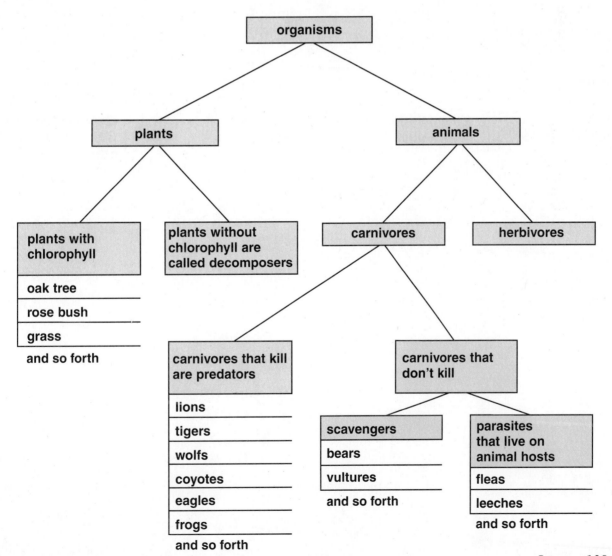

11. Study the chart below. Make sure that you can fill in this chart.

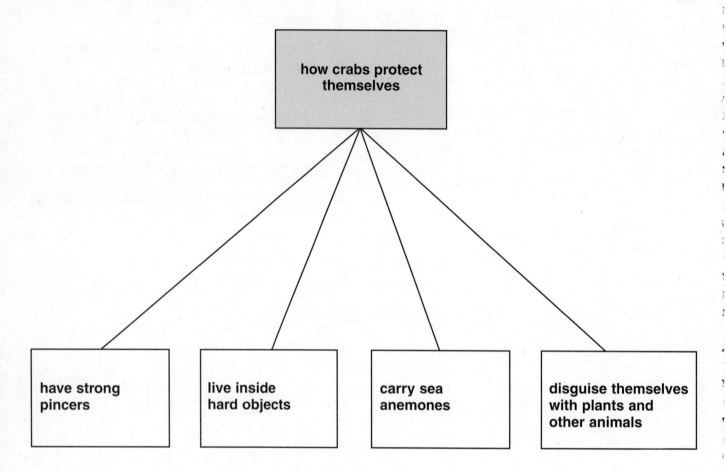

INFORMATION TEST. Answer each item. You have fifteen minutes.

1. How do lemmings reduce their population?

   _____

   _____

2. Where do lemmings normally live?

   _____

3. Why does the lemming population sometimes get too big?

   _____

   _____

4. What do we call trees that cannot survive in the shade?

   _____

5. What do we call trees that do not need much sunlight?

   _____

6. What does a shark do when a cleaner fish goes into its mouth?

   _____

   _____

   _____

7. What do cleaner fish eat?

   _____

8. What does inflation mean?

   _____

9. What do we mean when we say that an animal hibernates?

   _____

   _____

   _____

10. Fill in the chart on page 422.

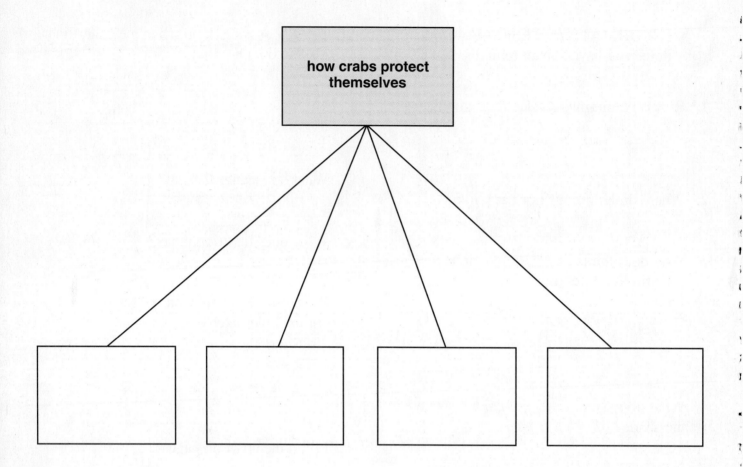

how crabs protect
themselves

11. Fill in the chart.

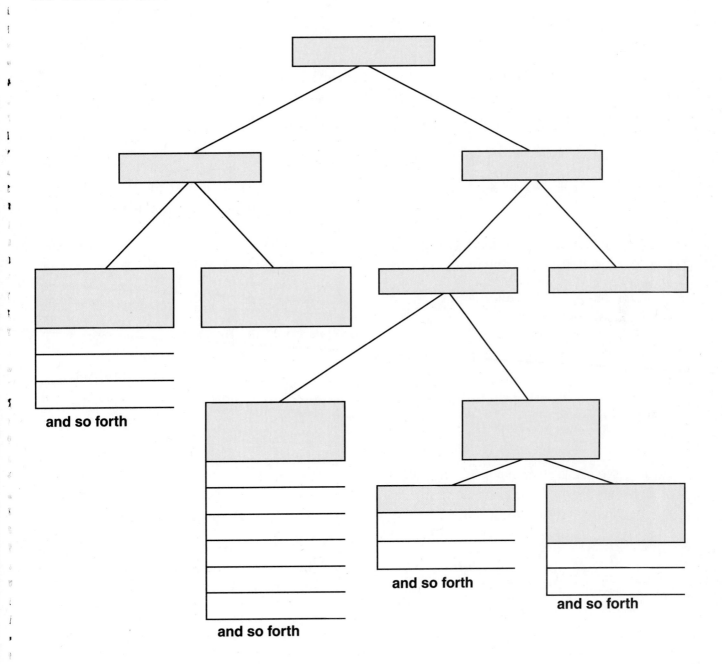

and so forth

and so forth

and so forth

and so forth

LESSON 140

★ **B** Select the right word for combining each pair of sentences below. Then write the combined sentence. Remember to punctuate each sentence correctly.

1. Jeff forgot to feed his dog last night. His dog was very hungry today. **and but**

_____

_____

_____

2. Jackie has always wanted to learn to play the guitar. She has never had enough money to buy one. **so however**

_____

_____

_____

_____

3. We wanted to see both movies. We arrived at the theater almost an hour after the first movie began. **therefore but**

_____

_____

_____

_____

4. The auditor found many mistakes in the books. The books were kept in the safe. **who which**

_____

_____

_____

5. People frequently talk with George. He is very open and friendly. **who which**

_____

_____

_____

6. The librarian told me that I still had six books checked out. He wouldn't let me check out any more. **so however**

_____

_____

_____

_____

C For each item, write a sentence that means the same thing by changing the underlined words.

1. The principal made up a rule that was based on the facts about school attendance.

_____

_____

_____

_____

2. He caused a great misunderstanding by giving an <u>unclear</u> <u>answer</u>.

_____

_____

_____

3. The manager has a <u>sound</u> <u>plan</u> for increasing production.

_____

_____

_____

4. In her proposal, Dr. Martin <u>argued</u> that she was not <u>hiding</u> the <u>reasons</u> for doing her research.

_____

_____

_____

_____

D Read the paragraph below.

When Jim arrived at work in the morning, his boss was in a foul mood. The next day Jim started work at another store.

1. The paragraph gives a clue about what caused Jim to start work at another store the next day. What caused him to start work at another store?

_____

_____

2. Name two ways that your answer to question 1 could cause Jim to start work at another store.

_____

_____

_____

_____

E Look at diagram 1.

Diagram 1

You can't see the dots in the picture, but **some dots are in the star.**

1. We're looking for a dot. What's the conclusion about where that dot is?

_____

2. Draw dots in diagram 1.

• Look at diagram 2.

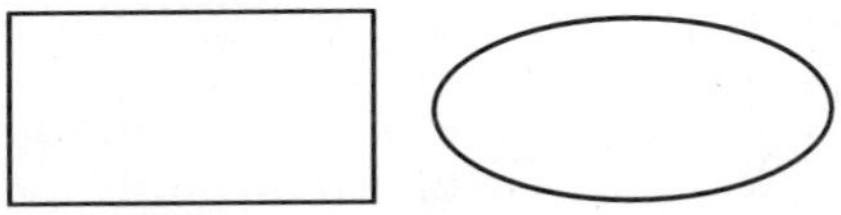

Diagram 2

You can see the rectangle and the oval, but you can't see the squares.

3. Complete the deduction.

All the squares are in the oval.
None of the oval is in the rectangle.

So, _____

_____.

F Each argument that follows is faulty. Read each argument and answer the questions.

- I thought I knew Charley really well. We've gone fishing together, and I can't tell you how many times I've visited his place. We used to play baseball together every weekend. As I say, I thought I knew him really well. You can't imagine how surprised I was to find out that he had a nervous breakdown. That doesn't sound like the Charley I know.

1. What does the author want us to conclude?

_____

_____

_____

2. How could you show that the argument is faulty?

_____

_____

_____

- The building repairer tried to tell me that our house has a crack in the foundation. Do you realize that the beams in our house are made from lumber imported all the way from northern British Columbia? And the windows are made of a special high-lead Italian glass. The roof is the best you can buy—red cedar shakes. How could there be a crack in the foundation?

3. What does the writer want us to conclude?

_____

_____

4. How could you show that the argument is faulty?

_____

_____

_____

_____

- We know that it rains an average of more than twenty-five inches during the winter in Drinmo, Washington. This means that during the winter season it rains nearly a quarter of an inch every day. When I go to Drinmo on February 8, I know that it will rain nearly a quarter of an inch that day.

5. What does the writer want us to conclude?

_____

_____

_____

_____

6. How could you show that the argument is faulty?

_____

_____

_____

FACT GAME SCORING CARD

1	2	3	4	5	6	7	8	9	10
11	12	13	14	15	16	17	18	19	20
21	22	23	24	25	26	27	28	29	30

FG   MT   BONUS   T

FACT GAME & MASTERY TEST **1**

AFTER LESSON 15

2. Tell if each line is **horizontal, vertical,** or **slanted.**

   a.

   b.

   c. _____

3. What do we call an event that helps explain a fact?

4. Combine these sentences with **however.**

   > **Here shoes were expensive.**
   > **They wore out fast.**

5. Fill in each blank with **is** or **are.**

   a. None of the dogs _____ eating.

   b. Some of the houses _____ for sale.

6. Here's the evidence:

   > **Some planets are very hot.**
   > **Venus is a planet.**

   What's the conclusion about Venus?

7. Fill in each blank with **was** or **were.**

   a. Each of the chairs _____ broken.

   b. Each girl _____ running.

8. Combine these sentences with **but.**

   > **The man had no money.**
   > **He bought a new car.**

9. Here's what we know:

   > **Gina runs every day.**

   Say **consistent** or **inconsistent** for each item.
   a. She is training for a race.
   b. She wants to stay in shape.

10. Say **relevant** or **irrelevant** for each event.

    > Fact: **Janet had a sunburn.**

    Events that happened before the fact:
    a. Janet spent all day at the beach.
    b. Janet liked to watch TV.

11. Name two words you can use to combine sentences that seem inconsistent.

12. What do we call an event that does not help explain a fact?

FACT GAME SCORING CARD

1	2	3	4	5	6	7	8	9	10
11	12	13	14	15	16	17	18	19	20
21	22	23	24	25	26	27	28	29	30

FG	MT	BONUS	T

AFTER LESSON 30

2. Here's what we know:

Tom had a headache.

Say **consistent** or **inconsistent** for each item.
a. He took two aspirins.
b. He turned up the radio as loud as it would go.

3. Name three words you can use to combine sentences that seem consistent.

4. Here's the evidence:

All teeth have roots.
Molars are teeth.

What's the conclusion about molars?

5. Say the model sentence that means this:

By pausing, she lost her chance.

6. Combine these sentences with **so.**

Pam earns money by cutting lawns.
She bought a new lawn mower.

7. Say the model sentence that means this:

His directions were unclear and repetitive.

8. Combine these sentences with **and.**

Fran has many books.
She is building a bookshelf.

9. Say the model sentence that means this:

They changed their Swiss money into Canadian money.

10. Combine these sentences with **therefore.**

Pete failed a test at school.
He plans to study more.

11. Say **relevant** or **irrelevant** for each event.

Fact: **It was midnight.**

Events that happened before the fact:
a. Most people went to bed.
b. The street lights came on.

12. Name two words you can use to combine sentences that seem inconsistent.

FACT GAME SCORING CARD

1	2	3	4	5	6	7	8	9	10
11	12	13	14	15	16	17	18	19	20
21	22	23	24	25	26	27	28	29	30

FG   MT   BONUS   T

FACT GAME & MASTERY TEST 3

AFTER LESSON 45

2. Here's the evidence:

> **Every bone needs calcium.**
> **The radius is a bone.**

What's the conclusion about the radius?

3. Say **relevant** or **irrelevant** for each event.

> Fact: **The man limped when he**
> **walked.**

Events that happened before the fact:
a. He had hurt his leg playing football.
b. He had hurt his arm playing football.

4. What kind of reference book would you use to find out:
a. Another word that means **gather?**
b. When the first rocket was used?
c. Which countries did not fight in World War II?

5. a. Name the earliest-known close relative of the horse.
b. What do we call the group of animals that modern horses belong to?

6. Fill in each blank with **has** or **have.**

a. Everybody _____ tickets for the game.

b. You _____ two chances to win.

7. Say the model sentence that means this:

> **The rule limited their parking.**

8. Tell **who** or **which** for each item.
a. A store clerk
b. A store
c. A thought

9. a. What do we call a machine that looks and does some things like a human?
b. What do we call a person who isn't part of the group?

10. Fill in each blank with **has** or **have.**

a. The grain _____ bugs in it.

b. Her family _____ three dogs.

11. Tell **who** or **which** for each item.
a. A dream
b. A taxi
c. A taxi driver

12. Say the model sentence that means this:

> **His directions were unclear and repetitive.**

FACT GAME & MASTERY TEST 4

FACT GAME SCORING CARD

1	2	3	4	5	6	7	8	9	10
11	12	13	14	15	16	17	18	19	20
21	22	23	24	25	26	27	28	29	30

FG	MT	BONUS	T

AFTER LESSON 60

2. Say **relevant** or **irrelevant** for each event.

Fact: **Jonas got a speeding ticket.**

Events that happened before the fact:
a. Jonas was driving to the store.
b. Jonas was going 80 miles an hour.

3. For each sentence, tell what's referred to by **who** or **which**.
a. Red River, which runs through our land, floods every spring.
b. He wrote a letter to Ann, who is his sister.

4. Tell **who** or **which** for each item.
a. The movie
b. The audience
c. The ticket seller

5. Tell what rule this argument breaks.

If I wear my red sweater when I go fishing, I catch big fish.

6. Here's the evidence:

**Some plants eat insects.
A sloth is an animal.**

What's the conclusion about a sloth?

7. Say the model sentence that means this:

Her <u>answer</u> was <u>filled</u> with <u>irrelevant</u> details.

8. Here's a rule:

Muscles need oxygen.

Tell if each piece of evidence is **relevant** to the rule or **irrelevant.**
a. The liver is an organ.
b. The deltoid is a muscle.

9. Tell what rule this argument breaks.

If Doris is such a wonderful dancer, everybody in her class must be wonderful dancers.

10. Combine these sentences with **but** or **therefore.**

**Tom broke his leg yesterday.
He was in school today.**

11. Combine these sentences with **so** or **however.**

**Mr. Ryse smokes too much.
He coughs a lot.**

12. a. What Greek word means **by the side of writing?**
b. What Middle English word means **thread?**

FACT GAME SCORING CARD

1	2	3	4	5	6	7	8	9	10
11	12	13	14	15	16	17	18	19	20
21	22	23	24	25	26	27	28	29	30

FG   MT   BONUS   T

FACT GAME &
MASTERY TEST

5

AFTER LESSON 75

2. a. Name the two parts of a herbivorous mammal that are well-designed for grazing.
   b. Do both eyes of a herbivorous mammal see almost the same thing?

3. Here's a rule:

   Trees give off oxygen.

   Tell if each piece of evidence is **relevant** to the rule or **irrelevant**.
   a. Poplars and maples are trees.
   b. Shrubs give off oxygen.

4. Look at the graph and answer the questions.
   a. The letter **A** shows pounds of apples for one year. What year?
   b. How many pounds?

5. Look at the graph and answer the questions.
   a. The letter **B** shows pounds of apples for one year. What year?
   b. How many pounds?

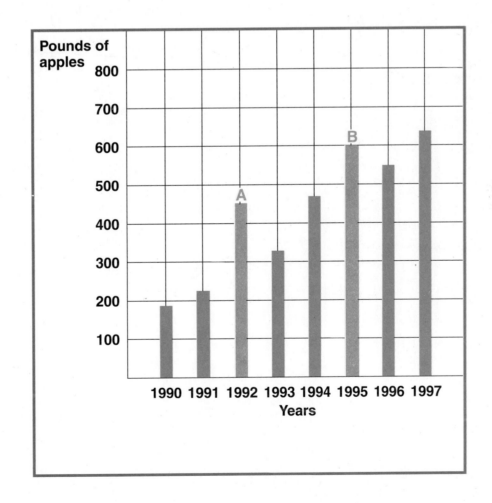

6. Tell which rule this argument breaks.

> **I know his car must have a good engine, because its body is in great shape.**

7. Say the model sentence that means this:

> **They <u>made up</u> a <u>fitting</u> plan.**

8. Tell which rule this argument breaks.

> **If that boy's club won the city swim meet, every boy in the club must be a great swimmer.**

9. Combine these sentences with **who** or **which**.

> **She wants to move that couch. That couch is very heavy.**

10. Tell which rule this argument breaks.

> **I know that Tom is a bully, because he told me he beat his little brother.**

11. Combine these sentences with **who** or **which**.

> **He wrote a paper about Alice Walker. Alice Walker is an author.**

12. a. What do we call the system of reading and writing that blind people use?
    b. What do we call it when people stop buying from a business or selling to the business?

FACT GAME SCORING CARD

1	2	3	4	5	6	7	8	9	10
11	12	13	14	15	16	17	18	19	20
21	22	23	24	25	26	27	28	29	30

FG   MT   BONUS   T

FACT GAME & MASTERY TEST 6

AFTER LESSON 90

2. a. How many days did it take to deliver mail from St. Joseph, Missouri, to Sacramento, California, before the Pony Express?

b. How long did mail delivery from St. Joseph to Sacramento take with the Pony Express?

3. Combine these sentences with **who** or **which**.

> **Josie wants to read this book.**
> **This book is about training for races.**

4. Tell which rule this argument breaks.

> **If Jolene is such a great athlete, everyone in her family must be a great athlete.**

5. Tell the conclusion for each piece of evidence.

> Rule: **All mammals are warm-blooded.**

Evidence
a. Snakes are not warm-blooded.
b. Polar bears are mammals.

6. Tell the redundant part in each sentence.
a. They moved to a remote house, far from town.
b. The diamond, which was very clear, had a lot of clarity.

7. Say the model sentence that means this:

> **A strange <u>event</u> caused the <u>fear</u> that she <u>showed</u>.**

8. Tell which rule this argument breaks.

> **If you don't want to have bad breath, use Rinso Mouthwash.**

9. Tell the redundant part in each sentence.
a. She was filled with sorrow and felt very sad.
b. He hesitated at the top of the stairs, pausing for a minute.

10. a. Name two parasites that live on plants.
b. Name three parasites that live on animals.

11. Combine these sentences with **therefore** or **however**.

> **All of his clothes were dirty.**
> **He didn't do any laundry.**

12. a. Name the three ingredients that plants need to manufacture their own food.
b. What do we call animals that eat other animals?

FACT GAME & MASTERY TEST 7

1	2	3	4	5	6	7	8	9	10
11	12	13	14	15	16	17	18	19	20
21	22	23	24	25	26	27	28	29	30

FACT GAME SCORING CARD

FG	MT	BONUS	T

AFTER LESSON 105

2. a. In what year did the first person walk on the moon?

b. In what year was the first coast-to-coast railroad in the United States completed?

3. a. What do we call any living thing?

b. Name 3 scavengers.

4. Tell the redundant part in each sentence.

a. He concealed the money by hiding it.

b. This weapon, which is lethal, could kill someone.

5. Fill in each blank with **has** or **have**.

a. Players on that team _____ practice every day.

b. Nobody in those houses _____ a TV set.

6. Say each sentence below, using **rarely, usually,** or **occasionally.**

a. He (almost never) likes to eat pizza.

b. She goes to the movies (once in a while).

7. Say the model sentence that means this:

> **The major <u>argued</u> that he had <u>sound</u> <u>reasons</u> for <u>hiding</u> the <u>facts</u>.**

8. Tell whether each statement is a **statement of fact** or a **statement of ought.**

a. People who smoke should try to quit.

b. Many people die each year from problems related to smoking.

9. a. Name the earliest-known close relative of the modern horse.

b. What do we call a species that is nearly extinct?

10. Combine these sentences with **so** or **but.**

> **He wants to buy a new bike.**
> **He is saving all his money.**

11. Look at the map and answer these questions.

a. How many countries border Bolivia?

b. Name those countries.

12. Brazil is bordered by five countries. Look at the map and name those countries.

FACT GAME SCORING CARD

1	2	3	4	5	6	7	8	9	10
11	12	13	14	15	16	17	18	19	20
21	22	23	24	25	26	27	28	29	30

FG   MT   BONUS   T

FACT GAME & MASTERY TEST   8

AFTER LESSON 120

2. a. The teeth and eyes of many herbivorous mammals are well-designed for

_____.

b. The teeth and eyes of many carnivorous mammals are well-designed for

_____.

3. Tell which rule this argument breaks.

> **If that company makes good cars, it must make good lawn mowers.**

4. The letter A on the graph shows the height for trees that are a certain age.
a. What age?
b. What height?

5. The letter B on the graph shows the height for trees that are a certain age.
a. What age?
b. What height?

6. Say each sentence with the word **especially.**
a. The dog was really happy to see its owner.
b. Summers in Arizona are very hot.

7. Make each statement more general by using the name of a larger class for each underlined part.
a. The <u>dogs, cats and goats</u> ate the <u>apples, steak and potatoes</u>.
b. The <u>car and the truck</u> stopped in front of the <u>store and the theater</u>.

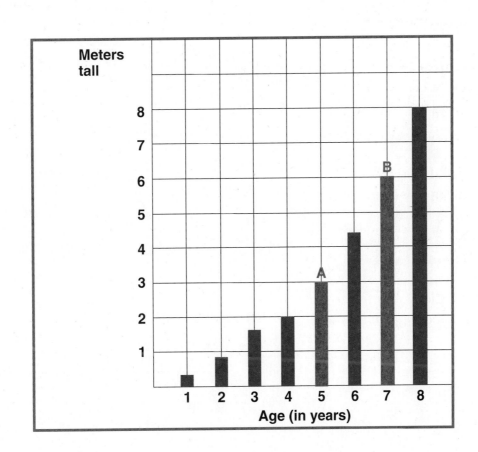

8. Say each sentence with the word
particularly.
   a. She is a very good singer.
   b. It rains a lot here, especially in the
      winter.

9. Tell which rule this argument breaks.

> **If that class won the attendance award,**
> **every student in the class must have**
> **had excellent attendance.**

10. a. What word comes from a Greek word
       that means **house?**
    b. What Greek word means **by the side of**
       writing?

11. Combine these sentences with **who** or
which.

   She is going to the movies with Pete.
   Pete is her neighbor.

12. a. What are the only living things that
       manufacture their own food?
    b. The teeth of a carnivorous mammal are

       _____ and the teeth of a herbivorous

       mammal are _____.

FACT GAME SCORING CARD

1	2	3	4	5	6	7	8	9	10
11	12	13	14	15	16	17	18	19	20
21	22	23	24	25	26	27	28	29	30

MT   BONUS   T

FACT GAME & MASTERY TEST 9

AFTER LESSON 135

2. Buffalo is close to two lakes. Look at the map and name those lakes.

3. What city on the map is not close to a lake?

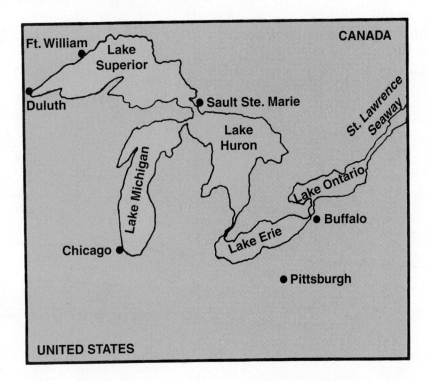

4. Tell which rule this argument breaks.

> If I put garlic under my pillow, vampires don't bother me during the night.

5. Tell the conclusion for each piece of evidence.

Rule: **Intolerant trees cannot survive in the shade.**

Evidence
a. Cottonwoods are intolerant trees.
b. Hemlock trees can survive in the shade.

6. Combine these sentences with **therefore** or **however.**

> She wants to go to college.
> She studies a lot.

7. Tell which rule this argument breaks.

> If he lied to me before, he'll lie to me again.

8. a. What do we call plants that don't have chlorophyll?
b. What part of plants helps prevent the formation of a desert?

9. Tell the redundant part in each sentence.
   a. He was frozen with fear and filled with anxiety.
   b. His ambiguous statement was unclear to everyone.

10. a. What do we call trees that do not need much sunlight to survive?
    b. Name the animal that removes parasites from a rhinoceros.

11. The letter **A** on the graph shows how much snow fell during a certain month.
    a. What month?
    b. How much snow?

12. The letter **B** on the graph shows how much snow fell during a certain month.
    a. What month?
    b. How much snow?

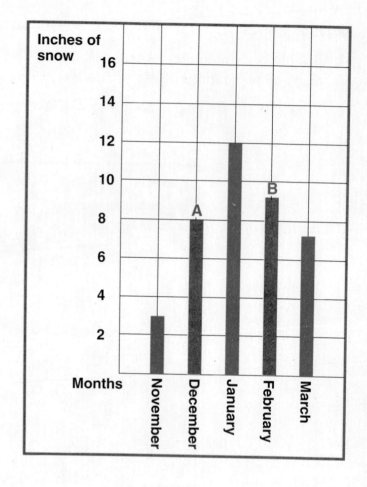

FACT GAME 1

2. a. Slanted
   b. Vertical
   c. Horizontal

3. Relevant

4. Her shoes were expensive; however, they wore out fast.

5. a. None of the dogs is eating.
   b. Some of the houses are for sale.

6. Maybe Venus is very hot.

7. a. Each of the chairs was broken.
   b. Each girl was running.

8. The man had no money, but he bought a new car.

9. a. Consistent
   b. Consistent

10. a. Relevant
    b. Irrelevant

11. But, however

12. Irrelevant

FACT GAME 2

2. a. Consistent
   b. Inconsistent

3. And, so, therefore

4. Molars have roots.

5. By hesitating, she lost her opportunity.

6. Pam earns money by cutting lawns, so she bought a new lawn mower.

7. His directions were ambiguous and redundant.

8. Fran has many books, and she is building a bookshelf.

9. They converted their Swiss currency into Canadian currency.

10. Peter failed a test at school; therefore, he plans to study more.

11. a. Relevant
    b. Relevant

12. But, however

FACT GAME 3

2. The radius needs calcium.

3. a. Relevant
   b. Irrelevant

4. a. Dictionary
   b. Encyclopedia
   c. Encyclopedia

5. a. Eohippus
   b. Equus

6. a. Everybody has tickets for the game.
   b. You have two chances to win.

7. The regulation restricted their parking.

8. a. Who
   b. Which
   c. Which

9. a. Robot
   b. Maverick

10. a. The grain has bugs in it.
    b. Her family has three dogs.

FACT GAME
ANSWER KEYS

11. a. Which
    b. Which
    c. Who

12. His directions were ambiguous and redundant.

FACT GAME 4

2. a. Irrelevant
   b. Relevant

3. a. Red River
   b. Ann

4. a. Which
   b. Which
   c. Who

5. Just because two things happen around the same time doesn't mean that one thing causes the other thing.

6. Idea: There is none.

7. Her response was replete with extraneous details.

8. a. Irrelevant
   b. Relevant

9. Just because you know about a part doesn't mean you know about the whole thing.

10. Tom broke his leg yesterday, but he was in school today.

11. Mr. Ryse smokes too much, so he coughs a lot.

12. a. Paragraphos
    b. Clewe

FACT GAME 5

2. a. Eyes, teeth
   b. No

3. a. Relevant
   b. Irrelevant

4. a. 1992
   b. 450

5. a. 1995
   b. 600

6. Just because you know about a part doesn't mean you know about another part.

7. They devised an appropriate strategy.

8. Just because you know about a whole thing doesn't mean you know about every part.

9. She wants to move that couch, which is very heavy.

10. Just because words are the same doesn't mean they have the same meaning.

11. He wrote a paper about Alice Walker, who is an author.

12. a. Braille
    b. Boycott

FACT GAME 6

2. a. 20 days
   b. 8 days

3. Josie wants to read this book, which is about training for races.

4. Just because you know about a part doesn't mean you know about the whole thing.

5. a. Snakes are not mammals.
   b. Polar bears are warm-blooded.

6. a. Far from town
   b. Had a lot of clarity

7. A strange phenomenon caused the anxiety that she exhibited.

8. Just because the writer presents some choices doesn't mean there aren't other choices.

9. a. Felt very sad
   b. Pausing

10. a. Mistletoe, dodder
    b. Any 3: Fleas, ticks, leeches, mosquitoes

11. All of his clothes were dirty; however, he didn't do any laundry.

12. a. Sunlight, water, carbon dioxide
    b. Carnivorous

FACT GAME 7

2. a. 1969
   b. 1869

3. a. Organism
   b. Any 3: Bears, porcupines, crows, vultures

4. a. By hiding it
   b. Could kill someone

5. a. Players on that team have practice every day.
   b. Nobody in those houses has a TV set.

6. a. He rarely likes to eat pizza.
   b. She goes to the movies occasionally.

7. The major contended that he had valid motives for concealing the data.

8. a. Statement of ought
   b. Statement of fact

9. a. Eohippus
   b. Endangered

10. He wants to buy a new bike, so he is saving all his money.

11. a. 5
    b. Brazil, Peru, Chile, Argentina, Paraguay

12. Peru, Bolivia, Paraguay, Argentina, Uruguay

FACT GAME 8

2. a. grazing
   b. hunting

3. Just because you know about a part doesn't mean you know about another part.

4. a. 5 years
   b. 3 meters

5. a. 7 years
   b. 6 meters

6. a. The dog was especially happy to see its owner.
   b. Summers in Arizona are especially hot.

7. a. The animals ate the food.
   b. The vehicles stopped in front of the buildings.

8. a. She is a particularly good singer.
   b. It rains a lot here, particularly in the winter.

9. Just because you know about a whole thing doesn't mean you know about every part.

10. a. Ecology
    b. Paragraphos

11. She is going to the movies with Pete, who is her neighbor.

12. a. Green plants
    b. pointed, flat

FACT GAME 9

2. Lake Ontario, Lake Erie

3. Pittsburgh

4. Just because two things happen around the same time doesn't mean one thing causes the other thing.

5. a. Cottonwoods cannot survive in the shade.
   b. Hemlock trees are not intolerant trees.

6. She wants to go to college; therefore, she studies a lot.

7. Just because events have happened in the past doesn't mean they'll always happen.

8. a. Decomposers
   b. Roots

9. a. And filled with anxiety
   b. Was unclear to everyone

10. a. Tolerant
    b. Tickbird

11. a. December
    b. 8 inches

12. a. February
    b. 9 inches